John Wilson's
1001
TOP**ANGLING**TIPS

This book is for my best friend.
My wife Jo.

This edition first published in the UK in 2007
By Green Umbrella Publishing

© Green Umbrella Publishing 2009

Publishers Jules Gammond and Vanessa Gardner

The right of John Wilson to be identified as Author of this book has been asserted by him
in accordance with the Copyright, Designs and Patents Act 1988.

Printed and bound in China

ISBN 978-1-905828-93-7

John Wilson's
1001
TOP**ANGLING**TIPS

Green**Umbrella**
Publishing

ACKNOWLEDGMENTS

All angling writers have special people or a particular person to thank. My wife Jo for instance, (who took the barbel cover photo incidentally) puts up with my profession like a trooper, knowing full well that at times I really do not always 'have' to go out fishing. I could perhaps draw on experiences past, and old photos to illustrate a particular article. But then she also understands my personal 'needs' to keep experiencing my sport. And with a string of good friends, some young, some my age, who are always providing me with reasons enough for leaving a warm bed in the early hours, like Martin Bowler, Dave Lewis, Simon Clarke, Terry Houseago, Nick Beardmore, John (Jinx) Davey, and others, how can I possibly refuse? Frankly, I don't think I ever want to.

A good, illustrative angling book just doesn't happen without much design and thought from an accomplished artist and editorial team, which is why I should like to express my appreciation to both designer Kevin Gardner and illustrator Andy Steer for their painstaking contributions.

Writing this mammoth collection of top angling tips has given me a wonderful opportunity of putting down just about everything I've learnt in getting on for 60 years of fishing, whilst simultaneously providing some lovely memories, past and present, along the way. And the plain fact is, if I personally have learnt anything from this volume, it is that we really never actually stop learning. Each and every day out or trip abroad, or opportunist, two hour session grabbed after work or at the drop of a hat, maybe just an hour spent in search of a particular monster, provides us all with such invaluable and unique individual experiences and memories. Even those hard lessons learnt of what not to do next time; because we tried in the wrong place, or took the wrong bait along, got the tide wrong, or misread current patterns, are all part and parcel of this fabulous field sport of ours called angling. And it 'is' a 'field sport' you know.

Surely no other pursuit is so full of contradictions, hearsay, luck, pleasure, indecision and contemplation. I know one thing for sure. No other outlet or 'calling' allows a grown man to draw on that boyish enthusiasm for decade after decade which finds him rising at a time when fish are most likely to feed, be it a February morning with a thick frost on the ground and chub are the quarry, to facing the full force of the Atlantic and punching out a lead that the wind promptly throws back at you, when there is a remote chance of a fat codling.

Lastly, I should like to point out that this volume is not in any way designed to be the be all and end all of angling advice, nor any kind of encyclopaedia. It is merely a collection of my own, personal 'top tips' covering some 50 subjects within the framework of angling in the UK today. Nothing more, nothing less. But I truly hope that some of you might catch more or larger specimens from reading it.

Good Fishing!

John Wilson
Great Witchingham, 2007

CONTENTS

FRESHWATER SPECIES

FRESHWATER BOAT FISHING

FRESHWATER TACKLE

FRESHWATER BAITS

SALTWATER SPECIES

SALTWATER BOAT FISHING

SALTWATER TACKLE

SALTWATER BAITS

Barbel

1 To stop chub from hooking themselves and disturbing the swim when barbel fishing with 'bolt-rig' style tactics, use a 12 inch hook length and a long (1-2 inch) hair, in conjunction with a heavy 2-3 ounce 'running' flat-bomb. Use a rubber cushioning bead between hook trace swivel and lead. They will then freely move away across the current or turn immediately downstream with the lower of your two 15-18mm boilies, large boilie or halibut pellet pursed in their lips, but usually spit it out at the last second. So only lift into a fish when the rod tip slams round and stays round, indicating a barbel has found the bait. Ignore all other pulls.

2 Have you ever wondered why a 'sand-papery' feeling happens to the line when you are touch ledgering for barbel, or the rod tip vibrates momentarily before 'hooping over' as a fish runs off with the bait and actually hooks itself? Well, as barbel are equipped with four long sensory barbels (hence their name) an under-slung mouth and a long snout, unlike fish such as chub, roach and tench, they actually lose visual contact with what they are about to swallow before opening their mouth. So they gently move their snout from side to side in an agitated manner, in order to centralize the bait once their mouth is open. And in so doing, their barbels must inevitably do a 'plink-plunk' against the line.

3 When baiting up a swim, either loose feeding by hand from a spot several yards upstream to allow for the pace of flow to ensure the food is deposited exactly where you want it on the river bed, or by using bait droppers full of maggots, hempseed or 3-6mm pellets, possibly the three most effective attractor 'loose feeds' for barbel, try not to fish immediately afterwards. Action is invariably more hectic and lasts for much longer if you first allow the barbel to move into the swim and over the bait, gaining confidence in their feeding, for at least an hour or so, before your hook rig is presented to them. Try it and see.

4 During the warm summer and autumnal months barbel are far more likely to move across the flow and intercept a moving bait, even one being 'trotted' through at current speed, than later on in the year when temperatures start to plummet, and they will only suck up static baits from the bottom. So get to enjoy catching some barbel on the float, using a powerful 13 foot trotting rod and centre pin reel holding 6-8lbs test. Keep a selection of both heavy 'Avon' and 'Chubber' floats in your waistcoat, and be sure to split their bulk shotting capacity of say 3-5 swan shots, into a line of AAs fixed

onto the line 12-16 inches above the hook, with a small shot or two in between. *See Grayling Tip 1.*

5 To get the most out of your river, especially when exploring those barbel-holding runs beneath willows and lines of alders along the opposite bank (I bet certain, previously unattainable swims immediately spring to mind here) you need to get in with the fish, at least into the centre of the river, in order to trot a bait through steadily and directly downstream. This means splashing out on a pair of lightweight, chest-high, waders. The best are 'breathable' and come with hard-wearing neoprene reinforcement at the knees and built-in neoprene socks. You then simply slip on 'felt-soled' wading shoes for maximum stability over slippery stones and boulders. Anyone who fly fishes for salmon or sea trout or who long trots for grayling during the winter months, will no doubt be equipped already. Either way, quality chest-high waders are a sound investment for enjoyment, allowing you to also kneel and sit down on the bank anywhere along the river without the need for a stool.

6 When ledgering at close range 'bolt-rig' style for barbel (or carp) in really clear water where they can be viewed moving all around the bait to

inspect it, even above your ledger rig, it pays to incorporate a 'back-lead' positioned on the line two to four foot above the bait. Simply and 'loosely' pinch onto the line two 3x swan shots, or sleeve a coffin ledger onto the line and secure with a rubber 'sliding float stop' at each end. This ensures that the line above your ledger rig is ironed flat to the river bed, thus alleviating any chance of lines bites and fish spooking through their fins touching the line, It is especially important when having to fish from 'high-bank' swims, where the line would otherwise angle down sharply from rod tip to ledger rig.

7 If like me you welcome the rest provided by the statutory closed season for rivers, but after a few weeks start to get itchy to be beside water, why not pay your favourite 'barbel' stretches a visit. From around the beginning of May onwards (depending upon water temperatures) barbel congregate upon the gravel shallows in readiness for spawning, and so there is no better time for 'fish-spotting', and ascertaining to exactly what size they grow along a particular part of the river. So don't forget the Polaroid glasses.

8 When clear-water barbel do not play ball and move up into a pre-baited swim, pushing smaller fish species out of the way, as they usually do, then plan to fish for them during the hours of darkness. This reluctance to feed aggressively during daylight hours is common place in stretches of river where the barbel are targeted daily, particularly with small groups of 'known' or 'specimen-sized fish' that have been repeatedly caught and know all the tricks. So plan to start an hour or so before dusk, expecting no small level of response once the light has totally gone, and be prepared to fish on for some while until they do respond. Those first few hours of darkness are usually best. But don't forget a trip during that first hour or two before dawn, which can so often produce, especially during the warmer months.

9 For depositing any kind of loose feed straight down to the river bed of close range swims (say up to a rod length and a half out) regardless of current force, bait droppers, which come in all shapes and sizes, are worth their weight in gold. Monster droppers holding half a pint of hempseed, maggots or pellets etc, get the job done in no time at all and minimize disturbance, though you do need a long, stiff rod to swing a large 'full' dropper out. And droppers must be 'swung' out and not 'cast', otherwise bait could get distributed all over the place. And you want it concentrated within a relatively small area over which the barbel will eventually move and start hoovering it up. Beware of the odd pike which appear from nowhere to attack the lid of the dropper when it hangs down and 'flaps' in the current as you lift it out.

10 One of the most satisfying and pleasing techniques for catching barbel occurs during the warmer months when donning chest-high waders and getting into clear-flowing, gravel-bottomed rivers allows you to carefully wade out to a position immediately below a shoal of fish, (which can often be seen hugging the bottom in the runs between long beds of flowing weed) and then to cast a chunk of luncheon meat upstream and slightly across, so it rolls back along the bottom directly in line with the shoal. And to do this you must allow an all-important 'bow' to form in the line between rod tip and bait.

Barbel

11 'Rolling meat', as the method has been dubbed, works effectively for one main reason. The free lined bait is brought down to the shoal at current speed, like all loose particles of natural food, so their suspicion is not aroused, and moreover, it comes 'directly' down river, tumbling along the gravel, and is not dragged 'unnaturally' across the fish's vision which is what the line would do if you were situated on the bank and not standing in the water immediately downriver.

12 To facilitate easy casting and to counteract the bait's inherent buoyancy when 'rolling meat' so it tumbles along naturally, catching momentarily here and there every so often amongst the clean gravel, just like all other tit bits brought along by the current, a slither of lead wire (roofing lead is exactly the right thickness) is super-glued to the top of the hook shank and firmly whipped over with black fly tying thread. Chamfering each end of the lead with your thumbnail makes for an extremely neat finish. *See Diagram.* The hook now looking decidedly 'shrimp-like' with its 'curved' back, will always present the bait with the hook point angled upwards, and is thus less likely to catch upon snags or weed. Generally however, large chunks of meat

are used in order that the hook is not actually visible.

13 You can make up several different 'weights' of hooks, (to cover all conditions from slow currents to turbulent runs) simply by using different thicknesses of lead wire. I suggest large sizes of 'wide gape' eyed hooks from 6 up to 2 will serve you best. And in addition to luncheon meat, tinned ham, sausage in skins, etc, etc, even good old bread flake and protein pastes will all make this method work and come alive.

14 For extra sensitivity when 'rolling meat', a braided reel line used in conjunction with a free running centre-pin reel is hard to beat, though you can manage with a fixed spool reel and monofilament. The secret being always to gently recover line as the bait is brought down to you by the current, whilst keeping that 'bow' in the line, which could suddenly 'tighten' or completely fall 'slack' as a fish hoovers up the bait and belts downstream towards you.

15 When 'bolt-rig' style ledgering for barbel (and chub) particularly when the river is in full flood and visibility is at an all time low, give your bait added attraction by

moulding a large dollop of soft, aromatic paste around your hair-rigged boilie or halibut pellet. As pieces break off or are pecked off by small fish and roll downstream, barbel will follow the scent up to your hook bait.

16 When smaller specimens pick up your ledgered size 10-15mm boilie or pellet hook bait, simply tie on a longer hair to accommodate two size 20mm boilies or a 25mm halibut pellet. The mouth of a double figure barbel can easily hoover them up.

17 If you have your sights set on a really big barbel, remember that a September fish for instance, could weigh as much as 10-15% heavier towards the end of the season in March. So providing the weather stays mild, concentrate your efforts during those 'precious' last two weeks of the river season.

18 There's no doubt about it, barbel love maggots. Trouble is, so does every other cyprinid species, so wherever small, nuisance fish share a particular swim with barbel you must be prepared to 'feed them off'. And that means having enough

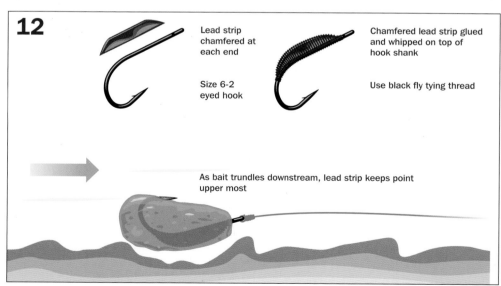

12

Lead strip chamfered at each end

Size 6-2 eyed hook

Chamfered lead strip glued and whipped on top of hook shank

Use black fly tying thread

As bait trundles downstream, lead strip keeps point upper most

16

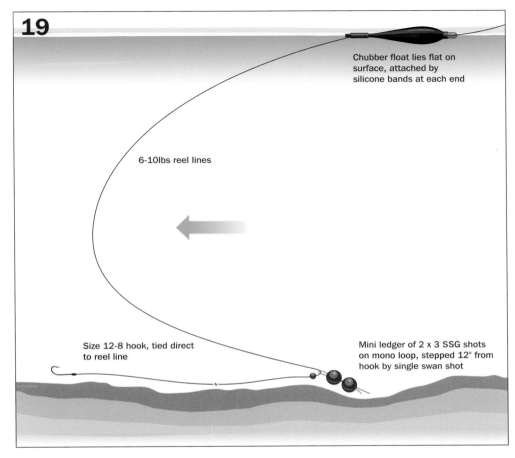

19

Chubber float lies flat on surface, attached by silicone bands at each end

6-10lbs reel lines

Size 12-8 hook, tied direct to reel line

Mini ledger of 2 x 3 SSG shots on mono loop, stepped 12" from hook by single swan shot

subsurface bow in the line between float and link-ledger. You simply set the float, a Chubber, Avon or large Balsa, fixed with silicon tubing at both ends, at least twice the depth of the swim (keep pushing it up the line till the set-up works) and cast directly downstream. *See Diagram.*

20 The secret of stret-pegging, once the mini ledger (in slow swims a single swan shot is sufficient) has anchored the bait to the bottom, is in allowing a little loose line, for the subsurface 'bow' to form and the float to settle 'lying flat', before placing the rod in two rests with the tip angled up a little. The float should now be swaying gently from side to side in the current, (literally any speed water may be fished in this way so long as your float is set far enough over depth) and when a fish takes the bait, it will cock and glide positively under all in one. A lovely sight to see, not only when barbel fishing, because any bottom-feeding river fish may be caught stret-pegging. *See Carp Tip 13.*

21 Though float fishing, the close-in technique of stret-pegging is best executed using a 11-12 foot Avon style rod, rather than a lighter 'waggler' rod.

maggots to keep loose feeding till all the lesser fish are literally full up, by keeping a steady stream going through the swim, either by throwing in maggots by hand or depositing them straight down to the bottom of really fast runs through continual use of a bait dropper. In small rivers a gallon of maggots is not excessive, while in rivers twice the size, you'll need twice as many maggots. But eventually, and it may take an hour or two, those barbel will be the only fish still munching maggots. Then you could clean up. And in clear-flowing swims where the fish are plainly visible, even select a particular specimen and watch it hoover in your bunch of maggots.

19 If you're planning to catch barbel from a deep, even-paced run close into the bank, then why not anchor your bait to the river bed using a mini link-ledger, but have a float to watch on the surface. This devastatingly

effective rig is called 'stret-pegging' and allows you to watch a float (which must lie flat on the surface) due to the exaggerated

20

Bream

Bream

1 Want to catch bream on the float that are feeding over weed or amongst 'cabbages' in still or slow moving water? Then 'float ledgering' is often the answer, using a peacock quill waggler float (attached with silicon tubing around the bottom end - not locked with shot) and set a foot or two over depth. But not with a small bomb stopped several inches from the hook by a small shot. This would drag the bait and hook length into the weed and minimize bites. Far better to use a 20-30 inch (depending upon weed density and height) 'weight link', joined to the reel line 20-24 inches above the hook using a 'four-turn water knot'. And simply pinch 2-3 large swan shot onto the end of the link. Don't worry about the float's actual shotting capacity.

2 Use buoyant baits when float-ledgering, like bread flake or crust, which will lie on top of the weed, and remember to angle the rod top upwards in a flow, in order to ensure that minimal line is on the surface, which will stop the float tip from pulling under. But when your rig is settled on the bottom, you can tighten

up so that only a small part of the tip is showing. Bites are registered by the float tip simply disappearing positively, though occasionally by it rising, if a bream 'lifts' the shots from the weed. Works well for tench, and carp too.

3 Rather than wait for 'difficult to miss' slammers which rarely materialize when quiver-tip ledgering rivers for winter bream, (summer fish are entirely different), be prepared to strike at any 'strange' movement on the tip. Keep

the rod angled up high (on two rests) to alleviate excess current pressure against the reel line, and you'll find that 'just' holding bottom (and this is the secret) with a couple or three 3x swan shot, is possible in the strongest flow.

4 'Drop-back' indications are often the bites to look for when quiver-tipping for bream, where the tip suddenly and seemingly without reason, momentarily 'eases' or 'jerks' back because the shots have slightly moved due to a bream inhaling the

bait. Forward pulls and vibratory pulses of the tip are also worth hitting, but those 'drop-backs' will put far more bream in your net. So juggle about with the amount of shots on your ledger link, ensuring that they only 'just' hold bottom. Anything more or less, is a bite.

5 The silver bream is in British waters extremely rare, and mainly confined to East Anglia and the Midlands. This decidedly 'delicate-looking' fish takes most small baits used for roach and rudd and prefers still and slow moving waters. It lacks the thick covering of mucus associated with common bream, and the scales are quite large and noticeably 'silvery', hence its name. It has a small head, large eyes and less of a protrusible mouth than common bream. When erect the silver bream's dorsal fin is unusually high, and its pectoral, pelvic and anal fins (unlike the common bream) show a tinge of orangey-pink, rather similar to the dace.

6 When 'slider-float' fishing for bream in deep, still waters, always use a 'bodied-waggler' float carrying more shot than would seem necessary. This is to ensure the reel line passes freely through the float's eye or ring, quickly taking the bait down to the bottom. Bulk most of the shot (against which the float will rest for casting) 3-4 feet above the bait, with two small shots in between, the lowest positioned 6-10 inches from the hook actually resting on the bottom. Using several inches of slightly 'finer' line, tie a five turn stop knot onto the reel line above the float at the desired depth for bait presentation, leaving both ends 1-1½ inches long, ensuring they 'fold' when passing through the rod rings. If the float's bottom ring or eye allows the stop knot to slip through, use a tiny (2-3mm) bead between it and the knot.

7 Remember always to dip the rod tip immediately after casting when slider-float fishing, and wind like crazy for a few turns, in order to ensure all

the line sinks between float and rod tip to counter act any sub-surface draw, and quickly open the reel's bale arm allowing line to peel freely from the spool and eventually through the float's bottom ring till the bait touches bottom and the float cocks. Lastly, remember to strike 'sideways' in order to pull the line 'through' the water and the hook into the bream, as opposed to losing striking power by trying to 'lift' the line 'against' surface tension; which is next to impossible!

8 When distance ledgering for big, still-water bream, hitting bites is always a problem. Taking a leaf from the carp angler's book however by incorporating a mini-shock, or 'bolt rig' into your end tackle, will result in those bream actually pulling a small hook into themselves. Method feeders with internal elastic are much favoured, (which alleviates snap-offs) to which a short 4-5 inch hook length of 10lbs test soft braid is tied with a size 12 or 10 hook on the business end. As for reel line, due to the long casting of a heavy ball of bait, do not go below 8lbs test.

9 The bait for distance ledgering for bream like a 10mm boilie, pellet, or three grains of corn etc, is then hair-rigged, and immediately prior to casting a ball of 'method-mix ground bait' (to which hempseed, corn, casters and chopped worms etc, have been added) is firmly moulded around the feeder, with the hook bait carefully hidden inside. After casting to the desired spot, (use a marker float cast out using another rod - so all the bait ends up within a relatively small area), the line is tightened up, and a heavy, 'swinger type' bite indicator clipped onto the line (on a short drop) in front of the bite alarm, so that should a bream swim towards the rod, the indicator will fall and indicate a drop-back bite.

10 When fishing the 'waggler' for bream in still water, one of the most common problems is avoiding the 'drift'. So here are three tips for beating it. Start by sloshing a finger full of washing up liquid around the line on your reel's spool, which will quickly sink the line. Second, use a really long,

Bream

straight peacock waggler with a bulk shot capacity of at least four to five SSG shots so all the locking shots are well beneath the surface and below the 'top drifting layer'. And lastly, fish over depth with one or two No 6 or 8 shots dragging along the bottom, which acts like a 'brake' to help keep the bait in position.

11 Feeder fishing for bream in still waters usually revolves around incorporating a clear plastic open-end or cage-type swim feeder made from wire mesh, into your ledger rig. A 'fixed paternoster' tied using a four turn water knot is best for this. And 'plugging' as it is often called, is the secret to this method, because you don't want feed coming out on the cast and baiting up areas you're not fishing. Start by pressing one end of your feeder into the ground bait mix (not over-dampened) gently pressing the ground bait inside to block that end. Then put in some loose feed, sweet corn, casters, finely chopped worm etc, but leave enough room at the opposite end for another plug of ground bait. Finally, squeeze tightly at both

ends using thumb and forefinger, immediately before casting, and providing you have not 'over-wetted' the ground bait, the feeder will explode its contents ONLY when it reaches the lake bottom.

12 When standard ledgering or feeder fishing for bream in both still and running water, regardless of whether you use a swing tip, a quiver tip or a hanging bobbin-type indicator, a 'running' ledger is not required. The simple 'fixed paternoster' is the best rig by far, and to make one simply tie an 8-10 inch length of line (could be reel line or thicker) onto your mainline using a four turn water knot. This forms the 'link' to which shots, bomb or feeder are attached. For feeders and bombs add a tiny snap swivel to facilitate quick changing. How far up the line from the hook you tie this link depends on whether you are presenting a 'static' bait, or are hoping to encourage bites 'on the drop'. For the latter, start with a tail of around 4-5 feet. For static baits 18-24 inches is ideal. If you wish to use a hook tail of a lighter breaking strain than your reel

line, for a more natural presentation of say slowly falling baits like casters and maggots, then simply tie this, again using the four turn water knot, say 10 inches from the end of your mainline, which itself then becomes the 'ledger link'. *See Diagram.*

13 When ledgering in still and slow moving rivers for bream, quiver tip and bobbin-type bite indicators are not only more commonly used than the 'swing-tip', but they are more versatile. The trouble with swing tips, though unbelievably sensitive, is that they wobble about too much when trying to cast any reasonable distance, causing the mainline to wrap around the rod tip and tangle. Swing tips do however have one redeeming feature, and that is showing the difference between line bites and true bites. 'Liners' cause the tip to twitch and jiggle about in short, sharp lifts. Whereas with true bites, the tip continues to rise until it points directly at the bream. Or, should the bream swim towards the rod, thus moving the lead or feeder, the tip simply 'falls back' dramatically. So in certain circumstances,

To initiate bites on the drop – make hook link 4-5" long and use slow sinking baits (casters etc..)

8-10" ledger link

Add a tiny snap swivel for quick changing feeders

especially for short to medium range ledgering, there is still good reason for using a swing tip indicator.

14 When feeder fishing for bream in shallow still waters, say less than six foot deep, put your faith in plastic or wire mesh 'cage-feeders' which ensure that the ground bait filling 'explodes' quickly and easily, forming an attractive cloud that doesn't spook the fish. But you don't want this to happen if ledgering a 20 foot deep swim in Ireland's fast flowing River Shannon, where a large, open end, clear, plastic feeder will retain the bait as it sinks and release only with impact with the river bed. Remember. Fishing is 'horses for courses'.

15 If you are distance-ledgering a still water that requires constant baiting with ground bait balls, add a few drops of oil-based liquid 'additive' to your feeder mix on the next cast, to leave a 'slick' on the surface, as a target for aiming your ground bait.

16 To catch big bream on 'static' baits that are situated within pole range in both wide, deep rivers (6-20 foot plus) and smaller, deep and fast flowing rivers, consider a 'Polaris' slider float set up. The wire-stemmed 'Polaris' slides on the 4-5lbs running line

(pinch a small shot at mid depth against which it rests while being shipped out) and automatically locks like magic (via the 'Frixon' device at the floats base) at the desired depth once the one ounce bomb has settled. Use a four turn water knot to attach a 12 inch hook link five inches above the bomb, and pinch on a tiny shot five inches above the hook to keep the bait anchored to the river bed.

17 If quiver-tip ledgering for bream in large, open waters remember that during extremely windy conditions, there will be a considerable 'subsurface tow' caused by the waves hitting one end of the lake which subsequently forces surface water down, and back up the lake. So for maximum line pick up on the strike, sit parallel to the bank actually facing wind direction, and make sweeping, sideways strikes.

18 You never know when you might be wanting to slider-float fish for bream in excessively deep still water, so always keep a few 'Polaris' floats in your box. Setting up these 'self-locking' floats is easy. Thread your reel line down through one of the two holes in the tubular 'Frixon' locking device at the bottom, and make up a fixed

paternoster end rig incorporating either a bomb or feeder rig. The small hole accommodates lines in the 3-6lbs range and the larger, heavier lines. Then pinch on a No 1 shot three feet up the line for the float to rest against when casting. It is imperative not to use less weight in the terminal set up than is recommended, otherwise the float's buoyancy will only drag the bait along the bottom when you try to tighten up.

19 Float ledgering using a 'Polaris' is the best way of beating that eternal problem experienced when ledgering for bream line bites. But because of the enormous 'right angle' of line that exists between bait and rod tip once the float has automatically 'locked', setting large hooks at distance can prove troublesome. So use smaller hooks and smaller baits when fishing the 'Polaris' and if you do inexplicably miss bites, try winding in fast for a couple of seconds before lifting the rod into a strike. This will effectively take up that slack line.

20 Having trouble getting the specimen-sized bream of rich and clear water lakes or pits to pick up your baits during daylight hours? Then simply fish for them during darkness when they naturally feed more ravenously.

Carp

1 One of the most simplistic and, consequently, most delightful ways of catching carp (any sized carp) at close range, is fishing the 'lift-method' with 4-6 inches of peacock quill attached bottom end only with a sleeve of silicon tubing, (locking shots result in the line breaking should a carp plunge through weeds), set slightly over depth. Using a reel line of around 8-10lbs test, with a single swan shot pinched on 5-6 inches above a size 10-8 hook, completes the rig. Bait can be pellets, maize or small boilies, hair rigged, with loose feed of the same or smaller, pellets or particles. The permutations are like carp fishing itself: endless.

2 When fishing the 'lift', the rod is best supported (no rod rests are used for this technique) beneath the forearm and rested upon your knee, after an 'underarm-flick' cast is made several feet further out than you have introduced 'loose-feed'. This is for good reason, because you need to quickly wind the rig back (with the float well clear of the surface) so the exposed hook does not catch up on bottom debris, or the shot bump into feeding carp, before allowing it to settle on the bottom directly amongst the loose feed. Gently tighten the line so the float is 'all but cocking' and wait, whilst holding the rod throughout. Line bites will make the float sway and jerk, almost dipping it under at times, as the tails or pectoral fins of carp momentarily catch the line. One reason why I like the float lying 'flat'. 'Lift bites' will still be recognizable however, whenever a carp 'lifts' the single shot up, by the float suddenly 'drifting' as though someone has cut the line with a pair of scissors. But most bites will consist of the float suddenly 'cocking and disappearing' all in one motion…lovely!

3 A 'marker-float' outfit is required whenever you intend distance casting to an area that has been pre-baited for carp (works for tench and bream

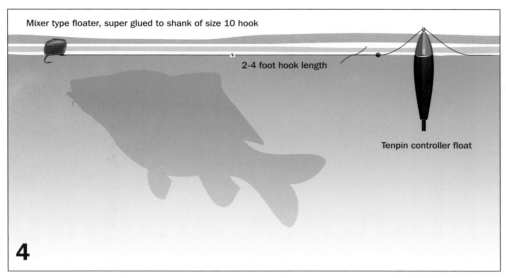

Mixer type floater, super glued to shank of size 10 hook

2-4 foot hook length

Tenpin controller float

4

fish, simply cut a shallow groove in the bait using a junior hacksaw blade, and super-glue along the hook shank. Once you have mastered this technique, very rarely will a bait come off during the hardest of casts. I even glue my pellet or biscuit floaters on when 'fly-rodding' for carp using powerful 'double-haul' casting.

6 Both clear and brown-coloured latex rubber 'bait bands', most of which come with a small, built-in dimple tab at the top through which the hook point is passed, are another excellent way of quickly attaching square-shaped floaters to your hook. Being tough and flexible, they come in varying sizes to accommodate virtually any sized floater.

7 At some time or another everyone is faced with the difficult task of extracting hooked carp out of lilies. The secret if there is one, and this works for me, is to watch carefully where your line actually goes into the pads, which we'll assume for argument's sake are both thick and extensive. Because you need to get the rod tip down low for some 'side-strain' hauling, following the exact 'angle' at which the carp is heading. And continue pulling with the rod nicely bent, in that direction till it is 'hauled' back, changing direction accordingly with your angle of pull each time the carp moves position. It is a strange but very effective technique. Obviously you need an all-through action rod that bends in harmony with the stretch in your line for this. It's simply no good heaving away with the rod held straight up high and fully bent if the fish has gone straight into the lilies and turned sharp right, winding the line at an acute angle around a clump of stems. The torque upon your tackle is immense. But steady and continual pressure from the right angle, will surprisingly, extract the largest of fish. One reason why I endeavour only to float fish or free line when tackling 'lily-bed carp'. The less on the line in the way of rigs, leads, tubing, anti-tangle this and anti-tangle that, the better. And as my float (a few inches of peacock quill) is

too) using a spod or radio-controlled boat. In fact, exploring with the marker float outfit is the very first task. Use an entirely separate outfit (to your fishing rods) such as a long 12-13 foot powerful carp or pike rod, a heavy (3-5 ounce) lead and a 30-50lbs test braided reel line. Simply thread a large rubber bead onto the end of your braided line, followed by the lead (which should have a large-swivelled eye) and another bead, and tie to the bottom ring of your marker float. Be sure to use one that incorporates a large, vane-type top that can easily be seen at a distance. After making an exploratory cast, if your rod 'locks-up' as you try to drag the lead back along the bottom, then you have located a weed bed. If you feel no resistance as the lead is being wound back, then you have found a weed-free area, with the bottom consisting of sand, mud or silt. If however you feel a little 'knocking' transmitted through the rod, your lead will be dragging over stones or a gravel bar. So select your 'fishing ground' and once the float is settled as a marker for both casting to and baiting up, sink all the line between float and rod tip by attaching a heavy 'back lead' close into the bank. With your entire marker float line now ironed to the bottom and the rod tip dunked below the surface and out of the way, you should not catch up on it throughout the session. And it can be simply wound in when you leave.

4 If you love catching carp off the top using small floating baits like mixer biscuits and floating pellets etc, here's a useful tip which allows you to quickly change from a 'floating controller' set up geared to fishing distances of up to 50 yards, to just the plain hook, for those times when fish move in ridiculously close, and you merely wish to suspend the floater directly below the rod tip, free-line style. Start by threading onto your 8-12lbs reel line a floating controller such as a 'Tenpin', followed by a 3mm, black, rubber bead, and then tie a five turn stop knot (using a few inches of reel line) before tying on a size 10 hook direct to the reel line 2-4 feet below the Tenpin. *See Diagram.* To quickly 'de-rig', simply work the rubber bead over the stop knot and all the way along the hook's shank and off the point, followed by the swivel at the top of the Tenpin. This literally takes seconds, and you are left with the bare hook. Repeat to be fishing with the controller again. Obviously, this can only be achieved when using a small 'rubber' bead. *See Rudd Tip 7, for fishing 'lighter'.*

5 To present small floaters to carp like mixer biscuits, sunflower seeds, floating pellets or even small boilies etc, use a small, but strong hook (a size 10 is ideal and will land the biggest carp) and so that it sits immediately 'below' the floater where it is less inhibitive to a 'taking'

Carp

always attached with a sleeve of silicon tubing, it immediately comes off as a fish enters the pads, as does the large single shot lightly pinched onto the line several inches from the hook.

8 Whether ledgering for carp at close or long range, due to varying bottom contours over which your line is bound to hang, 'line bites' can at times, prove a real problem, making the carp even more wary as they approach your bait. To alleviate this simply clip a 'back-lead' to your line immediately in front of the rod tip after casting and let it slide down to the bottom, thus pinning the line down between ledger rig and rod. Remember however, that this only works when employing 'bolt-rig' tactics where due to the weight of the lead, the fish more or less hooks itself.

9 For stalking summer carp, when carrying the very minimum of tackle invariably results in more fish on the bank simply because you haven't scared the fish away from the margins, it's worth investing in a 'stalking belt'. Designed to be worn around the waist with a variety of pockets at the side and at the rear, these 'bum-bag' type belts are capable of holding scales, a compact camera, baits, plus hooks, floats, shot and rig bits etc, leaving you free, clutching just rod and net, to crawl stealthily through dense vegetation in order to creep up on the whoppers slurping amongst the tree roots.

10 When the carp inhabiting large sheets of deep still water are cruising in the warm upper layers, sometimes topping, sometimes a few feet below, seemingly aimlessly moving about, one technique that can really sort them out is the 'Zig-rig' which on a size 8 hook, is used to present a small, rectangular, hair-rigged piece of buoyant cork, about the size of a mixer biscuit ('yes' cork!) at any depth from the surface to several feet down. It resembles a pop-up boilie or imitation floater like a

10

Start with cork bait suspended 2 feet below surface

Rectangular (mixersize) piece of cork, hair rigged

Size 8 hook and 10-15lbs reel line

Clear plastic subfloat

3-4 ounce running lead

Semi-fixed 3-4 ounce lead

mixer biscuit, and is, believe it or not, readily taken. The rig comprises of a heavy in-line, semi-fixed 3-4 ounce lead, through which the mainline passes before it is attached, via the swivel, to hook a length anything up to (assuming you are casting with 12 foot rods) 12 feet long, (you're fishing deep water remember), which means that the imitation, buoyant cork bait can be presented two feet below the surface (by far the best 'taking' distance) in a maximum of 14 foot of water. After casting, putting the rod in its rest and tightening up, hang a weighted swinger-type bobbin on the line and be ready for strange,

'drop-back' bites which sometimes just keep dropping. But do not strike yet. Wait for the fish to pull the indicator up tight before setting the hook. A most 'versatile' variation to this set up is to use a 3-4 ounce 'running lead' with a rubber 'cushioning' bead between lead and a buoyant, plastic sub-float. To the opposite end of the sub-float tie on a two foot hook length and hair-rigged cork bait already described. Then upon the lead settling on the bottom, free line is slowly given till the sub-float and floating bait pop up to the surface. Now slowly wind till the sub-float disappears, adding just four feet of line to the reel, if you wish the cork to be presented two feet below the surface. But it can of course be fished at any depth from two feet above bottom upwards, all the way to the surface. And there are days when it pays to experiment. So clip on an indicator and set the bite alarm. If bites do not materialize, slowly wind the sub-float and bait down to four, six or eight feet, and so on below the surface until a 'taking' depth is found. Most fish will hook themselves whilst moving off against the buoyancy of the sub-float, and give screaming runs.

11 Here's a handy tip for presenting your bait using a 'bolt-rig' set up to carp amongst dense weed beds when you have no option. Firstly step up your reel line breaking strain accordingly, and match it to a powerful 'all-through' action rod, which collapses into a 'full bend' and absorbs all the lunges of a big carp thrashing and crashing through weed beds. For the best presentation of your rig and bait, everything needs to be tucked away carefully into a clear PVA bag including a 2-3 ounce lead (to get you easily through the weed) plus some loose feed like small pellets etc, (secure the top of the bag using PVA string or tape, so that after casting through the weed and the bag dissolves, both hook bait and freebies are in plain view and nothing is 'hung-up'). Lastly, don't go far from your rod. It actually needs to be to hand, in order that you can respond immediately to a bite by bending into a fish and hauling it around before it travels too far.

12 Contrary to popular belief fuelled by the hype of 'pre-made' bait manufacturers, plain old 'maggots' are one of the most effective of all baits to catch carp. Trouble is, when used in ones, twos and threes, maggots are not SELECTIVE, and just about every fish in every water, from a two inch roach upwards, love them. The answer therefore is to present a real 'mouthful' if you only want to catch larger species like carp. And a method devised exactly to this end, is the 'Korda maggot clip'. A cunning device that permits dozens of maggots to be threaded onto a fine wire ring without bursting any of them, which in turn is then attached (via a quick-change clip) to the loop of a 'hair-rig'. You can even add slithers of rig foam cut to the shape and size of maggots should you wish to present your bunch of maggots 'pop-up' style above bottom weed. Clever, isn't it?

13 With more and more carp these days making their way into British river systems from adjacent gravel pit fisheries during flood time, including some 'whoppers', do you fancy catching them on the float in running water? Well, then the technique of stret-pegging is simply unbeatable. And you don't need heavy tackle either. Stret-pegging in rivers is a 'close-range' method, so a heavy Avon-style rod coupled to a centre pin or fixed spool reel holding 8-10lbs test monofilament is quite adequate. Fix onto the reel line several feet deeper than the swim, (with a band of silicone tubing at each end) an 8-10 inch straight waggler float, or unpainted length

13

of peacock quill. It matters not because they are the same thing really. Ten to 12 inches above your hook (all baits and hair-rig options are open here) pinch on a single SSG shot, and above this fold a short length of mono (could be reel line) and secure as a 'running ledger' by securing with two or three 3X SSG shot, leaving enough gap so the 'mini-ledger' can slide up the line. Now, cast the rig directly downstream over your baited area, and once the rig has touched bottom, allow a little slack for the float to come around and lay 'flat'. If it doesn't, push it further up the line till it does lay flat. Angle the rod on two rests with the tip pointing upwards and wait for events. From swaying gently in the current, the float will suddenly cock and slide under, all in one glorious moment. *See Diagram in Barbel Tip 19.*

14 Should you witness the sad sight of a freshly killed, partly eaten carp lying up on the bank or in the margins of your local fishery, (as shown in the accompanying photo here, it was unfortunately from my own two-lake fishery) then inform the owner immediately. Such devastation is caused by otters released into a river environment where due to cormorant predation upon silver shoal fishes combined with a much reduced annual run of eels, during the

winter months especially, they roam far and wide (up to 10 miles from their home) to enjoy the easy pickings of carp stocked into still water lakes and pits, because the rivers are bare.

15 Contrary to popular belief, whilst otters may be perceived by the public as cute and cuddly, they are in fact indiscriminate killers, which during the warmer months in addition to feeding upon frogs, toads and the spawn of both, plus newts and the eggs and young of moorhens and mallards (they also take the adult birds

incidentally) when pickings are scarce in the winter, they maul or actually kill (though they never consume the entire carcass) specimen-sized carp weighing far heavier than themselves. Otters have in fact been responsible for killing carp to over 40lbs up and down the country.

16 When stalking for carp around really 'overgrown' lakes and pits or rivers, don't put pressure upon yourself by carting around the typical 'session-type' landing net comprising of a short pole and large, 42-45 inch arm, triangular net. Not only will it get easily tangled up whilst creeping about, beaten carp cannot always be hauled in close enough. A strong, telescopic pole however, allows you to net fish that cannot be hauled close in through weed or lilies for a big net, and with a lightweight 24-30 inch round or spoon-shaped (deep-mesh) net on the end, you can capture fish of up to at least 40lbs when they lay beaten beyond the snags and marginal screen.

17 For targeting carp off the top when a fair amount of loose-fed floaters will get used during a lengthy session, invest in a 'bucket-organiser'. Mine has two strips of Velcro around the sides to which an organizer wallet is quickly fixed. This holds spare

hooks, floating controllers, hair needles, mini hacksaw blades, super-glue and scissors etc, while the bucket itself contains several pints of mixers or floating pellets, plus catapult, and a few tubs of 'alternative' hook baits.

18 When hair-rigging with particles, pellets or boilies, remember, (it takes but a few seconds) by using your thumb nail, to press the Dumbell-type, hard plastic hair stop completely into the bait so that it is hidden. With hard pellets, simply scrape out a depression with the end of your hair needle. Carp (and barbel) have been purposefully-equipped with four ultra sensitive barbels which have minute sensory taste-pads on the end, in order to probe through gravel, sand and into deep silt to locate small, soft items of natural food. And if a carp can locate items such as midge larva, 'bloodworms' by feeling them with its barbel-tips, it is quite capable of reacting to hard, alien objects like a hair stop, and possibly refuse your bait as a result.

19 There is a clear case for wearing shorts and a pair of old shoes or trainers when stalking summer carp amongst lilies and from amongst the branches of partly submerged trees. You can then quickly get in there to apply pressure from a different angle or to untangle a snagged fish, which you might otherwise lose, without second thought.

20 To suit all your carping (tench and barbel) rig requirements during the summer ahead, tie up a selection of eyed hooks of varying sizes, each with varying length hairs to accommodate a variety of bait combinations. Use a soft Dacron or braid for the hair and after forming the loop using an overhand knot, tie on using my spade-end 'barrel' knot, *(see Hooks and Rigs Tip 8)* adding a spot of super glue beneath the whipping so they do not slide up and down the hook shank.

18

Crucian Carp and Grass Carp

Crucian Carp and Grass Carp

1 With massive introductions of king carp and carp hybrids to a large proportion of still water fisheries in the UK during the last 20 years, particularly 'commercial fisheries' as they are known, finding waters containing true crucian carp is now exceedingly difficult.

2 Most 'thought to be' record crucian carp submitted to the British Record Fish Committee, are in fact found, on close inspection, to be either crucian/king carp crosses (paler, slimmer fish than true crucians with tiny barbels, sometimes referred to as F1 carp) or brown gold fish/ king carp/ or crucian crosses.

3 True crucian carp do not of course have barbels and rarely exceed 5lbs in weight. But they do have a slightly upturned mouth, are extremely deep-bodied, with rounded fins (which are an even, warm, grey-brown colour) and are distinctly 'buttery-bronze' in colour with flat-lying scales. If the fish you catch do not conform to all these characteristics, then consider them not to be true crucian carp.

4 As crucian carp need to almost stand on their heads (just like a tench) to inhale a bottom fished bait such as

sweet corn or bread flake, pinching on a small shot somewhere (it pays to experiment till bites become positive) between one and two inches from the hook, and to strike when the float tip 'lifts' momentarily. A scaled-down lift-float rig as used for tench (which are equipped with

identical, slightly upturned mouths) using a smaller float, less shot and smaller hooks, is the way to catch the often 'shy-biting' crucian. Bites do not always take the float under.

5 Looking very much like a chub in the water *(see Chub Tip 6)* grass carp are immediately told apart by their low-set eyes, and dark grey anal fin. They characteristically 'hover' differently too, just beneath the surface on warm days with their head slightly upwards. And most importantly, in so far as the angler is concerned, they have a much smaller mouth.

6 Grass carp do not aggressively engulf their food like a chub. When seen sucking in small floaters from the surface they make a point of always 'pursing' the bait momentarily between their lips, before sucking it back a second later. So never be in too much of a hurry to strike. If through clear water you can observe your bait in the fish's lips, always wait until it totally disappears.

Crucian Carp and Grass Carp

They will therefore not hybridize with other carps or ever 'over-run' a fishery. Moreover, because they feed on vast quantities of soft plant tissue and do not compete directly with king carp, both can reach specimen sizes in the same fishery. What could be better?

8 Originating from lowland rivers in China such as the Amur, the fertilized eggs of grass carp need to float along the surface of running water at a temperature in excess of 65°F for many miles to stand any chance of hatching. Which is hardly likely in the UK.

9 Though fishing 'punched bread' is normally thought of as a winter technique for clear water canals, during the summer months it is deadly for the shy biting crucian carp. Use a 13 foot light, fine tipped stick float rod, dot the float tip right down, and using size 18-14 hooks, nick on small pieces of fresh white bread, removed from a medium slice with a bread punch head (most punches come with four or five different diameter screw-

7 Here's a tip for fishery owners. Grass carp are the perfect fish for stocking into British waters, because they can not reproduce in our temperate climate. So what you stock (less predatory losses) is exactly what you end up with.

Crucian Carp and Grass Carp

15

on heads)of the appropriate size. To complement punched bread on the hook, loose feed with 'liquidized bread' on the 'little and often' basis.

10 Vastly more effective than rod fishing, is to 'pole fish' using a light float rig to create a slow, natural fall of the bread during those last few inches above bottom. Shot the float right down to the merest 'blimp' so you can pull into the slightest sign of a bite.

11 Next to catfish and pike, grass carp are, pound for pound, the UK's longest freshwater species. How long will a 20lbs fish be? Possibly over three feet in length. Anything over 40lbs could measure four feet plus. Monsters of over five feet and

weighing over 100lbs have been recorded in Europe, Africa and Asia.

12 Be most careful when handling grass carp out of the water. They are renowned for continually jumping and flapping about on the bank, often with more vigour than during the fight. So play each one till it is exhausted before heaving out and then cover securely with the wet mesh of your net till the hook has been removed.

13 When grass carp can be seen just beneath the surface or are suspected in the upper water layers but cannot be tempted to suck in a floater from the surface film, present a buoyant bait such as a pop-up boilie or floating pellet, bread crust even, (don't use

anything larger than size 8-10 hooks) suspended between one and two feet below the surface. A scaled-down 'Zig-rig' *(see Carp Tip 10)* is perfect for this situation. Use a 'two rod' set up and try altering depths at which each bait is suspended, by recasting every half hour or so until a bite materializes.

14 Where the crucian carp of small, pea-green ponds and commercial fisheries average on the small side (say up to a pound in weight) it's great fun catching them in real close using just the top three or four joints of a lightweight pole or 'Whip', with a running line of say 2lbs test tied directly to the Whip's end ring. Their 'dogged' fighting capabilities are more appreciated without pole elastic to suppress and cushion their

Crucian Carp and Grass Carp

runs, and will give your forearm a good workout. Use an ultra light float rig and shoot the bristle tip down to a mere 'whisker' in the surface film before accurately plummeting depth immediately below the tip of the Whip. Feed in maggots on the 'little' and 'often' basis (half a dozen around the float with every cast) after first introducing a few maggot-laced balls of cereal ground bait to concentrate a shoal of fish, and present a single maggot on a size 18 to 22 to a 1½lbs test hook length, exactly half an inch above the bottom.

15 Take a trophy photo of your big grass carp immediately after unhooking when it is at its most knackered. Hold it horizontally between your two hands, its head towards you not the water, 'upside down', yes 'upside down' (which immobilizes most fish incidentally) all ready for the photo and only turn it the right way up, once you are in position, a second before the shutter is released. Don't be tempted to let it recover in a sack or tube. Or you'll never be able to hold it still long enough for a photo.

16 Adding a single caster to your maggot hook bait, often makes crucians 'hang-on' that much longer. Also worth trying is half a red worm.

17 At all costs do not try and catch crucian carp by ledgering. Due to their gentle feeding routine and sensitivity to resistance, you'll not even see most of the bites, let alone hit them, regardless of what indicator is used.

18 Crucian carp when feeding from the bottom, can be told apart from king carp varieties even when they cannot be seen simply by observing their 'feeding bubbles'. Those of even quite sizeable crucians for instance, rise gently to the surface in small clusters of just 4-6 bubbles tightly grouped together, which do not burst, compared with those of

the king carp that are much larger, and which can be seen to burst after literally 'erupting' in the surface film.

19 As sweet corn is arguably one of the top hook baits for catching crucian carp, if you are uncertain about baits when tackling new crucian water, float fish corn with one large kernel on a size 14 hook, after adding the juices from the tin to some brown breadcrumbs to make a ground bait. Add a handful of 'squashed corn kernels' to the mix and feed on the 'little yet often' principle, keeping in mind that crucians are small carp.

20 Big, old specimen-sized crucian carp of say 2lbs and upwards can become extremely cagey if regularly fished for. The secret to catching them is to fish into darkness and well into the night, using the 'lift-method' *(see Tip 4)* with a 'luminous' chemical element sleeved onto a length of slim peacock quill attached bottom end only. Hold your rod throughout, ready to strike instantly as the float keels over flat. Some bites however will simply take the float under, sometimes quite fast, as the crucian characteristically 'runs' along the bottom with your bait. Bread flake, corn or worm are great 'after dark' offerings for big crucians.

Catfish (Wels)

1 For those wishing to land 100lbs-plus Wels catfish, the junction of where the River Segre joins the mighty River Ebro in the town of Mequinenza in North Eastern Spain is unrivalled. A two hour flight from Luton to Barcelona, followed by a two hour westerly drive from the airport to Mequinenza, gets you there. Contact The Bavarian Guiding Service whose offices and accommodation are adjacent to the river. Their website is: www.spanish-catfish-ebro.com and for email enquiries: mike@spanish-catfish-ebro.com

2 For impromptu sessions after catfish (or pike, eels and carp etc - any fish where 'positive' runs are expected to the method being used) if the banks are nicely flat to the water, or if the swim is too difficult for bank sticks, being fronted by stagings or a wall etc, then make your own 'bite alarm platform', simply by drilling and gluing the top two inches(hacksaw them

off) from a couple of old bank sticks into a 12 x 4 x ¾ thick piece of ply or softwood. These are placed eight inches apart, into which a couple of bite alarms are screwed. Should you require 'rear' rests, then add rod rest tops (an inch or two higher) to another wooden platform. These take up

far less room in your tackle bag than a collapsible 'rod-pod'.

3 Want to catch the hardest fighting freshwater species on this planet? Then the legendary Mekong catfish which has been netted to over 600lbs but is

thought to reach weights in excess of 1000lbs is the adversary awaiting you in Thailand. Specimens up to 200lbs are purposefully stocked into many of Thailand's 'commercial' still-water fisheries, where they have been weaned onto and are readily catchable on simple baits like bread. The most prolific of Thailand's 'Mekong' fisheries is famous Bung Sam Ran near Bangkok. For guiding details contact: info@kiwifishingbangkok.com.

4 Whether fishing at home or abroad for tropical freshwater catfish, all catfish (including Wels catfish) quickly home in on the 'blood content' of baits whether freshly killed meat, fish or fowl. Chicken heads for instance, (yes beak and all, catfish don't worry about the bird's head when sucking down a duckling or moorhen from the surface) and their livers make fine baits. As do the heads of freshly killed pigeon, partridge and pheasant. All plucked of course. Simply present by hooking once only through the gristle using a size 3/0-6/0 hook (depending upon the size of catfish expected) and either ledger or free line.

5 If you have a buddy who shoots regularly, or you shoot yourself, a supply of plucked heads can be frozen away during the shooting season which ends in February, for use throughout the summer months. Other 'hot' catfish baits, for the Wels especially, are live and freshly killed eels, trout and small tench, with chunks of mackerel or squid topping the endless possibilities of sea baits. And of course when used together with a pre-baiting plan, of regularly loose feeding halibut pellets into British still water fisheries, the same large 20-30mm sized pellets presented anywhere from two to six up on a long hair rig, (use a 'daisy-chain' when offering 'several' pellets, to deter carp from getting hooked) have proved to be one of the most effective catfish baits of all.

6 To find out where you can fish for Wels catfish within the UK, contact the Catfish Conservation Group, who not only control cat fisheries for their members, they list all still waters in the UK that contain the species. Their website is: www.catfishconservationgroup.com.

7 Offal, readily available from your local butcher makes fine and exceptionally cheap bait for catfish. An ox heart for instance, which is getting on for the size of a rugby ball will separate down into between 8-12 blood-filled chunks, while a pig's heart makes two great offerings. And of course the kidneys and liver of both animals are prime 'pussy-food'. Though significantly smaller, sheep's offal works well too.

Catfish (Wels)

8

drilled halibut pellets or soft baits like liver or squid, when normal boilie-type stops are simply too small.

11 By purchasing baby squid (calamari) in bulk, say several boxes at a time, from your local fishmonger or tackle specialist, there is no more economical way of ensuring throughout the summer months that you have enough suitable bait for both hook baits and loose feeding.

12 Presenting 5-8 inch live baits (rudd work well) just beneath the surface, especially during the hours of darkness, (using the 'Dumbell Rig') is one of the most effective ways of catching Wels catfish. As can be seen from the *Diagram*, after sleeving onto your reel line a 3-4 ounce lead followed by a large rubber bead, the line is threaded through a 'Dumbell Float' and a small but strong swivel is tied on. Presentation is improved if the swivel pushes firmly into the end of the 'Dumbell Float', thus making it semi-fixed. Lastly, add several inches of 'Catlink' braided trace material of 50-70lbs test and tie on a 2-3/0 hook, making sure the hook trace is slightly shorter than the length of the float, so that after casting and the lead

8 Whilst there is little point in trotting down live baits in British river systems to catch catfish, because stocking them into running water is illegal, throughout Europe, particularly certain Spanish rivers, The Ebro, The Segre and The Sinca, trotting is a 'deadly' technique because it covers so much water. Use a large 'through the middle' catfish float stopped 3-5 feet above the hook trace with a bead and power-gum stop knot. On the two foot 150lbs test trace, joined to an 80lbs braided reel line by a strong swivel, with a barrel lead immediately above, use a strong, size 6/0, wide-gape hook. An ideal 'live-baiting' pattern, and all-round cat fishing hook is the Eagle Wave big game whose unique shape in the middle of the bend allows the bait maximum movement and good penetration on the strike. Top trotting baits are eels and small carp.

9 Want to make your live bait even more attractive? Well, how about adding to your trace, two to three inches above the hook, a designer 'rattle'. These come in coloured plastic (white, red or yellow) and are fixed to the hook trace by laying the line in the hinge groove and snapping shut with ball bearing inside. A rubber float stop sleeved on either side, will prevent the rattle sliding. These incidentally have proved effective for pike, perch and for sea species.

10 To ensure your live bait stays on the hook, and this applies particularly to barb-less hooks, simply sleeve onto the hook after the bait, a designer 'Bait Shield'. Made from thick rubber, these unobtrusive discs, available from 'Catfish Pro' are also handy when using baits on a hair such as pre-

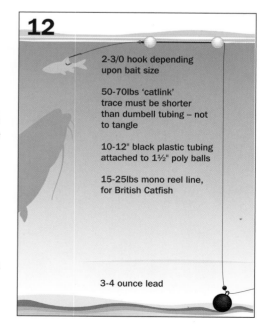

12

2-3/0 hook depending upon bait size

50-70lbs 'catlink' trace must be shorter than dumbell tubing – not to tangle

10-12" black plastic tubing attached to 1½" poly balls

15-25lbs mono reel line, for British Catfish

3-4 ounce lead

touches bottom, when you tighten up to the float rig (lying flat on the surface) it is impossible for the bait to swim around the reel line and tangle. This is the beauty of this particular set up. Always use in conjunction with an electric bite alarm and indicator, as you may not always hear that glorious 'smack' of a cat engulfing your bait on the surface. This technique can be most effectively used with *Tip 20*.

13 For retaining catfish to photograph, use a long (6 foot x 18 inch diameter) 'Tunnel' or 'Tube' made from soft, black material, which opens at both ends with toggles for tethering to bank sticks and tension to keep straight. Where really big fish are concerned, say 100lbs and larger, use a stringer made from soft, nylon cord. *See Freshwater Tackle and Lines Tips 6 and 7*, for correct tying of 'stringer loop' which cannot 'tighten' during the time a catfish, or other large fish such as a mahseer or Nile perch is retained.

14 For bringing big catfish into the boat when fishing abroad, especially in fast flowing rivers where landing nets are impracticable, wear a protective 'gripping' or 'chain mail' glove on each hand and with a firm two-handed grip of the fish's lower lip, haul it over the side, using the impetus of its own body movements to your advantage.

15 If you catch a Wels catfish which has just 'two' small barbels under its chin, instead of the normal 'four', you may not have caught a Wels, but an Aristotle's catfish (Silurus aristotelis) which originates from the Akheloos River in Greece, and which just might have found its way into British still waters (like so many alien species) through the ornamental pond-fish trade.

16 If you are limited in fishing hours or attempting to catch catfish from waters low in stock density, then 'prebaiting' can prove

the answer to success. Introduce, say every other evening, generous helpings (especially if carp are present) of pelleted food such as 'Halibut Pellets' (which break down and reduce to dust after 6-12 hours of being in the water) or 'Moggi Chunks' which come in both halibut pellet and fish-meal flavours, which break down somewhere between 24-48 hours.

17 Remember to set your rods 'well' back from the water's edge, and to be particularly quiet whilst fishing at night, as catfish love to hunt really close into the margins. So position one bait no more than a few yards out.

18 Watercraft plays an important part of targeting catfish during daylight hours. They love to lie up in the relative darkness and greatly reduced-light of beneath large, overhanging trees, sunken bushes and patches of lilies.

19 Fish care is so important when handling catfish. A giant unhooking matt is recommended as is a large, triangular landing net with 48-50 inch arms.

20 To present both live and dead baits at distances far greater than can be cast, (say 20 yards and beyond), try the unique 'Winching' method, which allows you to wind or 'winch' (hence its name) your bait out to wherever you wish. Start by making up a simple end rig on your 15lbs test reel line, comprising of a 3-4 ounce bomb to which a link clip and ½ inch diameter curtain ring have been added, running above a snap-link swivel, with a large rubber bead in between. But don't attach your hook trace and bait just yet. And here's the clever part: have an extra rod (butt end only) ready, propped up with the butt ring facing the lake, the reel filled with just 4lbs test line, and the bale arm open, and tie the end securely to the snap link on your main outfit. Now cast out the heavy lead to where you intend fishing so that both lines go out over the lake. Once your lead has settled place the catfish rod in two rests ready for action and open the reel's bale arm, so you can wind your snap link back using the half-rod, your 15lbs main line flowing freely through the curtain ring on the lead. Once the snap link has been retrieved, simply clip on your trace and bait and wind slowly back to the lead. And 'hey presto' your bait is now presented way out into the lake.

Chub

1 Learn to walk slowly, when stalking chub, as though you are creeping up on rabbits in a field, picking up each foot individually (like a chicken does when it's stalking a worm) because I rate chub, particularly big, educated chub, by far the spookiest to bank side vibrations, of all our British freshwater species.

2 Never go chubbing without Polaroid glasses. I much prefer those with HLT, 'yellow' lenses (high light transmission lenses) which make viewing in dull, overcast conditions noticeably 'brighter'. Only in extra bright sunshine would I swap them for grey or amber lenses. A cap with a 'long' peak stops you

moving your hand up and down to shield your eyes from the sun. Less movement whilst 'fish spotting' results in more chub in the net.

3 Invest in a good quality, lightweight, pair of waterproof over trousers. You'll need them when kneeling, and crawling along 'Indian style', even during those early summer mornings, when marginal grasses are soaked with dew.

4 Learn to keep a sharp look-out for slugs during early morning trips, especially when it's drizzling. During the summer and autumn, there is no finer, more instant chub bait than a big brown or black slug, hooked once only through either end on a size 4 hook tied direct to a 6lbs reel line, and free-lined (no additional shots) alongside those difficult 'snag' swims. Watch the line from the second the slug hits the water. Most bites quickly tighten the line like a bowstring. Such is the ferocity of the take.

5 Never put your finger down a chub's throat to ease out a large eyed hook. Your forefinger will come out (after a loud yelp of pain) looking like it's been hit with a 3lbs hammer. Why? Because chub have large, powerful pharyngeal (throat) teeth, that's why.

6 How do you tell the difference between a chub and a grass carp? The chub's mouth is much larger, and the eye of the grass carp is set very low, in line with its jaw hinge. In addition, the grass carp's anal fin is grey whilst the chub's has an orange hue. Otherwise at a quick glance, especially in the water, they appear similar.

7 Enjoy weedy, seemingly impossible river conditions during the summer months with chub by catching them off the top on floating plugs. Good patterns are Big S style plugs, Meadow Mouse, and Big Bud etc. Weedless models are particularly effective. Use a short wire trace to alleviate being bitten off by the occasional pike.

8 By far the best winter feed for chub is mashed bread. Use stale scraps soaked in the sink and squeeze most of the water out before mashing between your fingers into a pulp. Its secret is that if old bread is used, it will sink quickly and break up into a million tiny fragments; thus attracting but not overfeeding.

9 Don't be surprised if you catch a big chub on small live baits intended for pike, perch or zander. They are one of our most voracious freshwater predators. Try ledgering minnows or bleak, dead or alive, and how about half-inch chunks of eel or lamprey, which work well during the winter months. Loose feed sparingly with the same.

10 When long trotting for chub during the winter once the river bed has been scoured clean, use a wide-topped float (that can be easily see up to 30-40 yards) carrying a bulk shot of between 3-4 swan shot, but don't use swan shot. Instead bulk a line of AA shots 12-15 inches above the hook with a BB shot in between, so that just like a bath

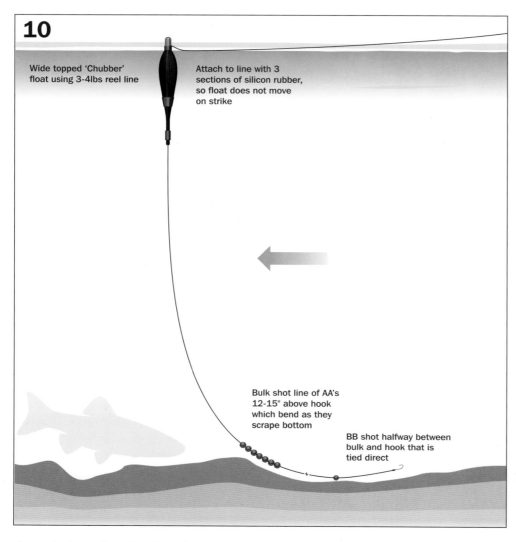

10

Wide topped 'Chubber' float using 3-4lbs reel line

Attach to line with 3 sections of silicon rubber, so float does not move on strike

Bulk shot line of AA's 12-15" above hook which bend as they scrape bottom

BB shot halfway between bulk and hook that is tied direct

13 When chub in a clear flowing river are particularly finicky during the warmer months, procure a whole wasp (or hornet's) nest. Try the pest control department of your local council, or get your own, but be careful (shop bought preparations are available) and slowly bring chub upstream into a feeding frenzy close to the surface by loose feeding chunks of £2 coin-sized wasp nest (called 'cake') which includes grubs. When most of the shoal is up on the surface inhaling every piece you drift down, (it floats), put your hook in the next and free line on weightless tackle. You can virtually 'select' which fish you want. Wasp cake is truly 'magical' bait, and the large, succulent, white grubs can even be long-trotted one or two up on a size 12 hook whilst loose feeding with maggots.

14 Summer chub are absolute suckers on the fly rod for large 'imitative' nymphs presented upstream into the gravel runs they occupy between long flowing beds of weed. Get well below a shoal and offer a mayfly nymph on a long leader, remembering to recover line whilst watching it drift downstream. Strike at any unusual movement of the leader where it enters the water.

chain, the line of smaller shots 'bend' without pulling the float under, whenever the river bed shallows up. *See Diagram.*

11 Be careful using long nosed artery forceps when unhooking deeply hooked chub. It is so easy to crimp and severely weaken the line immediately above the hook. If in any doubt, simply tie the hook on again.

12 For a simple way of constructing a fixed paternoster ledger (which suffices for most of my 'static-bait' chub fishing incidentally) use the four turn water knot. Cut off 10 inches of reel line (or

weaker if fishing amongst snags) and join to the main line 18-24 inches above the end. Tie the hook on last.

15 To bag up on chub using the bolt-rig style approach of a heavy running bomb, stopped

15

8-12 inches from the hook. Use a short ¾ -1 inch hair baited with a single 10-14mm pellet or boilie, or two size 10mm boilies or pellets, 3 grains of maize, etc, etc, while loose feeding with smaller attractor pellets, maize or sweet corn. For distance or really deep-water swims, pack loose feed plus the occasional hook bait sample into PVA tubing or bags and nick onto the bend of the hook, which will dissolve within minutes.

16 When ledgering across the flow in fast rivers, beware of those 'drop-back' bites where a chub moves towards you and thus makes the quiver tip spring back. In most cases it is not your bomb, feeder or link ledger shots re-settling on the bottom. It is a chub. So strike instantly.

17 Don't bother using a separate weigh sling to weigh your specimen chub. If in the landing net it is already in a perfect receptacle. Simply unscrew the net top and hook it onto your scales, remembering to deduct its weight afterwards. What could be easier and less harm to the fish?

18 When downstream quiver-tipping or rod top ledgering, angle your rod pointing downriver with the flow at around 45 degrees to the bank, as opposed to out at right angles. You will then pick up much more line on the strike, and even connect with tiny indications that would otherwise be missed.

19 When chub become suspicious of floating crust, step down to smaller offerings like 'mixer biscuits' that you would use for carp. And simply present one super-glued onto a size 10 hook, (don't forget to cut a small groove in the biscuit with a junior hacksaw blade first) using a small controller float 3-4 foot above for casting distance, stopped by a small rubber cushioning bead and a 5 turn stop knot tied on with a few inches of reel line. *See Carp Tip 4.*

20 Concealment, stealth and camouflage are not just well worn words of hype from angling writers. They are the basic requirements to successful chubbing, particularly when exploring and slowly

stalking clear and shallow, overgrown rivers and streams. So always creep about below the skyline, using the screen of tall grasses, shrubs and trees to full advantage. And above all, move slowly. It is that sudden 'movement' which instantly puts a wary chub on its guard.

Eel

1

1 With large eels in mind, one of the most successful baits, particularly in lakes or pits situated miles from the nearest river which contain only small numbers of adult eels, (often referred to as 'prison waters') is a couple of lobworms presented on a size 4 hook . It was in fact this very bait that produced the long-standing British record eel of 11lbs 2oz back in 1978 to the rod of Steve Terry.

2 As large eels are most sensitive to resistance, incorporate a large bore run ring into your running ledger rig, and use a lightweight indicator such as a simple coil of silver (kitchen) foil on the line between reel and butt ring, with an electric bite alarm as the front rod rest. Strong runs should then develop from an open bale arm.

3 Hot, humid, pitch-black, thundery summer nights, provide the best opportunity of contacting sizeable

eels, which at such times, often go on a feeding rampage.

4 In running water by far the best locations for targeting larger than average sized eels are weir and mill pools. But you'll need substantial tackle in pools where the bottom is full of junk, beneath which eels have their hideouts. This is 'hit, hold and wind' fishing at its most exciting.

5 During the autumn, vast numbers of eels 'silver-up' in readiness for their down river migration and journey to procreate their species way across the Atlantic in the depths of the Sargasso Sea. Apart from a distinct change in colouration from yellowy, greeny-brown, to bright silver, their jaws noticeably broaden and become more powerful. They 'thicken-up' too.

6 Big eels can at times chew through even 10lbs test monofilament. So construct your hook traces from one of the new soft, multi-strand, Kevlar-twisted materials marketed especially for catfish enthusiasts. Alternatively, use a thin, multi-strand wire that is so supple it can be knotted.

7 Though not a 'sports-fishing' technique, 'Babbing' as it is commonly referred to, can provide a few hours fun during the hours of darkness, for anglers boat fishing during the summer months on eel-rich waters such as the Norfolk and Suffolk Broads.

8 To 'Babb' effectively, you need several dozen large lobworms, a ball of wool, ('Worstead' is best), and a long darning needle. Thread the worms onto the wool and wrap around your hand to form a 'wrap'. Secure the ends tightly around the wrap and tie onto 10-12 foot of strong cord (100lbs test braid is ideal) with a 2-3 ounce lead fixed a foot or so above the worms. Then tie to the end ring of an 11-12 foot (light to hold) shore rod.

9 When 'Babbing', the wrap of worms are lowered down to the river bed, followed by the rod tip vibrating continually once eels are chewing on the worms. And, because their teeth 'catch' in the woollen yarn, they can be gently heaved out and lowered, all in one smooth, movement, straight into a large plastic bin. Don't worry about those which fall off. It's all part of 'Babbing'. You then have the choice of eating them immediately (simmering in milk in a saucepan produces a succulent meal of eel sections once they have been skinned) or freezing down for later use, either as sea baits for bass and tope, or for pike and zander.

10 If you happen to be friendly with a professional eel netsman (unfortunately they are a dying breed) there is no better or more informed person to point you in the direction of a 'big-eel water': a still water containing catch able numbers of specimen eels which for argument's sake, are in the

Eel

waters may not have been reached by many eels during their upstream migration, but those which made it, are likely to grow to a very large size, due to minimal competition for food.

14 Many 'prison' waters, especially small pits and farm ponds etc, give their best results during your initial few trips simply because they contain so few (albeit large) eels . So if results dwindle rapidly after say two or three trips, accept the fact that you may well have either caught, pricked, lost or simply scared virtually the water's entire eel population. So move on.

15 To weigh your specimen eel (and anything from 4lbs upwards is a 'target fish'), simply unscrew the landing net top and hoist onto the scales after removing the

hook. Grip the eel firmly behind its head on the outside of the net, using the mesh as a gripping agent when extracting the hook. Then deduct the net's weight afterwards. It's so much easier and much less slime is transferred from eel to you, than by attempting to transfer it into a separate weigh sling.

16 To take a trophy shot of a specimen eel do so immediately after capture and unhooking when it is at its most knackered. If you leave in a sack or tube till dawn, by which time it will have recovered, taking any kind of decent photo will prove almost impossible.

17 In really large still waters where feature, hideout-habitats such as bridges, old boat houses, islands, dam walls, sunken

4lbs plus category. Purchasing a batch of smaller eels from him to freeze down as winter pike baits, might loosen his tongue.

11 Whilst eel fishing is invariably much better at night when they come out to play, the eels inhabiting deep reservoirs and gravel pits are likely to hunt, and consequently feed, at any time of the day, particularly during low light conditions.

12 Use a powerful, but 'all through action' rod when targeting eels. One that will bend in harmony with a 10-15lbs test monofilament reel line, and so not cause the hook to rip out, or induce the trace to fracture when the eel comes close in under the rod tip, and is on a short line ready for netting.

13 'Prison waters' invariably contain the largest freshwater eels of all. Lakes or ponds, modest-sized irrigation reservoirs or pits (even the tiniest of farm ponds) that are miles from the nearest river or brook. Such

15

boats or cars, etc, are evident or known to you (in the case of sunken boats or cars) be prepared to move about and change swims regularly following every measure of success, because many of the very largest eels will occupy those 'choice' habitat hideouts.

18 Do not be tempted into using large hook baits simply because you are seeking large eels. Big baits can cause more trouble than they are worth when it comes to deciding 'when' to strike a positive run. Small, slim-bodied, freshly killed fish, (and 'freshly killed' is most important here) such as gudgeon, bleak, dace, roach or rudd of between three and four inches in length are ideal. Odd ball baits like the entire insides of a large swan mussel, or a baby 'calamari' (squid) are also worth trying.

19 To mount a small fish bait for optimum hook-ups, use a size 6-2 wide gape, strong hook, and push once only through the tail root. Work the hook along the baits flank (just beneath the skin) so it comes to lie immediately behind the gills with the point and bend of the hook nicely exposed. *See Diagram.* Just like pike, eels usually turn their prey to swallow head first so the fish's fins go down the gullet easily, and so a hook positioned immediately behind the gills usually finds purchase, despite the tail protruding from the eel's mouth. If you use a multi-hook rig, then use a wire trace in case a pike gobbles up your dead bait.

20 When striking, close the reel's bale arm gently (vibrations might travel down the line) and point the rod directly at the eel, waiting for the line to pull tight. Then, in one smooth, easy action, haul the rod back into a full curve and start winding. Big eels immediately pull back using that inherent 'snake-like' motion of their bodies, or actually run off. So make sure the clutch on your reel will yield line under pressure.

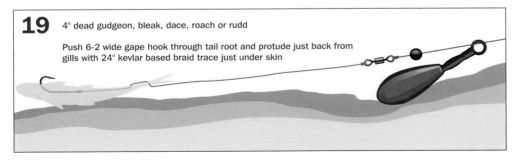

19 4" dead gudgeon, bleak, dace, roach or rudd

Push 6-2 wide gape hook through tail root and protude just back from gills with 24" kevlar based braid trace just under skin

Grayling

Grayling

1 When long-trotting for her ladyship the grayling, do not be tempted to fish with too light a shotting pattern, or dot the float tip down as though 'stick-float' fishing. Grayling are the boldest biters of all, even in the coldest weather. Wide-topped 'chubber-style' floats, that can easily be seen 30-50 yards downstream (yes you can hit bites at such distances in fast water) carrying between two and five swan shot are perfect for the job, but don't use swan shots. A line of AA sized bulk shot pinched on 12 inches above a size 14, forged hook with a No 1 or BB shot half way between is far better, because like a bathroom chain, it 'bends' when passing over stones and silt without pulling the float under, allowing the bait to drag bottom beautifully. *See Chub Diagram 10.*

2 Even in clear, really cold water, grayling will still pull the float down boldly so long as the bait is presented just above bottom, and within their line of sight. You can easily distinguish between male and female grayling by the different shapes of their dorsal fins. Males have a long 'sail-like' dorsal which when opened out almost touches their adipose fin, while females have smaller, almost 'square-shaped' dorsals when opened out.

3 The only conditions when grayling won't play ball and bite confidently in cold weather is when the river is swollen over the banks full of dirty, milky-tea floodwater. They then seem loathe to move towards a trotted bait, perhaps on account that it cannot be seen clearly anyway. Switching over to stret-pegging tactics with a couple or three maggots, or a small red worm anchored hard on the river bed, and introducing loose feed directly down to the bottom by way of a 'bait-dropper', will sometimes produce, as will quiver-tip ledgering in conjunction with a small block-end feeder rig.

4 After grayling, trout, pike, chub and dace (in that order) are the most likely species to bite in a freezing river. Remember that in sub-zero temperatures their metabolism will have slowed down to a snail's pace, and with chub and dace only tiny bite registrations are expected even to small 'static' baits on tiny hooks, which is why trotting enthusiasts love grayling so much.

prized trout fisheries along rivers such as the Test and the Kennet, where grayling abound, actually encourage responsible anglers to enjoy this winter pursuit between the months of November and March. Simply enquire at tackle shops in towns like Stockbridge and Andover in Hampshire and in Newbury and Hungerford in Berkshire.

7 As with big dace, there is very often a segregation of the sexes with grayling towards the end of the coarse fishing river season, in preparation towards their eventual spawning during April, with the big males, being either loners or grouped in twos or threes, and now noticeably darker in colouration, dominating many of the choice lies.

8 Summer or winter, grayling are always great fun to catch on the fly rod. With smaller, more intimate rivers in mind where short casting will cover most runs, a two ounce, wand-like carbon brook rod coupled to a lightweight reel and size 4 weight-forward floating line, allows the grayling to really show you what it can do. Use just a 2½ -3lbs test tippet and plan to plop your artificial in at the head of each run (exactly where you would start trotting a float) from a position directly downstream. So plan to wade swims that demand it.

5 If you cannot get to a tackle shop in time for some maggots or fail to find red worms in the compost heap, and you have a day's trotting for grayling already booked, then worry not. Grayling are real suckers for sweet corn, trotted down just like maggots. Some think that sweet corn's resemblance in size to the eggs of salmon, upon which grayling gorge at times (which is why the species is so unwelcome on prize salmon beats and treated with disgust) is what makes grayling accept it so readily. So it's always worth keeping a tin or two in the boot of the car, particularly coloured sweet corn, which in 'orange' looks uncannily like salmon eggs. Red works effectively too.

6 Long trotting for grayling in clear-flowing southern chalk streams is not, as many seem to think, only for

the privileged or the rich. The fishery managers and keepers of many highly-

Grayling

9 When fly fishing upstream for grayling, weighted patterns like the leaded shrimp and tin head or gold head nymphs on size 10 hooks are favourite, and you need to be continually retrieving the loose line as the nymph comes back downstream towards you with the current, your eyes 'glued' to where the leader enters the surface, because sometimes, you'll get little more than a quick 'forward twitch' to pull into.

10 Many fly fishermen attach a buoyant, highly visible 'sight-bob' to the leader 2-6 feet above the fly (depending on depth of the run being covered) which in effect acts just like a float and registers a bite instantly a grayling inhales the artificial.

11 Whether long trotting or presenting the upstream nymph to grayling during the winter months, so you can sit comfortably low down on the bank side, kneel when required, or easily wade into a prime casting position, even wade fully across the river in order to cover choice swims along the opposite bank, its worth investing in a pair of good quality, lightweight, breathable chest waders which have neoprene feet as opposed to rubber boots. Brogue-type leather or canvas wading boots with felt soles are then worn over the neoprene, sock feet, providing excellent support for either wading over slippery stones in fast currents, or wandering along the banks.

12 The wandering, exploring grayling angler carries neither holdall nor tackle bag. All tackle sundries such as fly boxes, floats, silicon float bands, hooks, shots, disgorger and forceps etc, are carried on his person in a waistcoat. A waistcoat with a tab and D ring on the back to accept the clip of a collapsible flick-up type landing net suits both the fly fisherman and long-trotter alike. There are times, however, when predominantly bank fishing over wide beds of reed and sedge, that a separate long handled landing net is required by the long trotting enthusiast.

13 An indispensable item of tackle when long trotting for her ladyship the grayling, is a simple two division 'bait pouch'. One for maggots and the other to hold red worms or sweet corn. This belts around the waist and alleviates the necessity of continually having to open bait boxes with freezing cold finger tips, to say nothing of carrying said boxes. When tackling wide rivers, a catapult is handy too.

14 Southern chalk streams have hatches of flies just about every day of the calendar year, and you can differentiate between a trout and a grayling sucking down an emerging or floating adult insect by the type of splash it creates. Look for the perfectly 'round' ring of the grayling feeding off the surface.

15 Small dry flies, anything in the 'olive' range are readily taken as are sedges and mayflies. A grey wulff is one of the better 'larger' patterns when it comes to sizeable grayling.

16 A small lightweight plastic bait dropper is very handy for ensuring that loose feed goes directly down along the bottom of deep and extremely turbulent gravel runs, which would otherwise send hand-fed maggots off in all directions and at all levels, scattering the shoal in the process.

17 The nice thing about grayling is that once the float has been set at the correct trotting depth to present the bait trundling along just above the river bed, there is little point in making any more than three or four trots through before moving on to the next run. Because if grayling are present, a bite will usually come at the first or second run through.

18 When tackling the grayling of shallow and clear flowing chalk streams where everything can be clearly seen, a positive plan of action which always works for me, is to first walk the entire fishery upon arrival starting from the downstream boundary up, making note of those swims which contain the most or the largest fish and where big trout or the odd salmon are lying, in order to avoid them. All the way upstream to the top boundary. Then walk and fish the entire fishery downstream along which everything will by now have settled.

19 Top chalk stream features much loved by larger grayling, are tiny, but deep hatch pools, deep runs close into the bank, even those of just a few yards in length, and those long, even paced, even-depthed glides with a clean sandy bottom.

20 Be prepared during an exhaustive day's long trotting to change your hook several times. The tell-tale sign of your hook becoming blunt is when a maggot becomes difficult to impale or bursts as you nick it on.

17

Perch

Perch

1 Of all top techniques for catching perch during the winter months, once the weed in lakes and rivers has died back, particularly those wily old 'big perch', 'back-ledgering', is the most deadly, because through 'minimal casting' it creates less disturbance. Go for a two rod-approach, employing a simple 'fixed paternoster' ledger rig on each, with a couple of 2x or 3x swan shots (depending upon casting distance or current strength) on the 10 inch weight link, and a large, gyrating lobworm nicked onto a size 4, on the 20 inch hook length.

2 For 'back-ledgering in rivers (quiver-tip rods are actually recommended here because the fine, forgiving tips are less likely to pull the hook from a lightly hooked perch) cast one rod as far downstream as you can, and the second around half the distance. And catapult in several helpings of broken lobworms down the entire length of the swim between the far bait and the end of your 'near' rod, to get the perch in a feeding mood. And continue introducing broken worms

throughout the session when fish are coming regularly.

3 When back-ledgering, both rods should be 'almost 'pointing at the baits. I say almost, because if set in the rests at a slight angle, gentle pulls and the start of a bite is often shown on the

quiver tip before the bobbin actually moves. And so striking can be pre-empted. Then clip on a lightweight bobbin-type indicator between reel and butt ring. An electric bite alarm used as a front rod rest incidentally, comes in very useful when sport is slow, and you don't want to miss out by day dreaming.

4 The secret of 'back-ledgering, is every 10-20 minutes or so, to remove the bobbin and gently lift up each rod whilst winding the reel's handle between one and a couple of turns, thus moving the worm off the bottom (it will 'flutter' down beautifully) towards you. Then put the rod down, wind up slightly and clip on the bobbin. A drop of around 12-14 inches is ideal. But sometimes you will barely have time for this because a perch will have nailed your lobworm 'on the drop'. Remember to keep those 'broken' worms going in throughout the session, or bites may dry up.

5 Where do big perch live? Well, due to 'summer weeds' dying back, when fry shoals tend to mass together for protection in deeper holes and gullies, larger perch then subsequently tend to group-up in catchable numbers close by. So in still waters such as lakes and gravel pit complexes, if you are not aware of the water's bottom topography, spend some time plumbing the depths to locate those choice, deeper areas. Marginal features such as an old boat house built adjacent to deep water, beneath overhanging and part-sunken trees and dam outlets, are also worth exploration.

6 In river systems, with the biggest perch in mind, look for 'top-habitat swims', where large bushes and trees overhang the water, especially where willows dunk their lower limbs below the surface, and keep an eye out for those big perch-swims par excellence: beds of dense bull rushes. Both habitats harbour perch because they provide great ambush points. The dark, vertical stripes of the perch blend in perfectly with the stems of the bulrush and with the subsurface stems of the willow. Around lock gates, beneath road bridges and beside pilings are also favoured, as are the 'holes' on acute bends and 'cut-backs' along thick beds of sedges hugging the margins. *Also, see Tips 12 and 13.*

7 Serious big-perch specialists are very selective about when they fish, and keep a keen track of winter weather patterns. Because while perch are possibly likely to feed at any time regardless of temperatures, by far the 'hottest' feeding periods, in rivers especially, occur during spells of extra-mild weather. Wait till temperatures do not fall below zero for several consecutive nights, rising to maybe 10 or 12 degrees during the day, and get out there pronto, making the most of conditions till the next cold snap.

8 When ledgering small live-baits for perch (gudgeon, dace, roach and little perch are best - in that order) I favour a reel line of around 6lbs test matched to an Avon-style ledger rod of 11-12 feet. On the business end is tied a wide-gape size 4 eyed hook, to 20 inches of reel line and a small swivel. Above this goes a 'cushioning' rubber bead and a running snap swivel with 4 inch heavy mono 'link'

6

and one ounce bomb attached. Any lighter and the bait might 'tow' the lead around.

9 Always angle the rod tip downwards supported on two rests and pointing directly at the bait to minimize resistance, when ledgering small live baits for perch. For bite indications hang a simple 'bobbin' on a 20 inch drop between reel and butt ring, pinching a swan shot or two on the retaining cord to counteract excessive movement from the bait.

10 To ensure the single hook is not impaired on the strike when live baiting, hook the bait fish once only through its chin membrane or both nostrils, and slip on over the barb, a ¼ inch square of 'rubber band'. This alleviates the bait flying off during the cast or at any other time.

11 That old saying 'that the best bait to catch a big perch, is a little perch', is on most

Perch

occasions, perfectly true. Next to gudgeon which seem to possess 'magical' powers of attraction to 'big stripies', a small live perch of around 4-5 inches long is indeed hard to beat because large perch become so, by consuming large quantities of their own brethren in addition to other small silver-shoal species.

12 Just like barbel, river perch adore bulrushes. Not those tall dark brown, cigar-like seed heads of the greater reed mace, often wrongly referred to as bulrushes, but the cylindrical, dark-green onion-like stems which protrude through the surface from a gravel bed and which can be seen 'quivering' often in huge marginal clumps as well as through the middle of a shallow river, as the strong current bows them slightly over. A few inches below their pointed tops are fragile, light-brown seed heads, so very different from reed mace.

13 It is most important to differentiate between the two plants above because they

each prefer different habitats. Perch love true bulrushes because their vertical stripes blend in remarkably well with the erect

stems, affording them marvellous ambush opportunities, from where they can attack small silver shoal species, using minimum effort. But if you cannot obtain small live baits don't worry. A juicy lobworm or dendrobena trotted along just above bottom beneath an 'Avon-style' or 'chubber' float produces the most gloriously positive bites. Free lining a big worm into gaps between the bulrushes, and allowing it to free-fall to the bottom as it drifts along will also produce aggressive 'chub-like' bites; the line 'zinging' tight after a preliminary twitch or two.

14 One of the best, or 'worst'-kept secrets about commercial carp-type fisheries, where the perch, if stocked often get neglected, is the size they grow to. Specimens over 3lbs being common place, due no doubt to the amount of loose feed in the way of casters, maggots and worms that are used to attract carp and silver shoal species. If you add the fry of silver shoal species that breed in these albeit small, but prolific waters, you don't have to be a rocket scientist to realize that 'commercial water' perch, are extremely well fed. Reason enough to be the odd man out by specifically targeting them.

15 A simple running paternoster ledger rig presented beneath a small (through the middle) sliding float is the best way of live baiting for big perch, because it keeps your bait continually working over the targeted area. Whereas free-roaming live baits all too easily dive into weed or beneath trees or vacate the area all together when predators show up.

16 To rig a sliding float (using a tiny bead and five turn stop knot above) set it a little deeper than the swim, with the 6lbs test main line threaded through one end of a swivel and tied to the hook link swivel (with a small bead between) and a wide gape size 4 on the business end of the 16 inch hook length. To the loose swivel above the bead (which now becomes the 'bomb

link) tie 20-30 inches of 8lbs mono and add a one ounce bomb. Small roach, rudd, gudgeon and dace etc, are ideal baits and work continually if simply hooked through both nostrils. Remember to angle the rod top high in order to keep as much line out of the water as possible.

17 To stand a chance with the largest perch of all, concentrate on the species during the last few weeks of the river fishing season leading up to the middle of March, when due to increased temperatures they will be looking to feed heavily prior to their eventual spawning during April.

18 Don't be tempted to hedge your bets whilst offering live baits to perch and incorporate a wire trace in case a pike happens along. Perch, the whoppers especially, are particularly sensitive to a wire trace. Besides, should a pike bite through your 6lbs reel line, it will either quickly get rid of

a large single, bronze hook, or the hook will rot and rust away within weeks.

19 During the warm summer months, below the churning, well oxygenated white water of a weir pool, immediately below the sill, and in the corresponding eddies on both sides, are areas much favoured by big, river perch. Vast shoals of newly hatched fry gather in such places and perch are only too aware of the fact. Try a small diving plug or float-fished live bait like a bleak or a gudgeon set around mid-depth. Your float won't be on the surface for too long.

20 Beware of striking float-fished live baits too hard. Simply tighten down once the float has disappeared and wind up tight till you can 'feel' the fish, before pulling the rod tip back and winding in one smooth movement, continuing to wind so the hook finds purchase as the perch tries to eject the bait by shaking its head from side to side.

17

Pike

Pike

1 To handle pike safely and carefully for both a trophy photo and during the process of unhooking, use a chain mail glove on your left hand (the Rapala 'Fillet Glove' is perfect for the job and will fit either hand) and gently slip four fingers into the pike's left gill opening, being very careful not to touch its gill rakers. When your fingers are fully in, press down tightly on the outside (against your forefinger) with your thumb. Don't relax your grip or the fish might escape. To remove hooks with long nosed-artery forceps,

(imperative) simply curl your left hand slowly, and 'hey presto' the pike's lower jaw will open. It has no option because being part of its bony skull the top jaw has little movement anyway. It really is so easy, and small fish can even be unhooked with most of their body still in the water, or when held vertically. For maximum support, big fish are best laid on their back on an unhooking mat during the unhooking process. Hooks deep down are most easily removed by going in with the forceps through the opposite gill opening.

2 When float fishing at distance in still water use 'hi-viz' sliding pike floats that incorporate dart-type, 'sight-vanes', and remember to use 3-4mm rubber 'cushioning beads' either side of the float, between float eye and trace swivel. And between float eye and a sliding stop knot, tied onto the reel line above the float at the required depth, using a few inches of 10-15lbs test, red (easy to see) power gum. Don't trim the ends too short (leave both 1½ inches long) or the knot will catch against the rod rings during casting, and inhibit distance.

3 To weigh 'trophy-sized' pike, it's far easier (especially on the pike) immediately after landing when they are still in the folds of a large (already wet) net. One with arms around 40-42 inches in length will accommodate the biggest specimens, and you simply detach the arms from the spreader block and roll the net up before hooking the scales on halfway along, remembering to deduct the weight of the

net afterwards. What could be easier? After which, the pike is laid onto a foam-filled unhooking mat, either still in or out of the landing net, and the hooks are removed. A separate weigh sling is really not required. Now is the time for a photo, following unhooking, immediately prior to release when they are at their quietest. Endeavour therefore, not to retain a large pike in a keep-sack or tube for any length of time in order to capture a picture of it. Unless of course torrential rain precludes this at the time of capture. Truth is, once pike have regained their strength by resting in a sack, they become unbelievably difficult to hold still. And at best you will become heavily covered in their protective slime as they wriggle about. So for the sake of both pike and angler, immediate release is always recommended.

4 Some anglers tend to think that because the pike is a marauding killer with an enviable array of backward-pointing teeth covering the roof of its upper jaw, in addition to the long, powerful canines set into the lower jaw and thus capable of engulfing, drowning and swallowing water birds as large as mallards, that it should be shown perhaps less stealth, than say the chub. But they would be wrong. So acute are the senses of pike, even totally 'blind' fish are confident at lunging into a shoal of bait fish or striking at an artificial lure. Smelling out static dead baits resting on the bottom is by comparison, child's play of course. This predator has in fact survived in British rivers and lakes for at least half a million years. Fossil remains found in Germany, date back to 20 million years ago.

5 Mill and weir pools are great meeting places for all river species. And because the occupants must keep moving in the fast currents, thus consuming more energy than still-water fish, they need to feed more regularly, even throughout the coldest winter conditions; pike included. In water running low and clear, best results usually come to trotted live baits just above

bottom, or working lures. A big spoon is my favourite, which with just the one treble hook at the rear, catches up on fewer snags than say, diving plugs. Wobbling dead baits is another extremely effective 'weir pool' technique which maximizes on time because you don't have to catch live baits first, and while a pike is likely to turn up anywhere except the main flush, I favour any slow back eddy close into the bank. Especially those lies beneath overhanging trees. Guaranteed hot spots these. Small areas of slack water beneath redundant hatch gates are also worth attention, as are any areas of slow, deep water. So, study surface currents seriously for several minutes before making that initial cast. Sometimes slacks occur in the pools centre, and to keep live bait out there use a float-paternoster rig incorporating a 'heavy' bomb, and angle the rod tip high to keep most of the line off the surface between float and tip.

6 For free lining dead baits to pike in both still and running water, even, and especially when boat fishing, the most effective bite indicator (used with the reels bale arm open) is a loop of line retained beneath an elastic band on the rod handle immediately opposite the reels

spool. This is 'sensitivity' personified because you can make the band as forgiving or as tight as conditions dictate (to combat fast river currents or a strong sub-surface 'draw' in still water for instance) and once the loop has pulled out, line simply peels from the spool without the slightest resistance. Always pinch a couple of swan shots onto the wire trace just below the swivel to initiate the pike moving directly away and giving a 'positive' bite indication.

7 If fishing 'tidal rivers' for pike, remember the most likely time for a spot of action particularly when sport is slow due to freezing conditions etc, is when the tide changes. Either from flooding to the ebb or visa versa, when all species including pike must change position in order to once again face the flow. And that period when fish are moving about just before the change, to when the river has swapped direction and is flowing in the opposite direction is not only critical, on a bad day it is very often the only occasion pike will find your baits.

8 If you are fed up with sitting frozen to the bone waiting for one of the baits presented on a multiple-rod set up to be taken, then here's a tip, based on

Pike

my preference to be continually moving, called my 'spoon and static' approach. A highly mobile technique I employ when searching previously un-fished rivers and lakes for pike, guaranteed to keep you warm. I use two 9 foot rod outfits, one of which sports a fixed spool reel (could be a multiplier) loaded with 12lbs mono, plus wire trace and a 5 inch spoon. The second reel is a 6501-sized (left-hand wind) multiplier loaded with 30lbs test braid and wire trace holding a duo of size 8 semi barbless trebles. I start by selecting a likely area, pinch on two 2x swan shots onto the wire trace immediately below the swivel, fix on dead bait such as a smelt, mackerel tail, or whole sardine, and cast it out. Once the bait has touched bottom I lay the rod on the ground pointing at the bait, without worrying about rod rests and bite indicators and wind the loose line reasonably tight. The reel is then clicked into free spool and the ratchet engaged. This is my audible bite indicator. I then search the surrounding territory with the spoon-outfit, retrieving it close to the bottom in an erratic, fluttering, wounded-fish action, with the rod tip pointing directly at the lure to maximize on the hooks going home when a pike lunges at it. I'll spend no more than say 15-20 minutes in any spot, before 'twitching' the static back (in case it gets grabbed on the move) and then move on to the next likely swim. There are days when pike really want a chase and the fluttering spoon scores, and times when only the static is taken, usually quite quickly too, within 5-10 minutes of being cast. And of course there are days when both methods produce.

9 Now here is a really top, top tip. That old adage of offering a 'big' bait if you are after a big pike, does not necessarily add up. What does happen in many cases is that with larger baits, the problems of hooking-up are far greater. Personally, whether live or dead baiting, I much prefer whole fish or half baits in the 5-7 inch size bracket. I can then point the rod at the pike and wind down till the line is completely 'tight', before striking

immediately, all in one progressive action, knowing that I have more than a fair chance of the hooks finding purchase.

10 For ledgering static dead baits in deep, fast, coloured rivers, use aromatic species such as the 'cucumber' smelling smelt and grayling, or blood-saturated fish like lampreys and eels, especially the head-ends that have huge blood content. Mackerel and herring heads also work very well. Initial 'knocks' on the rod tip (which should be angled up high to ensure maximum line is out of the water) signal a pike mouthing the bait, after which line will evaporate quickly from the reel. So either use a multiplier in free spool with the ratchet on, a loop of line set tightly

beneath an elastic band on the rod handle with the reel's bale arm open, or a 'bait-runner' reel. Alternatively, the rod tip might suddenly 'spring back' denoting a pike has dislodged the ledger weight whilst taking the bait, but if line fails to pull from the reel, it's because the pike has swum towards the rod. So wind down instantly, and 'feel' for that tell-tale 'knocking' of a fish already on.

11 When targeting the big pike of my local Norfolk Broads during the coldest, most featureless time of the year between December and March when the marginal cover of reeds and sedges has died back and their baitfish prey lack cover, a large

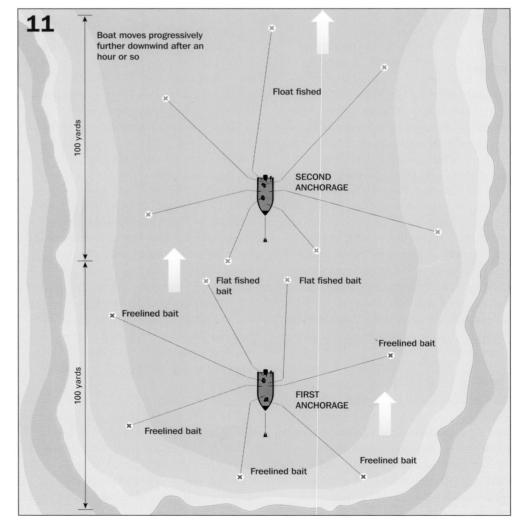

12

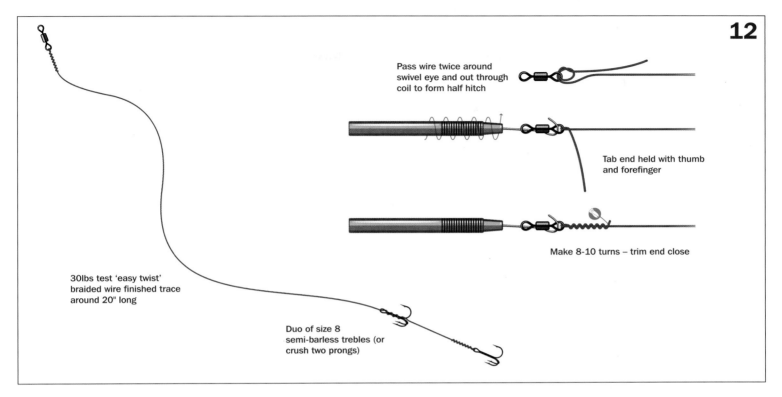

Pass wire twice around swivel eye and out through coil to form half hitch

Tab end held with thumb and forefinger

Make 8-10 turns – trim end close

30lbs test 'easy twist' braided wire finished trace around 20" long

Duo of size 8 semi-barless trebles (or crush two prongs)

percentage of the fish I'm after will be well out from the bank on the bottom of the 'bowl' (many of the shallower broads are like a saucer in cross-section) in the deepest section. And for this kind of pike fishing, I find that systematically 'grid-searching' the middle reaches of the broad, pays best dividends. After putting the mud weights down at the most 'upwind' area (with a view to subsequently simply lifting them and allowing the wind to take me down to the next position) rods are fanned all around the boat presenting static dead baits, using a mixture of float-fished and free-lined smelt and lamprey heads, with the tip of each rod pointing directly at the bait. The idea being to cover every angle of where a pike might be lying or approach the bait from. Then if nothing materializes within say an hour after repositioning each bait a couple or three times, then the mud weights are silently lifted to try the next area downwind. This technique certainly produces a high proportion of quality-sized double figure fish, (not to mention the occasional whopper) which show a distinct preference for static dead baits. *See Diagram.*

12 Fancy making your 'own' traces up for pike. It is not only cheaper than purchasing tackle shop 'pre-mades', you have total choice in what patterns of hooks and swivels are used, plus the type of wire they are presented on. And if the trace lets you down, you only have yourself to blame. But because making your own is so much cheaper, you will automatically replace each one immediately it becomes doubtful through 'fraying' or bent hooks, etc. Essential items include a selection of trebles and swivels (may I suggest size 10 swivels and size 8 semi barb-less trebles will suffice for most pike fishing) a roll of 30lbs test 'easy-twist' braided wire, and a small pair of quality wire cutters. A 'twiddle stick' which has a 'shepherd's crook' at one end for twisting the tab end of the wire around itself, to secure treble or swivel, (though this can be done with your bare fingers) not only makes constructing traces so much easier, but more professional-looking. *See Diagram.* Start by cutting off around 24 inches of wire and (assuming you are right-handed) holding a treble in your left hand,

with your right, pass one end of the wire through the eye, and then a second time to form a loop. Now pass the end through the loop to form a simple 'clinch' and gently pull evenly on both strands of wire to reduce the loop into a tight knot. Using your left hand catch the crook of the twiddle stick around one prong of the treble and slowly revolve towards you, whilst with your right hand (holding the tab end of wire between thumb and forefinger) carefully guide it around itself in neat coils. After a dozen or so coils, snip off the end. Slide on the second treble (through the eye) and secure two to three inches above the first treble by gently wrapping the wire three or four times around the shank. To complete the trace, repeat the 'twisting' procedure by adding a swivel to the other end. And there it is. Job done. Traces end up around 20 inches long (after twisting and trimming) so that should the bottom few inches of wire become 'kinked' or 'frayed' after catching a pike or two, cutting off the suspect length of wire and replacing the trebles takes but a jiffy. And your trace is still long enough for action, though a few inches shorter. Make

Pike

up 'spinning traces', (12-14 inches long) with a plain swivel at one end and a snap swivel at the other, in exactly the same way.

13 Here's a tip for catching cold-water pike in ultra low temperatures when they lie on the bottom (covered in double-sucker leeches on their fins and gill plates) and show not the slightest interest in food unless it passes within mere inches of where they lay motionless. To ensure your lure or wobbled dead bait works only within this critical, cold-water depth band, less than two feet above bottom, try adding a 12 inch 'stiff' mono link and running swivel immediately above the trace swivel (with a small bead between) with a half ounce bomb on the end. You can then twitch and wobble your dead bait or lure in ever so slowly, only tightening up when you feel a take.

14 When trotting down live or dead baits for river pike, use an in-line, sliding, 'Tenpin-style' buoyant float through which the reel line passes and is stopped at the desired

depth by a small bead and five turn stop knot, tied with power gum. Bulk shot in the way of two to three large swan shots or a large oval bullet (cushioned by a rubber bead) should sit on the main line immediately above the trace swivel. The beauty of using the 'sliding Tenpin' is that at any point along the swim where the bottom is known to shallow up or there is a snag, you simply ease the stop knot a few feet above the float by holding the rod tip high, and then let it go again when depth resumes. In addition, this is the perfect rig for 'stret-pegging' dead baits static on the bottom of fast flowing rivers.

15 To rig the sliding 'tenpin' or any other 'through the middle' pike float for 'stret-pegging', simply exchange the shots or oval bullet for a running 1-2 ounce bomb, and slide the stop knot up to several feet deeper than the swim. Then cast directly downstream, and allow a 'subsurface bow' to form in the line between float and terminal rig, so that the float actually lies 'flat' on the surface. The 'flat float' creating minimal resistance to a pike sucking up the bait.

16 Want the most durable of all baits to use for a day's 'wobbling' for pike where continual and long casting are prerequisites? Well, look no further than 5 to 7 inch rainbow trout which have unbelievably firm bodies and last for ages. You can purchase them frozen from specialist tackle shops, or, and you may well be obliged to buy these in bulk, enquire at your local trout farm or fishery where small disfigured and freshly dead trout are removed daily from the stews. When mounted on a duo of size 8 semi barb-less trebles (the top in an eye socket and the lower down the flank) with a slight 'bend' set in the trout's body a lovely action is produced.

17 For 'popping-up' light, smallish whole dead baits such as roach, smelts or sprats, etc above bottom silt and weed,

simply twist a 2-3 inch link of soft multi-strand wire onto to the shank of the lower treble on your standard two-hook wire trace. Then, at the other end, twist-on a 'green' ¾ inch diameter 'Pro Popper' soft foam buoyant ball to raise the bait's head and torso off the bottom. Pinch a 2 or 3x SSG shot onto the wire trace a few inches from the bait's tail, (to ensure it rises the exact distance required above bottom) and another next to the trace swivel. It works an absolute treat, and pike are not put off, because the foam ball is 'soft'. For popping up larger baits simply use two small foam balls, instead of one larger one, which could impair striking.

18 When after the huge pike of trout reservoirs, there are two kinds of fish-holding features to look for: visual features such as valve towers, the dam wall and around the cages where trout are fed daily in the floating stews, and unseen features, which only become apparent when using an echo-sounder/fish-finder unit. These might consist of anywhere that dense shoals of baitfish gather such as around an old stone wall (many reservoirs, remember, are flooded farmlands) or group of buildings, or the 'deeper' bed of a stream or river, rocky outcrops, defunct farm machinery, etc. The possibilities are endless, and all will show up on the finder.

19 Have you ever thought about fishing for pike at night? In some cases, particularly on waters heavily fished for pike, in both rivers and still waters, results can actually surpass those made during daylight. Dead baiting using simple ledgering tactics, presenting static baits on the bottom is by far the easiest and most productive method. Pretend you are carp fishing at night by using electric bite alarms and indicators, and by taking along hot drinks and warm clothing (if fishing in the depths of winter) plus a powerful torch and other necessities such as a towel and head lamp etc. Actually pre-baiting during the hours of darkness, areas that are popular during the day *(see Ground baiting Tips 6 and 7)* can make an enormous difference to your results. Try it and see.

20 Ever tried fly fishing for pike? I should say 'fly-rodding' really, because with pike, and to a much lesser extent other predatory species such as chub, perch and zander, flies are tied up to represent small fish, frogs, newts or small rodents, etc, not flying insects. You need a fairly long (10 foot is ideal) powerful rod capable of throwing 9 and 10 weight lines, plus a large diameter fly reel, preferably with a sensitive disc drag. Add a floating, sinking and fast-sinking line, and you are there, but for a few short, supple wire traces (which become the leader tippet) plus an assortment of large flies and bugs. It's great fun too, and in shallow water especially, the turn of speed and subsequent tail-walking action from a fly-hooked pike can prove spectacular.

18

GRAFHAM WATER

Roach and Dace

Roach and Dace

1 Being a shoal fish, roach are forever watchful of changing situations and circumstances that affect their brethren. Which is why the entire shoal often stops feeding confidently at the drop of a hat (as though a switch has been pulled) when danger occurs. Like the sudden appearance of a pike in the swim, with its fins quivering (a sure sign of its intention to attack) or simply the sun suddenly hitting clear water at an angle that immediately illuminates everything. The shoal is merely relating to its vulnerability. This is why the biggest, wiliest roach of all, those over that magical 2lb bracket for instance, whose fellow shoal members have diminished in numbers over the seasons, through predation and disease, usually only feed with the utmost confidence in conditions of low light: at dusk and into darkness, and again at dawn. Because time has taught them they are far less vulnerable

and subsequently less likely to be attacked and eaten, when their pursuers cannot see so well. A point well worth remembering.

2 When you cannot buy a bite from river roach in cold, winter conditions, it is because their metabolism has slowed down and they refuse to move quickly in order to intercept food on the move, no matter how juicy your maggots. Fact is, roach hate changing position every few seconds in really cold water and expending unnecessary energy. They much prefer to slowly suck up small particles of 'static' food such as maggots from the river bed. So switch over to quiver-tip ledgering, using a small block-end feeder (to deposit loose feed with extreme accuracy beside your hook bait) and offer two maggots on a size 16 hook, stepping down to smaller hooks and a single maggot if bites are not forthcoming.

3 Want a really big dace? Something between say, 12 ounces and that magical one pound figure. Then here's a good tip: concentrate trotting maggots or small cubes of bread crust, close to the bottom in the deeper, 'roachy-looking' swims of smaller rivers, particularly chalk streams, during the last two weeks of the river fishing season in early March. Dace are often segregated by sex at this time as an early grouping process prior to their eventual spawning during April, with the big, pigeon-chested females resting up in the deeper, slower swims, while the males, (already covered in spawning tubercles) decidedly wiry and sand-papery to hold, mass together along the fast, shallow reaches.

4 When ledgering using basic rigs with small baits presented on small hooks for roach and dace, particularly

3

during the cold, winter months when bites are far less aggressive, it's imperative to employ the most sensitive of quiver-tip indicators. For those who do not own built-in, or push-in quiver tip rods of varying tip strengths, invest in a selection of screw-in quiver tips starting at one ounce test curve for really slow currents, going up to 2-2½ ounces for rivers like the full-flowing Severn.

5 There is something extraordinarily satisfying about watching a strong flow whisk your red-topped float

smoothly downstream. The current draws the 2lb-2½lb test line steadily from a free-running centre pin reel, while you gently brake the side of the drum with thumb pressure, ensuring the bait is presented as near as possible to the actual current speed down there close to the bottom. Yes, searching for specimen-sized roach in running water is arguably the most rewarding of all ways to see a big one come sliding over your net. And by big, lets say roach of around 2lb and upwards, because being in a minority and rather scarce in these times of chronic 'cormorant

predation', such fish are now extremely highly prized. And to encourage one to intercept a moving bait (maggots, casters or a piece of fresh white bread flake) mild conditions coupled to a 'coloured' river are imperative. If long trotting, and the river's running crystal clear, you're unlikely to get a bite until the light fades, and then you have but a few casts remaining to score. But catch the river immediately following heavy flooding when visibility just starts to improve, but where you still lose sight of a maggot a foot below the surface, and those roach, if they exist in a large enough shoal,

5

Roach and Dace

could well feed for at least a couple of hours. So make the most of mild spells and coloured water.

6 To alleviate the annoyance of debris, both surface and down the line, when ledgering for roach and dace in a swollen river, you have two options. Either to fish 'static' mill or over-shoot pools that have backed up - which can be 'full' of fish in the right conditions. Or, to select swims immediately behind wide bridge supports, behind sunken trees or on the inside and immediately downstream of acute bends. In short, wherever fish group up to seek respite out of the main flow, and where the full force of the current is deflected away from your ledgered bait.

7 To catch roach and dace using the 'waggler' float, it is important to bulk most of the shotting capacity (say 75-85 percent) on each side of the bottom ring, leaving a ½ inch gap between for the float to 'fold' smoothly on the strike. This not only allows 'dart-like' accuracy when casting because the shots pull the float through the air, but also only the very minimum of shots are then required 'down the line', to create a natural fall of the hook bait, which is most important when fishing in still waters. This leaves you free to add just a few small shot (No 6 and 8 shot are perfect) starting midway between float and hook. Then, if the rig happens to 'fold' at the highest shot, the hook won't be able to touch the float or

locking shots and tangle. For trotting in running water, larger shots can be used down the line, and an overall 'heavier' bulk shotting in order that the bait trundles along close to or actually 'dragging' bottom.

8 Remember to have a 'peaked' base ball-type cap or visor in your kit when float fishing for roach and dace in bright conditions. It is essential to stop you from squinting all day when concentrating upon the float tip.

9 When 'waggler' fishing for roach in waters where you may need to change from straight to tipped or insert floats, or to models carrying a greater shotting load, or maybe you simply wish to

11

switch from a red top to a black top for 'silhouette' situations, attach the float to your line using a silicon float adaptor. Switching from one float to another then takes seconds.

10 When you're float fishing or ledgering for roach and dace and your maggots or casters repeatedly come back 'crushed', you have actually missed and perhaps not even seen, a 'positive' bite. All cyprinid species including roach and dace are equipped with powerful 'pharyngeal' teeth in the back of their throats, for masticating their food, and

so to wind in 'sucked maggots' means the fish has actually had your hook well inside its mouth. To remedy this so you can identify a bite, keep shortening your hook tail if ledgering, or if float fishing move the lowest shot closer to the hook till bites are registered. Also, (and this is imperative in cold conditions) shoot the float tip down so it's a mere 'blimp' in the surface film.

11 When ledgering for roach and dace in fast flowing rivers during the cold winter months using a block-end feeder rig, and you don't want maggots or casters emptying

too quickly, here's a useful tip. Keep a roll of black electrician's tape in your kit, so you can slow down the rate of release by taping up some of the holes. Simple, but effective.

12 Regardless of which type of feeder you start the day with, make sure it is attached to your lead-link via a tiny snap link swivel. Then you can change the size and type of your feeder, literally within seconds.

13 When using bread flake on the hook do not pinch it on 'too' hard, especially when long

Roach and Dace

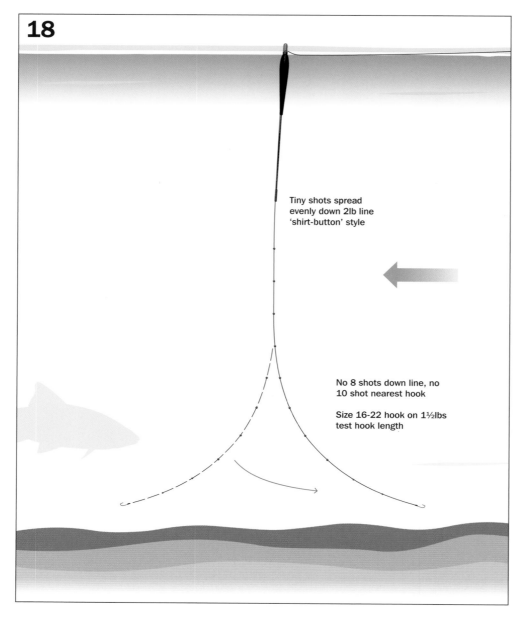

18

Tiny shots spread
evenly down 2lb line
'shirt-button' style

No 8 shots down line, no
10 shot nearest hook

Size 16-22 hook on 1½lbs
test hook length

fitted in seconds, accommodates elements between 3.0 and 4.5mm in diameter in a short length of clear tubing and keeps the two halves of the unit (which actually 'hinges and folds around the quiver tip) held tightly together. These adaptors come two to a packet, one large and one small. The larger will also fit on rod tops up to 2mm in diameter.

16 If luminous elements fail to hold your attention for ledgering at night, then simply illuminate a 'white-painted' quiver tip or rod top with a narrow torch beam. Position it from downstream, to angle outwards and upstream, thus illuminating 'only' the quiver tip. It will then not impair your night-time vision, nor shine into the water and scare the fish.

17 To quickly construct a mini ledger, pinch a shot onto the line 10-18 inches above the hook, and immediately above fold a short length of 'slightly thicker line' over the reel line. Pinch onto this sufficient shots to hold bottom, leaving a gap slightly narrower than the stop shot, so the ledger slides freely up the line.

18 To fish the 'stick float' correctly, you need calm conditions, (a gentle upstream wind is sometimes advantageous) and all the shots should be evenly spaced (shirt-button style) between float and hook. For the most subtle presentation of small baits like a single maggot or caster, make the two shots closest to the hook smaller than the rest. *See Diagram.* The stick float works most effectively in depths from 4-10 feet, but only at short range with the tip dotted down to a mere 'blimp' in the surface film, if held back gently when being run through, so fish it no further out than an under arm flick. A rod length and a half out, say. Do not allow any loose line between rod and float tip and get used to counting down and observing how many seconds it takes for all the shots to dot the

trotting, otherwise hook penetration at distance becomes a problem. Pinch only a small area of the flake (around the eye of the hook) on hard, allowing the rest to swell into an attractive 'carnation' around the hook.

14 For 'quiver-tip' ledgering at night, here is one easy way of watching a powerful 'beta light' element, or one of the extra-bright 'chemical luminous elements', both of which can be sleeved into a short length of clear tubing pushed onto a 'Tip-sight'

holder which itself is sleeved into silicon tubing on the quiver tip immediately below the tip ring. First of all a length of clear silicone tubing is sleeved over the tiny tip ring to accommodate the holder. For a more permanent fixture, the holder may be whipped to the quiver tip.

15 An even easier way of adding a 'luminous' element for night fishing, is by attaching an 'Enterprise Tackle' nightlight adaptor. This ingenious piece of kit which can literally be

tip of the float down to its final position, and strike instantly when it takes too long. One big shot may very well cock the same float instantly, but up to a dozen tiny shots will take several seconds, and this is your period for interpreting and striking into bites on the drop.

19 Of course not all bites will come on the drop when fishing the stick float. Some will occur when the float is allowed to run through totally unchecked and actually preceding the bait. Holding back steadily however will encourage the bait to fish almost directly beneath the float, thus instantly indicating the tiniest of bites from the wiliest big roach or dace. Those who trot using a centre pin reel and brake the line by applying gentle thumb pressure to the reels drum, enjoy superb control for easing a stick float downstream. There is in fact no finer reel to use for this technique.

20 To locate big roach in our smaller, richest rivers, walk the river at dawn and again at dusk with binoculars. Even during the colder winter months big roach love to porpoise on the surface, especially during those frosty mornings, instantly giving away the whereabouts of the shoal, which tend to occupy the same, even-paced runs and glides all winter through. Seeing that large, red dorsal fin, followed by a red tail as the roach rolls is a lovely and quite unmistakable sight.

19

Rudd and Golden Orfe

1 Although most anglers tend to associate catching rudd with offering free-falling baits close to the surface during the summer months, in shallow lakes averaging 3-6 feet which tend to warm up quickly during mild winter spells, estate lakes in particular, rudd, and large rudd at that, are a very targetable species.

2 For 'winter rudd' try at the deepest end of an estate lake (close to the dam) and put out a dozen or so tangerine-sized balls of bread-based ground bait at a short to medium casting distance. Say 30 to 50 yards out from the dam. Then, using a two-rod ledgering approach (Avon style rods are ideal for the job) simply ledger thumbnail-sized lumps of fresh white bread flake covering size 10-8 hooks tied direct to a 4lbs reel line.

3 For bite indication when ledgering for rudd, and this applies both summer or winter, rely on simple 'bobbin-type' indicators, and whilst many bites will give positive 'lifts' or 'drops' of the bobbin, don't be afraid of striking at 'two-inch' movements. Fishing lighter with smaller baits will only attract 'smaller' Rudd. And you could be looking at beautiful golden-sided specimens close to or even exceeding 2lbs. So don't settle for less.

4 Whilst rudd regularly hybridize with roach wherever both species occur, only rarely in England do rudd/bream hybrids (they are common in Southern Ireland) exist. Rudd/bream hybrids are actually a fine, hard fighting fish displaying the finer qualities of both species. They are thick-set with muted, golden-bronze flanks (quite unlike any other fish) and have scales noticeably larger than a true bream. The fins however are red-brown and the lips usually level.

5 Catching rudd on the fly rod during the warm summer months when they cavort regularly on the surface in the pursuit of hatching flies is a true delight. An 8 or 9 foot 4-weight outfit with floating line and a fine leader tapering to just a 2-3lbs tippet is perfect for the job and allows rudd of all sizes to show their sporting value. By their splashes, identify whether fish are sucking down adult insects on the surface or insects emerging from their pupas in the surface film and match your artificial accordingly.

6 Good patterns of dry flies to tempt rudd are black gnat, (which represents many adult midges), all the olives and particularly small sedges. They will also move aggressively to lightly leaded imitations presented 'on the drop' such as a mayfly nymph or a shrimp pattern, when nothing is happening on the surface.

7 Targeting rudd that are feeding close to or actually from the surface is most effectively practiced using the 'flat-float' controller technique. The 'controller' which adds both weight for casting in addition to a visual indicator, is simply a 2-5 inch length of unpainted peacock quill (what could be more natural floating flat on the surface than a bird quill) common reed, or (for fishing at greater distances) rd of an inch diameter stained, (use green garden

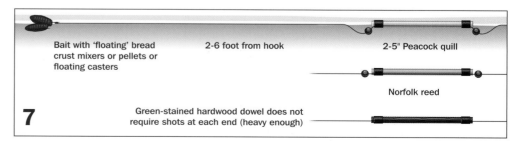

Bait with 'floating' bread crust mixers or pellets or floating casters

2-6 foot from hook

2-5" Peacock quill

Norfolk reed

7 Green-stained hardwood dowel does not require shots at each end (heavy enough)

fence stain) hardwood dowel. Each of these three floats is attached to the reel line with a wide band of silicone rubber at each end, 2-6 foot above the hook, with a shot close up to each end. *See Diagram.*

8 Using a heavier 'dowel' controller, additional casting weight is usually not required. But for peacock quill and reed, simply pinch a BB or AA shot onto the line at each end. Surprising distances can be cast with flat controllers, using naturally buoyant baits like casters, bread crust, or pellets presented in the surface film. Alternatively, a crust and bread flake cocktail, or a caster and maggot cocktail, etc can be offered 'on the drop'. Gloriously 'positive' bites result from fishing the flat float technique, with it suddenly sliding across the surface or actually being dragged under. So hold the rod throughout.

9 A lightweight, 13-14 foot 'waggler' rod coupled to a baby fixed spool reel filled with clear, 3lbs test mono, is the perfect combo for surface rudd fishing. And you'll need a catapult for regularly

putting out floating casters way up wind to get the rudd up on the surface and active.

10 For taking rudd off the top at long distance (30 yards plus) swap the 'flat-floats' for a small 'tenpin' floating controller, stopped by a five turn stop knot and tiny rubber bead, 2-4 foot above the hook. For catching carp/rudd off the top, *see Carp Tip 4.*

11 To distinguish between a true rudd and a roach/rudd hybrid first look at the fish's lips. The true rudd has a noticeably protruding lower jaw, showing it was purpose built for feeding effectively near the surface, while with 'hybrids' the lips could be level. The body of a true rudd is noticeably deeper than that of either a 'hybrid' or roach and the colour is of burnished, highly reflective, buttery-gold enamel along the flanks, fusing upwards into olive-bronze along the back. Its fins are bright orange-scarlet, and there is a distinct 'keel' to the anal fin, which is overlapped in a vertical line by the dorsal. 'Hybrids' are of a more even, muted, far less intense colouration. So if you are in any doubt on

Rudd and Golden Orfe

12

any of the above counts about the fish you have just caught, discount it as a true rudd. For rudd/bream 'hybrids' *see Tip 4*.

12 To stand a chance of catching numbers of specimen-sized rudd (fish between two and three pounds) which by the year are becoming less common in England, Ireland, in both the north and the south, throughout its canal, river and inter connecting lakeland waterways, offers superlative rudd fishing. Contact The Irish Tourist Board, or top Tour Operator like Anglers World Holidays, tel 01246 221717.

13 In lakes and pits where carp, tench or bream predominate, species at the end of the food chain like rudd, especially big rudd, are at their most catchable when the other species are not. So concentrate on locating the rudd shoals during the middle of the day when they love to bask close to the surface.

14 Big rudd also feed in earnest at dusk and dawn, giving away their whereabouts by cavorting and porpoising in the surface film as they inhale emerging insects. They can however at such times be encouraged to accept large bottom baits such as a thumbnail-sized piece of bread flake covering a size 8 hook (rudd have large mouths) ledgered over a few handfuls of mashed bread ground bait. But once fish start disappearing from the shoal sport is often short-lived.

15 Like roach, rudd are covered in protective mucus which is easily removed by holding them in dry hands. So always wet your hands (quickly grabbing the wet landing net mesh will do) before picking one up to unhook.

16 Rudd are equipped, as are all cyprinids from gudgeon to the mighty mahseer, with a pair of powerful 'pharyngeal (throat) teeth'

for masticating their natural food into a pulp prior to swallowing. Which is why worm or maggot baits often come back 'crushed', when you have either missed or not even seen a bite, but your hook must have been sucked back into the fish's throat just the same.

Rudd and Golden Orfe

17 To remedy missed or unregistered bites from rudd, either shorten your hook length if ledgering, or move the bottom shot much closer to the hook if float fishing.

18 For targeting small groups of big rudd which are loath to leave the sanctuary of lily pads during daylight, 'free lining' a slow-sinking bait 'on the drop' often scores where 'static', bottom-fished baits do not. Try a large piece of fresh white bread flake, 'lightly' pinched onto a size 10 or 8 hook, so that upon landing on the surface it very slowly descends. Experiment in the margins to ascertain exactly how hard you need to pinch the bread on so it sinks slowly, before casting amongst the lilies. And then watch the line like a hawk as the bread slowly sinks, striking instantly into any unusual movement. Fortunately, rudd amongst lilies are invariably bold biters, with the line fair 'zinging tight' or dramatically 'falling slack', should a fish swim towards the rod.

19 Golden orfe are not dissimilar to rudd in that they are always on the move, darting about and forever looking upwards in order to intercept 'falling' food items, or one floating on the surface. And everything mentioned in *Tips, 7, 8 and 10* for catching rudd, will also account for the beautifully coloured golden orfe.

20 Golden rudd, are quite a rarity in fisheries, although they are a popular pond fish. Their overall 'salmon-pink' colouration is much like the golden orfe, and they are no different to catch than naturally coloured rudd. Because of their bright and distinct colour they feed quickly when close to the surface. It's almost as though they realize that they are brightly coloured and thus an easy target to predatory birds like the heron and of course pike. One reason perhaps, why it is that whenever golden rudd are stocked into a fishery with naturally coloured rudd, with which they interbreed freely, incidentally, they never seem to last too long. They are simply too visible to predators like albino fish.

19

Tench

Tench

1 To help 'dour' tench fishing come 'alive', try actually wading into shallow, weedy swims (wearing chest-high waders of course) and with a long handled garden rake give the bottom detritus a really good going over whilst creating (if the weed is that bad) a wide channel to fish in. In less than a hour's work (there is nothing to stop you preparing two or three spots) a swim can be cleared and the bottom subsequently stirred up with all manner of natural food items left in suspension ready for the tench to turn up in a hungry mood. Which they will do quicker than you can imagine with colour in the water. For deep swims, purchase one of those wide, heavy rake heads to which rope can be tied for throwing out.

2 Learning to understand the distinctive 'feeding' bubbles of tench will result in more fish in your net. Small clusters of say four to ten small, non-fizzy bubbles rising to the surface come from the fish itself, (through its gills in fact) which is what happens when all cyprinid species masticate their food with their powerful 'pharyngeal' (throat) teeth. Whereas those long lines or patches of larger, 'fizzy' bubbles come from 'methane' trapped immediately below the bottom detritus rising to the surface. You can sometimes actually see bits of twigs and leaves accompanying bubbles into the surface film. The result of vegetation such as leaves and weed that has rotted down, and subsequently been released by a tench standing on its nose and deliberately running along the bottom to dislodge items of natural food such as shrimps and bloodworms, etc.

3 To duplicate the kind of 'fizzy' bubbles tench send up via the bottom detritus when feeding aggressively, just run a rod rest or the end of your landing net handle along the bottom of any 'silty' swim, especially those directly beneath trees and you will immediately create the same effect.

4 When fishing at 'close range' float fishing the 'lift method' is phenomenally successful due to the way species like tench (also crucian carp,

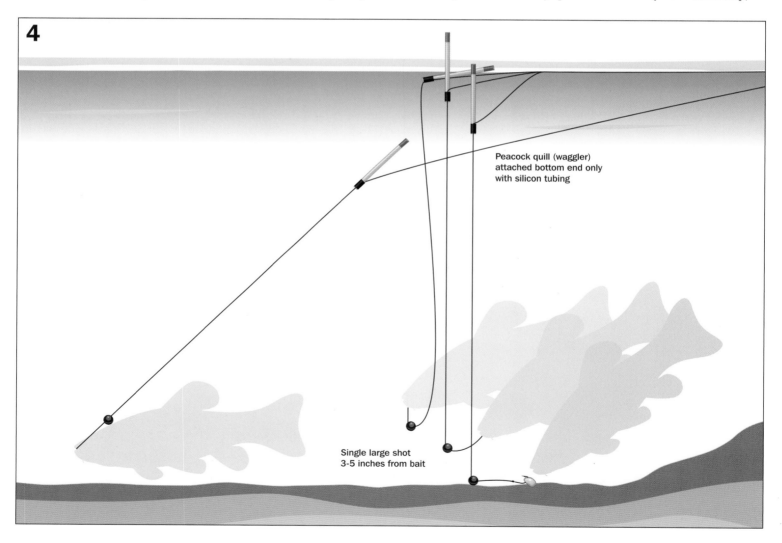

4

Peacock quill (waggler) attached bottom end only with silicon tubing

Single large shot 3-5 inches from bait

Tench

5 Unlike most cyprinids, male and female tench can be told apart easier than any other species. The smaller, often darker, more 'dogged-fighting' males have crinkly, spoon-shaped pelvic fins which when spread out cover the anal vent, with lumpy, protruding muscles or gonads above. Whilst the pelvic fins of the female are smooth, of normal shape and do not cover the vent.

6 To facilitate quick and easy attachment of 'bobbin' indicators to your bank sticks when ledgering for tench, simply whip on a tiny rod ring at the top of the bank stick. Then add a snap-link swivel to the end of your 'bobbin' retaining line. Incidentally, a two foot length of 80lbs test Dacron is the perfect material for 'bobbin' retaining lines. Possessing minimal stretch it will not 'twang' back like heavy monofilament on the strike.

7 In summer lakes which have a covering of filamentous weed on the bottom, tench really respond to ledgered baits that are popped-up just above the weed and in plain view. Try baiting with a large lobworm and inject a little air into the head end, fixing a large shot on the line several inches from the worm so it floats up just above the weed in an attractive, gyrating manner. Alternatively, try a cube of luncheon meat on a hair, to which a piece of buoyant rig foam (cut to the same width of the meat) has been added. Make sure this is threaded on last so it floats uppermost.

8 If when ledgering for tench using small hooks and maggots the maggots come back 'crushed', (indicating they have in fact been sucked back to the fish's pharyngeal teeth for mastication) keep reducing your hook (shorter and shorter) length till 'hittable' bites are registered on your indicator. Alternatively, keep your eyes glued to the line where it goes into the water immediately in front of the rod tip, and strike at any lift or twitch, no matter how slight.

and to a lesser extent bream and king carp) feed naturally, by standing on their heads to suck up baits from the bottom. By using a slim stem of 'buoyant' peacock quill (waggler float) attached with silicon tubing at the bottom end only, which not only 'lifts' (hence the method's name) but actually supports a single large shot fixed on the line 3-5 inches from the bait, during the

time it takes the tench to right itself back into to a horizontal position, a firm strike can be made at any time before the float actually lies flat. Once it does, the tench is of course supporting the shot and may eject the bait. So never wait for the float to go under before striking. This applies to all species targeted with the 'lift-method'. *See Diagram.*

9 To counteract subsurface tow when ledgering for tench using 'bobbin-type' indicators such as the 'Tenpin', simply pinch one or two 2, or 3x SSG shots onto the retaining line immediately below the bobbin.

10 Wherever clear water tench are unbelievably 'spooky' during the hours of daylight, float fishing at night using a luminous 'chemical-element' tip which is sleeved onto a waggler-style float via a piece of clear tubing, is often the answer. Bites not only happen, as the light starts to fade, but are most positive. The 'lift-Method' works well here. *See Tip 4.*

11 There is no favourite or best method for coming to grips with the rare, 'golden tench'. This beautiful creature, with a 'black eye' often called 'banana fish' due to its bright yellowy, sometimes orangey body, flecked all over with small black markings, (just like a banana) appears not to hybridize with the common green tench, and exists in only a few isolated fisheries within the British Isles.

12 If you wish to specifically target a rare golden tench, then visit the complex of lakes at the 'Anglers Paradise' fishery in Devon, which contain good numbers of this breath-taking species to 7lbs plus.

13 When casting tight up to reed lines from the bank or an anchored punt or boat (surely one of the nicest ways of accounting for summer tench) use a bodied waggler float rig with most of the bulk shot grouped around the base (which precedes the bait during the cast) and have just two small shots down the line, the lowest 6-8 inches from the hook actually coming to rest on

the bottom once the bait has 'arced' downwards through the water to settle immediately below the float, mere inches from the reed stems along which tench patrol.

14 Ledgering 'method-feeder' style is a deadly way of taking summer tench, especially from distant swims. Use a ground bait mix that breaks down quickly (it's no good lying there clogged around the frame feeder for 30 minutes when tench are on the rampage) and use a short 4-6 inch hook length. Include hook bait samples like casters, chopped worm, corn or small feed pellets in your ground bait mix, whilst baiting with the same on the hook.

15 To complement a pellet-based feeder ground bait, soft hook pellets are especially effective whether hair rigged or side hooked. Alternatively, and this works great over filamentous bottom weed, hair rig artificial floating sweet corn, which floats up above the weed. Tench hit it like it's the only kernel of corn left in the lake. Artificial casters can score too.

16 Free-lining for tench may well seem an ancient technique in these days of hair-rigging and bolt rigs, but in certain situations it can still produce. Tench hugging the margins amongst reed mace or sedges for instance or those lying beneath the shade of overhanging rhododendron bushes or willows, where a heavy bolt lead rig 'sploshed' in amongst them, will put an instant end to any possible result. Tench moving through gaps in dense weed immediately below the rod tip, or simply tench moving very close in through clear water that can be easily seen and cast to.

17 In each of the above situations, free lined bait, especially a 'natural' bait like a big lobworm, is liable to be immediately inhaled without suspicion. Or you could try

a large piece of soft protein paste, a piece of 'slow-sinking' bread flake, or better still a bait of 'balanced' paste and crust that will come to rest on top of the most dense weed.

18 To free line effectively you need to be nicely camouflaged and kneeling or sitting well back from the water's edge so that only the end of your rod hangs out over the surface along the margins. You then simply watch the fish or the line between surface and rod tip for bites, and you'll enjoy the most glorious of uninhibited 'slow' indications, where you can almost pre-empt the line lifting and snaking out behind the tench as it moves away with your bait, before striking firmly. And what fights and long runs you'll enjoy as a

consequence! So use an Avon type rod and just a 6lbs reel line with a number 6 hook tied direct.

19 When 'immediate' bites are expected to a free lined bait, simply hook your forefinger around the line just above the bale arm, so that you'll still feel the line move should your attentions be elsewhere.

20 For long free lining sessions rig up both front and rear rod rests with the rod tip angled downwards, and loop a coil of silver kitchen foil around the line between reel and butt ring on a two foot drop. Fish with a closed bale arm so you can strike the instant the foil indicator either rises or drops back.

Trout

Trout

1 When sight-casting to monster rainbows and the big browns especially, of small exceptionally clear-watered, man made lakes, and they won't play ball, showing not the slightest interest in a sumptuous, weighted, slow falling imitative nymph no matter how attractively you 'twitch' it, try this. Observe closely the 'movement route' of the particular trout you're after (most big, small-water trout adopt a 'favoured' feeding route) and select an area where it usually comes close and is thus easily visible through the clear depths. Now, with your prize trout well out of sight, roll out a heavily weighted Czech nymph of a colour you can clearly see, tied to a long leader and allow it to free fall down to the bottom, obviously at a spot over which the trout will eventually pass. Keep your eyes glued to the exact spot and when the fish next comes round, twitch your Czech nymph up off the bottom clearly within its path. Bingo!

2 For an entirely 'different' slant on modern fly fishing for trout, which is really great fun, why not try 'float-tubing'? Many lake-land and reservoir trout fishery complexes up and down the country encourage this fascinating approach and even have equipment for hire. If you already own a set of diving fins and lightweight, chest-high waders however, you may even wish to purchase your own 'tube'.

3 To enjoy a days 'tubing' you simply walk backwards into the water (fins/flippers already on) with shoulder straps supporting the tube which has an open front, across which is stretched a webbing seat, and suddenly you're afloat, sitting most comfortably with legs dangling ready to work those fins. Most purpose-built tubes have zipped compartments on top to house necessities, and can be easily inflated (built-in tubes for blowing into) and deflated in minutes. You get to explore all those awkward to fish (from bank or boat), tree-covered spots around islands, etc and there is a wonderful sense of 'freedom' when out tubing. And subsequently playing fish when actually 'in' the water is pure joy.

4 Fancy some action with jet propelled rainbows and maybe even the occasional big brown or two during the cold winter months? It's fabulous fun! Gone, for some thank goodness, are the days when fly fishers packed away their rods throughout the winter because trout were perpetuating their spawning cycle, and hooking into skinny black cock fish with kype-like jaws, or gravid hen fish swollen

with roe, was just not on. Today however, progressive still water fisheries stock only with 'triploids', trout coming from eggs that have been subjected to a heat-shock treatment, making them 'sexless' adults which remain in tip top 'silver' condition all year round, and fighting fit, using all their energy packing on weight as opposed to producing eggs or milt.

5 And how do triploids fight in cold water conditions? If anything they actually battle harder and for considerably longer during the winter, particularly in deep, clear, still water fisheries. So what's stopping you?

6 Though individually 'small' in size, the family of 'midges' which we fly fishermen refer to as 'buzzers'

(because the hordes of egg-carrying females when gyrating over the water at head height audibly 'buzz') includes more than 400 species, and is easily the most important family of flies for the still water angler. But really, just a couple of imitations, say black and red standard buzzer patterns, and the same again in 'suspender' or 'emerger' versions, where flotation fibres at their heads (to represent gills on the naturals) suspend them in the surface film, with their bodies hanging vertically, are all the fly fisherman needs to fool most trout.

7 The midge larva, non other than the 'bloodworm' is arguably one of, if not 'the' most prolific and thus the most valuable source of natural food not only for trout, but for all our cyprinid species too, from rudd to the largest carp.

8 When out boat fishing huge expanses of still water like reservoirs, and fish are on 'buzzers', but due to bright conditions the trout are staying deep, the standard technique of 'drift fishing' does not always work. This is because by the time you have cast out and let the team of flies sink to the right depth before starting the retrieve, the cast is almost back to the boat and you have to recast. Far better therefore to anchor-up and let the flies sink to the required depth, then make the retrieve at your own pace.

9 Barometric pressure is something we all 'know' must seriously affect our sport, but rarely get to pin point when. Well, those who regularly fish small, man made, clear water trout fisheries where trout can be clearly seen repeatedly refusing

Trout

whatever fly is put before them, have noticed that the trout's mood changes 'drastically' in line with a change in barometric pressure. Whereupon they suddenly snap at anything for a few casts, before going back to being difficult again. And those whose wrist watch shows that pressure change, have subsequently bagged up. Food for thought, eh?

10 For catching 'cold water trout' in the early spring which are stocked into the deep water of reservoirs and gravel-pit fisheries where depths might shelve to 30 feet plus, then presenting a 'booby' fished on a short 3-5 foot leader and Hi-D, ultra fast sinking line, is one hell of an effective way of turning a 'hopeless' day into success.

11 'Boobies' are so effective because they work in reverse to all other flies. When you start to retrieve, having allowed enough time for much of your Hi-D line to be

laying on the bottom, 'boobies' (so named for the two extra 'buoyant' polystyrene balls - breasts no less) tied around the hook, will angle sharply 'downwards' as opposed to 'upwards' like all other artificials. So even the most wily, and fished-for trout has not the slightest reservation in gobbling them up. Most fish are in fact hooked way back in the throat.

12 If purchasing your first 'priest' for dispatching your catch quickly, then select one where one end unscrews and 'reverses' to become a 'marrow spoon' which when sleeved down the trout's throat and into the top of its stomach, will, after pressing its belly gently, tell you exactly what insects it has been feeding upon, so that you can match you're artificial to the natural.

13 To obtain the utmost enjoyment from catching trout, particularly large rainbows, from still water fisheries, invest

in a specialized 'smoker' which via a small metholated spirit burner heating hardwood, aromatic sawdust placed on top of the heating plate, cures, cooks and hot smokes your catch all in one. Try putting the hot-smoked flank of a large trout, wrapped in silver foil together with a large knob of butter and masses of coarse-ground black pepper, onto the Bar-B-Q. Lovely!

14 When casting a fly, always wear a hat, preferably one with a peak to alleviate glare and concentrate your field of vision (shield your eyes with your hand as if looking into the sun and you will see what I mean) plus

'Polarized' glasses. Together they greatly reduce the painful experience of a fly, travelling over 50 miles an hour, embedding in your head, or worse still, an eye.

15 If fly fishing from the bank, it makes more sense to spread your fly collection around your waistcoat in a number of small boxes, each holding different patterns such as nymphs, lures, dry flies, emergers, buzzers, and so on, as opposed to one large (wooden) box, favoured by many reservoir boat anglers . Upon leaving the car, you can then set off with exactly the types and patterns of flies that might be required during your day's fishing, instead of carting the kitchen sink, and its dog around.

16 Endeavour, even if it's only once in your lifetime, to be beside a top chalk stream trout fishery (to hell with the expense) with rod in hand, at 'Mayfly' time. The thickest 'hatches' of this extraordinary aquatic insect usually occur during the last couple of weeks in May, (global warming accepted) and trout gorge themselves silly. After getting your hand in with a couple or three 'easy' fish, you'll know whether trout are showing a preference for the newly-hatched fly or spent insects lying on the surface, inert with their wings stretched out. You can then take time in stalking one of those 'whopper' brown trout that only ever seem to present any chance of them sucking down an artificial, during the 'Mayfly' cycle.

17 For fly fishing all day in both large and small sheets of still water, without the undue fatigue of continually bringing your rod back and forwards, back and forwards, in order to get a long line out, learn the art of 'double-haul' casting. This entails roll casting, say a third of your line forwards, (following the retrieve) and momentarily pulling hard on the line during the back cast to accelerate its flight. A second downwards pull or 'haul' is then made (with your hand gripping the line immediately below the butt ring) prior to making the forward cast. And this acceleration will shoot out whatever line you have on the ground. It is in fact easier to do than explain because it's mostly all down to feel and timing. But turning round to watch the flight of your back cast will help enormously. And remember that the line must be as straight in the air as possible at the beginning of each 'haul' whether forwards or backwards. Try it.

18 Both 'golden' and 'blue' rainbow trout are not different species, merely coloured variants of the rainbow trout, whereas, a 'brown bow', is a sterile hybrid (little bred by fish farmers these days) resulting from the crossing of a rainbow with a brown trout. The 'cheetah' is another sterile hybrid, resulting from the crossing of a rainbow with an American brook trout. And the 'tiger' is a sterile hybrid resulting from the crossing of an American brook trout with a brown trout.

Incidentally, only into a handful of 'southern' chalk-stream fed lakes are any of these colourful trout stocked nowadays.

19 Never set out across a trout reservoir for a day's fly fishing without a 'drogue', which is employed in windy conditions to slow down the boat's drift so that you have more control over the way your flies are fishing. *See On the Drift and Trolling Tip 1.*

20 One of the most delightful ways of catching reservoir trout is to drift 'loch style', casting ahead of the drifting boat set sideways-on to the wind (with a drogue over the windward side) into the relatively 'calm' surface of 'wind lanes'. Long casts are generally made down a particular lane, and a team of three flies steadily retrieved back to the boat. Watch out for rainbows especially, which at the last second just as you start the backwards cast, appear from nowhere to shoot up and grab the point fly or sometimes even the' bob'.

18

Salmon and Sea Trout

1 Fancy catching a salmon on a 5 or 6 weight trout, brook-rod, and a leader tapered to just 6lbs test? Well, it is certainly not impossible, and guaranteed fun. You just need a little confidence and of course access to smallish clear-flowing rivers where salmon are known to rest up fairly close into the bank, because 'casting' is not in any order of importance here. The secret, having identified a lie close into the bank likely to hold a fish or two, immediately downstream from a croy, or beside pilings or behind a 'salmon stone' is to let a really heavily weighted nymph (a gold head for instance) quickly reach bottom following a short roll cast made square on, and then 'lift' it steadily upwards to the surface, where, every so often, a salmon, having followed it up through sheer curiosity, will nail it just before, or actually on the top. Sounds strange I know, but the technique really works well on small rivers, particularly southern chalk streams.

2 Selecting the right artificial to tempt Atlantic salmon that are periodically stocked into still water trout fisheries, is almost an impossibility. These particular 'oddities' do seem to feed on natural food items, and strangely, do not 'colour up' as might be expected, even when still uncaught in a lake for a year or more. A trait they do follow however is that even in large lakes they seem to favour definite 'patrol routes' which take them close into the bank, similar to the characteristics of large brown trout. So it's not so much the fly offered, but where and at what depth. Something that can actually be visually worked out in clear water fisheries.

3 When using 'Toby-type' spoons for catching salmon, a 'multiplier outfit' (6501 or 7001 sized left-hand wind) not only fits snugly into your hand (go for a 'trigger-grip' reel fitting, behind which your forefinger sits comfortably) counting the lure down to the river bed before clicking the reel back into gear is so much easier, than with a fixed spool reel. Start by casting directly across the flow and once the spoon touches bottom, simply put the reel back into gear and, holding the rod tip up, allow the current to bounce and wobble the spoon slowly across the river, occasionally touching bottom. Do not attempt to retrieve as the spoon comes around or it will rise and work too fast for a salmon to grab hold. It pays to have amongst your kit several different weights (from say 12 to 28, even 40 grams) of the same colour spoon, to work varying depths and current speeds.

4 When the lure reaches the end of its downstream ark and starts to 'dangle' just like a fly, then, and only then, start a slow retrieve. Then, when the spoon is back at the rod, take a short pace downstream and repeat the cast. In wide rivers make two casts at each spot before moving. The first short and the second long, to cover all potential lies.

5 One of the most famous salmon and sea trout lures, the 'Devon minnow' can really produce in cold water conditions. It is offered in the traditional, 'downstream and across' technique, either with a banana-shaped 'Wye' lead built into the trace 3 feet above the lure, which

bounces over a rocky bottom, or presented on a separate 3 foot link joined to a three way swivel, below which is a 1-2 foot mono link and bomb, or stick weight that literally 'bounce' over the river bed. A buoyant, balsa wood Devon, will then spin well above any snags. It's always worth keeping a few different patterns in your waistcoat.

6 In Sweden, a similar rig to the latter method is used in conjunction not with lures, but large tube flies. It catches plenty of sea trout and salmon too.

7 To cover runs or pools that can only be approached from downstream, one lure tops all others. So don't go salmon or sea trout fishing anywhere without a few 'Flying Condoms' in your kit. Referred to more reverently as the 'Flying C', which is really an elongated Mepp's-type spinner with a long, heavy, shaft and treble hook, over which is sleeved a coloured rubber tube, this lure works at its most effective when cast directly upstream and across. After touching bottom, it is then retrieved downstream and across with the flow. A technique which gives both salmon and sea trout a much shorter period of indecision, due to the angle and reduced length of time at which the lure cuts across their field of vision. And for this reason, the Flying C can prove deadly.

8 During the summer and autumn, long trotting for salmon in many of our smaller rivers, using a centre pin reel and a preserved shrimp presented attractively beneath a wide-topped float, will account for fish holding station in awkward, weedy, even impossible lies, which cannot be covered with the fly. Rig up an Avon-style rod with an 8-10lbs test reel line and a 'chubber' float carrying 4-5 SSG shots. Bulk this 18 inches above a size

8 treble hook with a 1½ -2 inch 'shrimping pin' threaded onto the line in between, so that it can be sleeved through the bait to keep it straight before nicking the treble into the head.

9 To present the preserved shrimp attractively, set the float to work the bait 1-2 feet above the river bed, and trot through at current pace, 'holding back' on the float every so often so the bait rises up attractively. And expect 'bold' bites, as though you were trotting for chub.

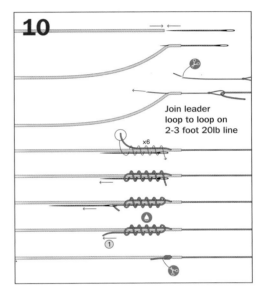

10
Join leader loop to loop on 2-3 foot 20lb line

10 For joining a full line or a shooting head to braided backing, use either the Albright knot *(see Freshwater boat fishing 'on the drift and trolling' Tip 10)* or the standard 'needle' knot. *See Diagram.*

11 There is no doubt, especially in low and clear water conditions, that fly fishing for sea trout throughout the hours of darkness, vastly improves your chances of hooking up. But even shallow, intimate, little rivers take on an entirely different character at night. So before you set forth into the night, walk your river slowly during daylight taking account of where trees and bushes are situated along each of the pools you intend covering and actually wade in to roughly

Salmon and Sea Trout

where you will stand to cast. Take a good look all around on the bottom for large boulders or tree stumps that might trip you up and work out your casting angles required to move steadily along the pool, taking into account that fish will often not be so far away under the cloak of darkness.

12 When tackling sea trout at night be certain that everything you might need, from a small torch to a pair of scissors, spare tippet material to a small pair of forceps, plus your fly boxes, etc, are all

stored and easily got at within the pockets of your waistcoat or wading vest. Realizing that your favourite flies are in a tackle bag back in the car when half way down a promising pool in the pitch black, is no laughing matter.

13 When tackling big, fast and boulder-strewn rivers for salmon or sea trout, where wading deeper than your knees, maybe up past your waist, is imperative to work yourself into a casting position for covering some pools, do not leave the bank without a

'heavy' wading staff, that is retained around your shoulders on a lanyard. You can then 'feel' your way downriver.

14 A pair of good quality, breathable, or neoprene chest high waders is an indispensable piece of kit to all salmon and sea trout fisherman, whether they Spey cast or throw artificial lures. To alleviate slipping on algae-covered stones and rocks and risk a ducking in freezing cold water, wading boots, which are worn over the integral neoprene socks, should have felt soles, as should waders with integral rubber boots. For really cold 'spring' conditions, 'all neoprene' waders' 5-6mm thick with integral, felt soled boots are recommended.

15 One important thing to remember about Spey casting is to always allow the 'bow' in the D to fully form and hang beside you, before roll-casting the fly out. It's then so easy.

16 Here's a handy tip that I picked up at the famous 'junction beat' on Scotland's River Tweed when Spey casting for salmon. Once you have cast downstream and across and rolled an upstream loop in the line to 'mend' it, whilst holding the rod parallel

British Isles, should you not wish to eat your catch, do not even attempt to net or especially, handle it. Using a pair of long-nosed artery forceps, slip the hook free whilst it is lying beaten on its side, and take great pleasure in watching it swim off.

19 If you are ever unsure about whether you have caught a salmon or a sea trout, or indeed a giant brown trout, grip firmly around its tail root. Salmon have a narrow tail root often referred to as a 'wrist', with a ridged and distinct 'keel' to their tail and so can easily be lifted up. Whereas both brown and sea trout (one and the same animal really) have 'soft' tail edges, against which your hand will slip. So they cannot be easily lifted.

with and low to the water as the line swings round, try moving the rod back say nine or ten inches, every few seconds, which moves the fly attractively at the other end in short surges. It induces takes on days when the fish are not really having it. Try it and see.

17 Remember that the exact height of a river will have a great influence on the chances of catching, whether fly fishing or working artificials. Ideally, a steadily falling river with the water clearing after a flood is most likely to induce salmon to lie-up in the pools for longer periods. Moreover, with the previous occupants nearly all having migrated upstream during the last spate, most fish in each pool will be newcomers and likely to hit the first angler's offering they see.

18 In these days of diminishing salmon returns from most river systems within the

20 'Worming' or 'prawn' fishing for salmon work when other methods do not, and especially in difficult times, such as the river being heavily coloured and out of sorts. So do not be put off by the stigma that some game fishermen like to attach to 'bait fishing'. A salmon does not fight any the less for being hooked on bait. It's down to how you value that fight.

Zvander

Zander

1 Zander are arguably, more sensitive to resistance, than any other British freshwater species. So when ledgering live or dead baits opt for a lightweight 'bobbin' indicator (that clip onto the line between reel and butt ring) hung on a two foot drop, as opposed to 'drop-off' indicators, which require significantly more pressure on behalf of the fish to register an indication. There are days when this makes all the difference between runs developing, and the bait being repeatedly dropped.

2 Even in heavily coloured water with mere 'inches' of visibility you can enjoy hectic sport with zander. Their large, light-reflecting eyes are purpose built for hunting in low light conditions when the eyes of their prey, such as small roach, rudd, dace and bleak, are not. Try working a 3-5 inch freshly killed bleak up and down 'sink and draw' style, close to the bottom mounted on a double treble trace. The most successful of all rigs being the 'Drachkovitch rig', (with which soft plastic shads and eels can also be used) invented by Frenchman Albert Drachkovitch, which comprises a lightweight, V-shaped sprung wire stem inserted down the dead bait's throat, to which at the top clip is attached a ball weight of between (depending upon depth, casting distance and current force) 4-12 grams. Also attached to the clip is around six inches of stiff copper wire,

which is threaded once through the bleak's slim body at the shoulder, and then wound firmly around the body. Two single trebles joined to wire or tough braid, one short and one long, are pushed into the fish's flank and tail root on opposing sides, to ensure a hook-up from whatever angle the zander grabs hold. Expect those juddery, snappy 'takes' from zander both on the drop, as the bait 'flutters', and whilst on the jerk, by working the bait constantly with your rod tip. Strike at anything 'positive'.

3 When is the best time to go zander fishing in the British Isles? When following a couple of weeks of intermittent, often heavy rain, the rivers are

well up and running the colour of strong tea. That's when! This enigmatic predator, with its huge 'glassy' eyes is superbly equipped for hunting out its preferred prey of small shoal fishes like roach, rudd, dace, gudgeon, bleak and skimmer bream, both during the hours of darkness and when flooded rivers offer minimal visibility. Exactly the kind of conditions you would not fancy for pike fishing, are exactly what zander prefer.

4 During the warmer months, at dusk and at dawn (again, during low light levels) are prime times for finding zander in a feeding mood, and of course, at any time during the hours of darkness, especially during mild spells of winter weather.

5 Whether you offer lures or use dead or live baits to tempt zander, you will catch infinitely more fish by striking instantly, certainly 'earlier' rather than later. As this predator is 'ultra sensitive' to resistance, the worst course of action is to allow several yards of line to evaporate from the spool as you might prior to hitting a run from other predators such as eels, pike and catfish. The further it runs off with your bait, the more resistance it will feel, especially if it runs off at right angles to the ledger bomb (zander living in

7 To catch zander on small live and dead baits choose roach, rudd or dace, (gudgeon work well too) between 3 and 5 inches long. Every so often a big zander will wolf down an 8 inch skimmer bream intended for pike, as they will the occasional sea dead bait, like a smelt or a herring. But generally speaking zander are not receptive to sea baits, nor anything over large. What they do seem to home into however and often with surprising speed, are small, indigenous, freshwater fish freshly killed that have been 'stabbed' a few times with a sharp knife, immediately prior to casting, which allows those attractive 'juices' to permeate quickly downstream with the current. Try it and see.

8 While there is just the 'one' species called zander in European rivers and lakes, two extremely similar species, sauger, and the larger, walleye, are found in North American freshwater. A small number of North American walleye, were in fact introduced into The Fens way back in 1925, long before the controversial stock of 97 zander were introduced into the Great Ouse Relief Channel in 1963.

9 There is actually a British record 'walleye' that weighed 11lb 12oz, caught from the River Delph by Mr F Adams in 1934, although as early as the 1870s, European zander were being brought across the Channel by boat to stock The Duke of Bedford's Lakes at Woburn. And there were numerous subsequent stockings of both European and home-grown zander into various southern waters during the 1920s, 1940s and the 1950s.

10 You'll catch far more zander, and enjoy their scrap much more, by not simply using the same tackle you do for pike. And it's all down to reducing 'drag' and 'resistance' to a biting fish. An 8lbs reel line matched to an Avon-type rod for instance is quite adequate, (double figure barbel come out on the same strength, and such fish fight far harder than zander) or 10lbs test at the most.

Fenland Drains have no option but to run along the drain) and eventually it will either eject the bait, or you will be unable to straighten the line out in order to set the hooks.

6 'Twitching' a small dead bait back just above bottom after waiting some time without a run, is often the 'trigger' to catching this finicky feeder. So above your wire trace and two-treble hook set up, with a large bead on the reel line in

between, use a 'bomb link-ledger' which ensures the bait won't foul bottom during the 'twitch' back. Eight inches of stiff rig tubing is threaded over 15lbs mono to form the link, with a bomb tied at one end and a ¼inch diameter ring and buoyant rig foam body at the top. This set up can be used in conjunction with a ledger bobbin, and the bait left static for a minute or two between bouts of 'twitching'. It will certainly keep you active alternating between two or three rods.

11 The same goes for trace wire and hooks. A 'soft', fine, multi-strand wire of around 15lb test twisted onto a size 10 swivel, is more than adequate yet strong enough for pike should one (as they regularly do) pick up your bait intended for zander. And with hooks, a duo of semi-barbed fine wire, size 10 fits the bill admirably.

12 If ledgering small live or dead baits for zander and the mono 'bomb' link which slides on the line above your wire trace repeatedly 'twists' around the wire, which it sometimes manages to do with surprising ease, then here's how to alleviate the problem. For starters, make the 4-6 inch bomb link from 'stiff' 20lbs test mono. And secondly, incorporate a 10 inch section of mono (same as reel line) above your wire

trace, the top swivel of which, (with a bead in between) the swivel of your 'bomb' link rests against. Tangles will then not happen.

13 When striking into zander be gentle. Simply wind down to take up any slack and slowly pull the rod back and upwards whilst reeling. Most times the hooks actually find purchase when the zander opens its mouth and shakes its head from side to side in order to eject the bait, just like a perch. And a heavy strike at this time will only pull out the trebles, especially from lightly hooked fish.

14 Learn to pull into mere one and two inch 'lifts' or 'drops' of the ledger bobbin when ledgering with small dead baits in clear water conditions and when zander are being

particularly finicky. Sometimes, any stronger indications simply will not happen before the bait is ejected.

15 Short, two to three inch sections of ½ - ¾ inch diameter eel or lamprey ledgered static on the bottom, can prove 'magical', and at such times zander will show a complete and distinct preference for them to all other dead baits.

16 In rivers and slow moving drains, trotting live bait downstream beneath a sliding float rig, into areas of low light such as beneath road and rail bridges can really prove productive. Such areas are inevitably quite deep (due to the excavation work and piling when constructing the bridge) and are usually prime zander 'hot spots'. So plumb

'Storm'. Available in just about every shape size and colour, many of these decidedly 'real to the touch' soft rubber and plastic, internally-leaded artificials are fitted with just a large single hook protruding from behind the dorsal fin. These models are ideal for working in and around weedy and snaggy areas without catching up.

19 Other types of rubber and plastic bodied lures, in addition to the large single also come fitted with a small treble protruding from the pelvic fins, and they all attract and catch zander 'big time' due to the vibratory, throbbing action from either curl or block tails. Some even have holographic flash foil, scented bodies impregnated with various oils. All have life-like swimming actions, and some are actually designed to be trolled. Try them all. But stick to the smaller 'zander' sized models of between 9-14cm in length.

20 An ideal combo for working 'rubbers', is an eight-nine foot, tip-actioned spinning rod coupled to a small fixed spool reel or baby multiplier, loaded with 12-18lbs test braid, for maximum sensitivity. Hits are often extremely gentle 'taps' and 'judders' of the rod tip, and you need to strike into any potential hit, no matter how slight the pull. Obviously, where pike are regularly encountered a short, (5-6 inch) but soft, multi-strand wire trace is imperative.

each run accurately and set the float to present the bait (a gudgeon or small roach, etc) two feet above bottom, with a swan shot pinched onto the wire trace just below the swivel to keep it down, and wind quickly down to pull into a fish immediately the float disappears. Wait too long and it will feel resistance and eject the bait.

River Severn, the Warwickshire Avon or the River Nene, locating them by going afloat and using a fish finder, can provide superlative daytime sport with artificial lures, particularly 'rubber shads'. Generally, the smaller sizes are best, when worked in a 'jigging', up and down action once bottom has been found.

17 On some of our larger rivers where zander have become well established, such as the

18 By far the best selection of synthetic rubber shad-like artificials is marketed through

At Anchor

1 There is nothing more frustrating, particularly when runs from pike are coming thick and fast, or the swim fills up with feeding bream or tench, than due to gusting winds, the boat suddenly drifts away and out of the action because your mud weights have lifted. So invest in the best and heaviest pair of mud weights that are available which you can lift, and shackle them (visit a boat chandler) to 'soft', half inch thick rope, at least 30 feet in length. Thin ropes cut into your fingers all too easily. I carry along a 'third' weight incidentally for extra stability in extreme winds and currents, which is lowered over one side amidships.

2 The 30-50lbs steel weights fitted to cruisers are the best mud weights money can buy. Being small for their weight they are easily transportable, mud or silt which clings to the bottom with surprising ease is easily shaken off before bringing them onboard by swishing from side to side (imperative when moving swims) and as you will 'hopefully' only ever purchase one pair, though expensive, they are money well spent.

3 To economize on mud weights, fill a couple of 2-3 gallon plastic buckets with cement. This provides a couple of cheap (boat-friendly) mud weights which benefit from already being covered in plastic. Remember to make a couple of small holes two inches apart in the top of each bucket-to take a U of ¼ inch diameter mild steel rod, for tying the rope to. And lay the bucket on its bottom (with two inches of your U of steel rod in the ground, with the ends bent back inside the bucket) before filling with a strong mix. Remember to smooth the cement over thoroughly when level with the lip of each bucket. Mud clings with ease to a 'rough' surface.

4 If you know of anyone on the railways, old steel railway track cut into 12 inch lengths, makes for formidable mud weights, and is easy to tie on.

5 When anchoring in deep and fast flowing water, such as the tidal reaches of my local rivers which feed the Norfolk Broads for instance, (and this applies whether targeting silver shoal species or predators) plan NOT to anchor sideways on to the flow. It is far better to put the bows of the boat pointing directly upstream before lowering down your first mud weight on a long rope, at least twice that of river depth. Three times for extreme conditions. Then once the boat has come to settle directly down river, lower your second weight over the transom on a short rope. This should keep the boat as steady as it's ever going to be in a current. A third weight put down at amidships will reduce any sideways yawing to a minimum.

6 When purchasing oars, it is well worthwhile investing in a quality pair of exactly the correct length for your boat and installing a pair of rowlocks which actually fit the protective rubber collar on the oars. There is nothing more frustrating - embarrassing even - should you tip over backwards within sight of other boats due to the oars pulling out of over-size rowlocks when leaning back into the rowing against a headwind.

7 Remember NOT to keep your oars on the boat if it is tied to a permanent mooring. Get into the habit of taking them home along with your engine and petrol tank.

8 Do you know that carp fishing from an anchored boat (in either river or lake) is not only 'possible (yes! using 'bolt-rig' ledger tactics and boilies too) but, where few other anglers ever bother to go afloat, sport can actually prove surprisingly good. Electric-even. Putting down a carpet of maize or wheat-based particle feed (which includes major attractors like well-stewed hempseed and tares or tic beans, etc) to which some hook baits like chopped up boilies and halibut pellets have been added, for a few days prior to fishing can only improve results (don't forget to mark the spot with an empty plastic bottle on a

cord tied to a house brick) which largely depend on being able to anchor your boat really steadily. Almost a technique in itself!

9 Flat bottomed craft like aluminium boats with semi-flat hulls are best, and wobble about the least, providing a wonderfully stable platform. However, and whatever your craft, the secret to carp fishing from a boat is having three really heavy mud weights (each of at least 50-60lbs apiece) with two of them tied to long ropes. And by long I mean at least five times swim depth. For fishing in rivers, put the bows of the boat into the flow and drop the front weight, paying out all the rope. Tie it off around a cleat and drop the stern mud weight. Now start pulling the boat back upstream on the bows rope while paying out rope at the stern. When you have equal lengths of rope in the boat which means you are anchored mid-way between the two weights, tie off both ends really tightly. Then put down your third weight amidships and tie off.

10 You now have the steadiest floating platform possible in both still and running water (it is the same process for anchoring in lakes and pits) from which bolt-rig ledgering, using the reel's 'free-spool' facility as your bite indicator, for carp or tench fishing, becomes immensely enjoyable. It's great for float fishing too. Try it and see. This way of anchoring was introduced to me by top angling guide Gary Allen who takes visitors after big carp and catfish along prolific stretches of the Rivers Segre and Ebro at

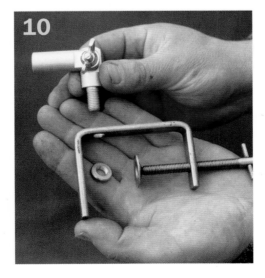

Mequinenza in north eastern Spain. Gary's e-mail address is: garyallenfishing@gmail.com. He can also be reached via his mobile on: 0034667455863. Whilst commercially produced boat-rod rests are available from specialist tackle shops to suit both trolling and at anchor fishing, homemade front rod rests for float fishing and special keep net angle locks for gunwale fixing are easily constructed by the DIY enthusiast. To make a gunwale bracket simply drill a ⅜th of an inch hole through the top of a small steel G clamp which is readily available from any hardware shops. This then accommodates either a front rod rest head of your choice, or the special angle top tilt built into top of the range keep nets, allowing the net ring to lie horizontal to the surface. For nets not fitted with this device, simply screw an 'angle-lock' into the G clamp and secure, as with the rod rest top, by a ⅜th BSF nut.

11 Don't wait till you are close to or actually anchored up over your favourite spot before laying all your equipment out within the boat in an organized manner. A quick getaway at the moorings by dumping everything in haphazardly could cost you

At Anchor

dearly in lost sport later on due to all the moving and scuffing about. So take time while the boat is still tied up to store everything where it won't slide or bang about. Set the landing net up and position the mud weights at exactly the spots from where they are going to be lowered at the bows and stern. Make up all the rods and rigs required (I take mine along already made up and broken down with elastic bands holding them together at both ends) storing them lengthways inside the boat (banks of 3-6, tubed, 'vertical' American-style rod holders are indispensable for this) so that as you approach the intended fishing area (wind permitting) the boat can be positioned side-on and both mud weights lowered simultaneously with the absolute minimum of noise thereafter. An old piece of carpet underlay laid on the bottom of the boat will help to deaden most of your shuffling about.

12 Boat fishing really does open up a 'whole new world' to fresh water anglers, whether pike fishing remote parts of the Norfolk

Broads and their connecting tidal rivers, or tench, bream, or carp fishing amongst the tranquillity of a secluded estate lake, mere, reservoir or gravel pit. You get to explore areas and swims never fished from the shore, and thus fish which rarely have bait offered to them. And even ledgering can be enjoyed from a boat properly anchored. *See Tip 9.*

13 A lightweight but stable (flat bottomed) car-top dinghy will get you started in boat fishing. Alternatively, there are several lightweight pack away-foldaway, one and two man boats from which to choose, such as the Samalite Discovery, foldaway dinghy and the 'folding' Portabote. And if you really catch the 'get away from it all' bug then it's well worth investing in a pucker 12-14 foot aluminium fishing boat and trailer which can then literally be taken anywhere. Aluminium hulls require absolutely no maintenance and thus hold their price. And they are available with extras such as rod holders, swivel seats and water tight compartments for stowage etc, to make life afloat all the more comfortable and enjoyable.

14 A good quality pair of binoculars (mine are size 10 x 42, and about the most

powerful you can hold steady using one hand) are indispensable when boat fishing. You can see from afar, before getting too close, the feeding bubbles of tench, bream or carp, and thus lower the mud weights long before scaring them. You can see fish swirling on the surface and capitalize by moving to the same spot. You can observe the floats and direction to which other anglers pike fishing the same water are fishing, so a wide berth can be given when on the move. And of course watching our native and migrant birdlife when out afloat adds an enchanting aspect to the world of angling.

15 When boat fishing at anchor in the depths of winter, as my experiences of spending close on 40 years pike fishing the windswept and lonely waters of the Norfolk Broads have proved, you should always set out well equipped against the elements. Even if it's warm and sunny when you arrive and think twice about leaving the thermal gear in the car. In addition to a good quality waterproof ¾ length coat with a built-in hood, (I wear a separate, peaked hat anyway so I don't have to sit on a sunny day forever squinting) and layers of warm clothing beneath, don't just settle for waterproof trousers. A tall, salopette-type/ bib and brace combo with shoulder straps, and long zips down the

waterproof trouser leg bottoms that go easily over, wide, thermal boots, are worth their weight in gold. Alternatively, some prefer a one-piece waterproof suit, (over a thermal under suit) which certainly keeps all the draughts out. Though should the weather turn warm later on in the day, you can always remove your top coat, if wearing separates. The choice is yours.

16 Everyone has their very own favourite food to take boat fishing. And while I guess 'Pot Noodles' are not everyone's idea of real food, we are talking about something hot and nourishing here with the least amount of fuss when sitting in a rocking boat, possibly in the rain or snow miles from nowhere. So simply taking along a flask of boiling hot water for adding to instant meals like 'Pot Noodles' (you get enough water for at least three 'Pots', from the average flask) plus some crunchy, pre-buttered rolls for 'dunking' (sorry I have heathen tendencies) requires little forethought. They are far more warming than cheese sandwiches, anyway.

17 There is nothing worse than going afloat pike fishing with a mate and both whacking out

say three rods apiece all around the boat, only to find all the floats and consequently the baits, huddled together in just one small area of the lake in due lee of the boat, mere minutes later. It's not exactly making full use of the potential area around the boat, which is the whole idea of going afloat in the first place. And of course it's all due to the wind dragging your lines and floats along. So for starters, plan only to place float-fished baits directly down wind of the boat. All the rest can simply be free lined (which are unaffected by wind drift) with a couple of swan shots on the trace so the pike has something to 'pull against' and thus move off directly away from the boat and requester a 'positive' bite. Also, to determine there are no arguments as to who should be fishing where, draw an invisible line either down the boat lengthways, or across the middle (depending upon which way on to the wind you have put the mud weights) and stick to your own half.

18 For securing firm anchorage in deep water when pike fishing the Scottish Lochs or in trout reservoirs, galvanized steel anchors of the 'hinged type' are imperative. 20 to 30 foot of chain is attached at the lower, hinged end of the anchor shaft, before being run along the shaft and secured to the other end with a length of weak cord, (that will

break easily under pressure) before it is joined with enough rope to accommodate at least twice the depth of water beneath the boat. To retrieve the anchor, motor upwind and pull heavily to break the cord, after which, the anchor is easily lifted from the roughest ground.

19 A deadly method for catching both pike and zander in really windy weather from large sheets of still water, using both sides of an 'anchored boat', is to cast directly across the wind (assuming you have anchored up with the bows into the wind) and allow a 'bow' to form between your float fished live or dead bait and rod tip. Then, by paying out line gently, the float will work the bait 'directly' down wind. Start with a cast close to the boat, and if nothing materializes along that particular drift, (you can work the bait as far as the float remains visible) slowly retrieve and make the next cast a few yards further out and try another drift. It's a great way of systematically searching large sheets of especially, 'feature-less' water.

20 Whether casting lures or wobbling dead baits for pike from an anchored boat close to rocks incorporate a 20 foot 'thick' mono rubbing leader between your wire trace and mainline.

On the Drift and Trolling

On the Drift and Trolling

1 Anyone who loves to boat fish on the drift using surface tow or the wind, whether fly fishing for trout, or casting dead baits or artificial lures for pike, will at some time or another find themselves at a distinct disadvantage without a drogue. This relatively inexpensive item of tackle is usually constructed from rot-proof nylon or canvas and is attached around amidships to the windward side of the boat by rope or strong cord, often with a short length of galvanized steel chain at the drogue.

2 Once your drogue is sunk below the surface and acting just like an underwater parachute (which of course it is) the boat's passage is considerably slowed down, so that fishing is done in a less hurried, more controlled manner. Thus the water is covered much more effectively.

3 Here's a tip for would-be drogue users. When the drogue is tied on slightly off centre, more towards the stern or bows, the boat will 'crab' across the wind, enabling it to run parallel with a particular feature such as a reed bed, island or the shoreline, rather than straight onto it.

Its great fun, and makes for vastly more interesting and calculated fishing. Try it and see.

4 'Back-drifting', presenting small, live fish or fish strip bumping merrily along the bottom 20-40 yards behind the boat (drifting along sideways on to the flow) is a most popular technique in tropical Africa on clear-flowing and clean, gravel-bottomed rivers like the Nile and the Zambezi, for both tiger fish and several species of catfish. Along particularly deep reaches, a large swan shot or two are added to the wire trace immediately below the swivel to ensure the bait is presented just above or actually bumping the river bed. And generally, because the bottom is largely made up of clean shingle or sand, baits rarely become snagged.

5 The same technique of 'back-drifting' also scores along many of our clear-flowing British rivers with pike and to a lesser extent, zander, when presenting dead baits, particularly where the bottom consists mainly of gravel or silt, and a non stretch, braided reel line (which allows you to feel every bump of the river bed) is used in conjunction with a

multiplying reel, so that free line can instantly be given to a 'taking' fish by a simple 'click' with the heel of your thumb. You need however to row or motor quickly upriver to release your terminal gear whenever the bait becomes snagged. Enormous lengths of river can be explored in this manner.

6 Back-drifting along with the current presenting float-fished live baits 10-30 yards behind the boat is another most effective way of accounting for pike. To keep the boat 'side-on' to the current throughout the drift, one angler sits on the centre seat and gently works the oars. Remember to keep a mud weight at the ready so it can be instantly lowered within seconds of a pike grabbing one of the baits,

10

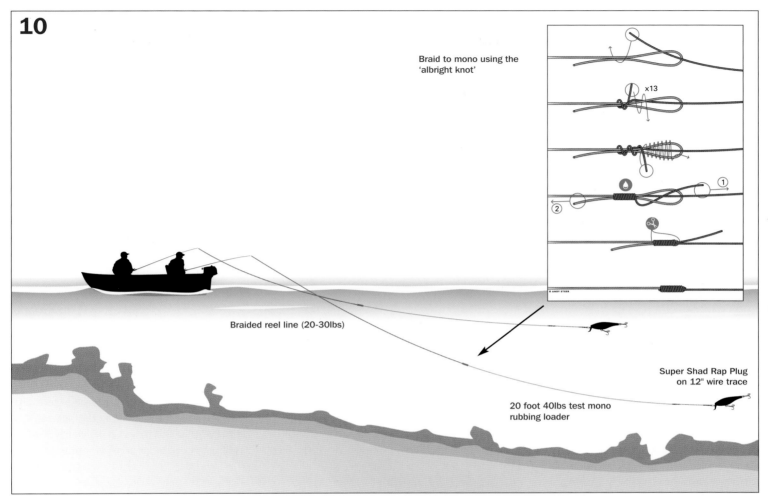

Braid to mono using the 'albright knot'

×13

Braided reel line (20-30lbs)

Super Shad Rap Plug
on 12" wire trace

20 foot 40lbs test mono
rubbing loader

© ANDY STEER

so a more thorough search of the area can subsequently be made. Pike do tend to 'group-up' in rivers in 'choice' lies, so make the most of these situations.

7 Freshwater trolling, save for reservoir and loch fishing, is not regularly practiced in the UK. It is not (understandably) permitted for instance on the Norfolk Broads, or throughout our networks of rivers and canals. But wherever you are allowed to pull an artificial lure behind a motor-powered boat, remember that due to its much thinner diameter, a braided line (used on a multiplier reel as fixed spool reels are useless for this technique) will allow any given artificial lure to dive significantly deeper than it would being attached to monofilament of identical breaking strain.

8 When trolling artificial lures, spoons, diving plugs, etc and regular taps and short bangs on the rod tip fail to develop into solid hits, take the rod from its rest and immediately following the next tap, click the reel out of gear (multipliers are the 'only' reels to use for trolling) and give a couple or three yards of line (so the lure in effect momentarily 'stands still') before winding back into gear and cranking the lure forward 'fast'. Whether you're after pike or big trout, or abroad targeting Nile perch or the legendary tiger fish, this ruse often results in a 'slamming' take. So be ready.

9 Holding the rod when trolling often produces 'bonus' fish which would otherwise not be caught. Rod holders can make you lazy. Get used to continually

fishing shorter or longer lines, especially around headlands for instance, where fish tend to congregate at the corners and dropping the lure back, or shortening the line accordingly whilst watching the fish finder read out. Similarly, if you are holding the rod when trolling a lure close to or amongst snags, you'll have a much better chance of subsequently landing the fish.

10 When trolling in freshwater over a rocky bottom using a braided reel line, incorporate a 20 foot 'thick' mono rubbing leader between your wire trace and mainline. Tie braid to thick mono using the Albright knot: a super-neat and strong knot which passes easily through level wind of multiplier reel. *See Diagram.*

On the Drift and Trolling

11

In clear water conditions you will actually be able to see pike following a lure or wobbled dead bait, etc right up to the boat, and observe areas of dense weed.

15 For bright and sunny conditions when the surface is calm, wear grey or amber lens Polaroids for reducing reflective glare, and a peaked cap.

16 Keep a mud weight at the ready even when trolling or drifting, and slip it over the side immediately you hook up and start playing the fish. You can then cover the area thoroughly by casting around, trying a variety of lures before restarting the drift or the motor for trolling.

17 Electric motors that work from a heavy duty battery and via their G clamp can virtually be clipped on anywhere around the boat, especially flat bottomed craft, are indispensable for correcting the line of drift every so often, and particularly for trolling over popular areas where the fish

11 Wherever you fish in the world, one way of ascertaining whether water levels are up or down, even in a 'flooded desert' environment such as Egypt's Lake Nasser shown here, is to study the shoreline. Look at the different lines of grasses and bushes that have sprung up from seeds washed up on the shore when the lake was at previous heights.

12 Try not to troll a mixture of mono and braided reel lines. If they come together, long, twisted tangles will result.

13 When letting out floating/diving plugs, keep them in your sight (floating on the surface behind the boat) whilst line pulls freely, without any 'thumbing' from the spool, till each is the desired distance behind the boat. Then click the reel into gear and allow each lure to dive. You then know their exact distance from the boat. If you 'thumb' whilst they are going out they will dive and you'll lose sight of them, not knowing how far behind the boat each is running.

14 Don't forget the Polaroid glasses when out afloat, especially in dull and extremely overcast conditions. Yes, especially when light values are low, for which HLT yellow lenses are indispensable.

15

On the Drift and Trolling

wind in immediately to inspect. The tiniest strand of weed can impair the lure's action, resulting in no hits.

19 Whilst it's nice and immediately instils confidence to mark fish congregated around sunken features when trolling using a sonar/fish finder, pay most attention to the actual depths prior to and immediately after each feature shown on the display screen, and work your lures at according depths. There is inevitably a 'hot' zone where one of the lures is grabbed as you pass through. Finding it is more important than relying on fish symbols shown on the display screen.

20 If out for a day pike fishing in gentle winds and you do not own a drogue but fancy a go at trying 'drift fishing', dangle your keep net (with a rock inside) behind the boat on the windward side, tied on firmly around the rowlocks. It will slow the boat down considerably.

become used to and consequently 'spooked' by the sound and vibrations of petrol outboard motors.

18 Whenever one of the rod tops stops vibrating to the particular lure it is trolling,

Rods and Reels

1 For some really exciting, opportune-style, wandering, pike, zander, perch and chub fishing invest in a little 'American-style', pistol grip, bait-casting outfit. Rods are tip- actioned and one piece, just 6-7 feet long, and work beautifully using a single-handed casting action, with a baby multiplying reel. Such an outfit allows you to place plugs and spoons, etc close alongside weed rafts or beneath overhanging trees, or along reed-lines etc, with extreme accuracy. This technique relies on mobility, stealth and observation and is particularly suited to small still waters and particularly river fishing during the summer and autumn months. So wear Polaroid glasses, drab clothes and take along only the bare essentials stored in your waistcoat. Then you'll enjoy walking for miles.

2 Snapping the top two or three inches of a finely tapered quiver tip rod, is in all probability the most common breakage amongst every type of freshwater rod. This is because the reel line usually becomes wrapped around the second (tiny) ring prior to casting whilst baiting up because the line goes slack. To alleviate this get used immediately before each and every cast, to gently pull on the line between reel and butt ring. If the line is wrapped you will feel it. Simply lower your end rig onto the ground and shake the rod tip while gently pulling the line between reel and butt ring, till it comes free. Alternatively, ensure the line is tight and your quiver tip slightly bent whilst baiting or filling the feeder, so the line cannot 'coil' around the end of the tip.

3 To obtain optimum performance in terms of 'lure action' and subsequently 'hooking-up' when working 'jigs' and 'jerkbaits' you need a specialized rod and reel outfit. The ideal rod should be 'stiffish', no longer than 6-7 feet with an acute tip action. Such rods are designed to be used with a 6000-6500 sized multiplier and therefore held upside down. This means that if you are right handed, you need a 'left-hand wind' reel, so that your strong arm works the rod. To ensure every flick of the rod tip is transferred to the artificial lure, a non-stretch, low diameter braided reel line of between 30-50lbs test is imperative. This may seem excessive, but some jerk baits are both heavy and large and the continual casting demands a lot of your reel line. And as braid is so much thinner than mono (less than half the diameter) it's better to err on the safe side. Besides, with stronger reel line, it is easier to pull an expensive lure free from most snags without the fear of breaking off.

4 Should you snap a few inches off the top of a built-in quiver tip rod, you'll need to replace the solid glass or carbon tip. Start by carefully removing the whipping around the junction with a razor blade or craft knife. This will reveal if the tip is sleeved through the rod's top joint and pulled out the end, or is merely pushed in from the top. Some manufacturers actually glue the tip in, in which case you'll need to cut back the end of the joint to remove the two to three inches of glued-in quiver tip, and then gently chamfer the end with a file to facilitate an even whipping, before fitting a new quiver tip. Keep all the rings of the old tip so they can be whipped onto the replacement. You will however, like as not, need to buy a new, tiny tip ring which simply pushes and glues on. Most manufacturers produce replacement tips, but for those who do not, buy a 30-36 inch solid glass 'Donkey top' and sleeve through the top joint till it protrudes from the end. Pull gently through and twist till it locks into place, then mark the spot with a pencil. Judge how much needs to be cut off from the thick end (use a fine tooth hacksaw blade for cutting) by coming back around two inches from your pencil mark and gently saw through. Pull through and twist again to 'lock' into position, before making a whipping over the junction, and then whip on the rings. If the tip is too fine, gently cut back to your requirements before obtaining a new tiny, push on tip ring and fixing with a touch of superglue. Now, should you ever break the new tip, it can be removed easily and a replacement fitted without having to cut the tip back again and alter the action of the rod. To finish, paint around 18 inches of the tip in matt white, with a two-inch band of bright red at the extreme end, for maximum visibility of tiny bite registrations in dull conditions.

5 When fishing abroad and several flights in light aircraft are imperative to reach secluded locations, three and four piece spinning and fly rods packed in a protective tube are worth their weight in gold.

6 Many rods are marked in their respective 'test-curves', which provides you, the customer, with an idea as to their power and what strength lines should be used. The late Dick Walker devised this useful guideline, which works

simply by multiplying the rod's test curve by the number 5. So a rod with a 2lbs test curve for instance, works perfectly in harmony with a 10lbs test monofilament line. Braided reel lines incidentally, do not come into any of these equations. To find the lowest breaking strain monofilament line that the rod will comfortably handle, multiply by 4 (8lbs test), and for its upper limit multiply by 6, which is 12lbs test. This does not naturally mean that lighter or heavier lines cannot be used in particular circumstances. It merely provides a useful guideline.

7 Due to their light weight, neat, smallness of size (compared to many fixed spool monstrosities) silky-smooth clutch and the fact that the line is wound directly onto the spool without passing around a bale arm roller (like a fixed

spool reel), small 'multiplying reels' are an absolute joy to use. And not only for lure fishing, the purpose for which they were initially devised. All manner of freshwater situations are arguably 'improved' by opting to use a baby multiplier instead of the traditional fixed spool reel. I use multipliers for much of my pike fishing for instance (the ratchet becomes an instant 'bite alarm' when the reel is in free spool, as it does when 'bolt-rig' ledgering for carp) and for both float and general ledgering tactics for carp and barbel, even tench.

8 To catch carp on the float at close range using a multiplier, line is simply pulled (using two fingers) from either side of the butt ring as I would do with a centre pin reel, and an underarm or sideways cast is made to where bubbles or tail patterns are erupting on the surface. When on, a big carp can be played noticeably closer to the breaking strain of the line, using a heavy drag setting, than with a fixed spool reel, because the line comes directly off and is wound straight back onto the spool (no line twist either incidentally) without travelling at right angles around a bale arm. Try it and see for yourself.

9 Psssst! Here is the best 'reel' tip of all. For most close range float fishing techniques in both running and still waters get yourself a 'centre pin' reel. For long trotting it is simply unrivalled and provides direct and perfect control over any float because you can easily slow down the float (and your bait) by applying gentle thumb pressure to the revolving drum. Quality centre pins are even fitted with a 'micro adjustable disc drag' (which puts pressure upon the spindle) for mechanically slowing the reel down in really fast currents, and have a built-in line guard to stop coils of line slipping behind the cage when fishing in slow rivers during windy conditions. And for playing big fish, because the line leaves the reel in a straight line (as opposed to going at right angles around a bale arm as with all fixed spool and closed face reels) line twist is never a problem.

JOHN WILSON'S
1001TOPANGLINGTIPS

Rods and Reels

10 Line clips, nowadays fitted into the side of the spool on the majority of fixed spool reels, are not always reliable. A big fish can easily steam off and snap the line when it is 'clipped up'. The answer? Well it may be old hat, but a simple 'tight-fitting' elastic band slightly smaller in diameter than the spool and placed around it, will not only prevent you casting beyond the baited area from which bites are coming (the reason for 'clipping up' in the first place) it will permit any whopper to keep on going and rip line off without the fear of breakage.

11 Here's a most important tip if you are considering purchasing, or indeed if you already own, a free-running centre pin reel. Because depending upon how you intend casting, either 'Nottingham' or 'Wallis' style, reflects the type of reel and even the rod, that you require. With 'Nottingham' casting for instance where fingers of line (like a spider's web) are pulled from between reel and butt ring and from between up to each of the first three rings above, (depending upon how far you wish to cast) you need a reel that has a built-line

guard. This stops line flapping behind the cage in windy conditions when trotting a float along 'slow-moving' rivers. Choose a float rod therefore, already fitted with three rings set close together on the butt section to accommodate centre pin fishing. Or whip a couple more on the rod you own.

12 For the 'Wallis' cast, originally devised for casting directly from the reel and trotting a heavily shotted float down fast rivers, a line guard is not required because the constant pull from strong currents stops line from flapping behind the cage. The impetus required however for starting the Wallis cast using a firm sideways swing of the rod and heavily shotted float rig, to send it distances of 20 yards or further across big rivers like the Hampshire Avon, for which the cast was developed, demands a reel line of at least 5lbs test. A 2lbs reel line for instance would instantly snap. So while heavy lines of say up to 12-15lbs test can be used on both types of reel for catching carp or pike, if you wish the facility of stepping down every so often to just a 2lbs reel line for sensitive float fishing in slow moving rivers as well as fishing heavier, then choose

a centre pin with a built-in line guard. If however you will not be stepping below lines of 5lbs test, and mainly fishing fast flowing rivers, a centre pin without a line guard is perfect for you.

13 Now that relatively compact fixed spool reels (size 3000 downwards) are available with a 'bait-runner' or 'free-spool' facility, and competitively priced too, it makes sense, whatever your preference in fishing methods, to use them. The free-spool switch, usually located at the rear of the reel, instantly disengages the spool's drag, so that line can be stripped from the rotating spool at a tension of your setting (via a calibrated knob) by a pike or a carp having belted off with the bait (hence the original term 'bait runner') without the rod being dragged in. And as you might be using this sensitive facility for any number of techniques such as ledgering for perch, pike or zander, free lining for catfish or eels, bolt rig ledgering for carp, tench, chub, bream or barbel, or simply float fishing for carp and you don't fancy the rod disappearing into the lake when you stand up to make a call of nature, any slight extra purchase cost seems irrelevant.

14 When casting with a fixed spool reel and whether ledger or float fishing, get used to the art of 'feathering' the line against the side of the spool using your forefinger, in order to brake the cast and bring the float or feeder down exactly where you want it. Feathering also makes the bait precede the float so it comes to land ahead of the float in exactly the desired spot. Practice makes perfect here.

15 It's a fact that fixed spool reels with front drags (with tension nut on the spool itself) though they might not look so 'space age' are actually smoother than those with 'rear drags.

16

16 Whether you choose a rod with a light (1¼lbs) test curve, or a heavy (2½lbs) model, those with an 'all-through' action, will not only allow you to enjoy the fight more, but also put your fish on the bank surprisingly quickly without the risk of the hook pulling or the line snapping when the fish is under the rod tip on a short line and decides to make a last ditch dive. Which is why fly rods are so incredibly effective. They just keep bending and bending to the lunges of the largest fish. So be careful when selecting a new rod. Decide whether you want it for close to medium range fishing, or for out and out distance work.

17 'The' most versatile tool covering most aspects of fresh water fishing is the 'Avon-style' rod, which has a test curve of around 1¼lbs. It will handle monofilament lines ranging from 5 up to 8lbs test and as such will easily subdue, due to its 'all through action', all but the most heavyweight of carp, pike and catfish.

18 Get used to holding your rod and (fixed spool) reel firmly and comfortably so it becomes part of your forearm. Start by laying your strong arm along the rod butt and placing your hand around the reel stem with two fingers gripping on either side. Your forefinger will now be perfectly situated for picking up the line when you open the bale arm to cast, for applying pressure to the side of the spool when playing a big fish, and for 'feathering' the line down when casting.

19 To hold your rod steady for fishing the 'lift and waggler methods' whilst sitting down, without use of a rod rest, the bottom of your reel should be touching your knee, whilst your forearm presses the rod's handle along your thigh. If held correctly, you can actually ease up on your grip around the reel fitting, as it is your forearm which keeps everything steady. Your hand

will certainly 'tighten up' quickly enough when the float moves.

20 When playing big fish using a fixed spool reel, you will probably need to alter the setting of the slipping clutch several times during the fight. Really ease up (slacken off) when that monster is on a short line under the rod tip and your left hand is busy wielding the landing net, because if the fish makes one last dive on a firm clutch setting either the line will break or you will rip the hook out. A non stretch, braided reel line only accentuates this potential problem.

Sundries

Sundries

1 If I were to choose the most beneficial, of the countless sundries that in one form or another have a real and valuable use in my fishing, it would be the simple 'bait dropper'. Constructed from a variety of materials including high density plastic, brass and stainless steel, including tiny models no larger than a matchbox for depositing half a handful of maggots or casters down to the river bed when I'm roach and grayling fishing, to monsters that can drop half a pint of hempseed onto the gravel bottom of a fast flowing river when barbel are the target species, bait droppers are truly invaluable.

2 A comparatively modern material that I also find invaluable is PVA. I use both bags and the mesh tubing for ensuring that my hook bait lies on the bottom surrounded by free offerings. And in achieving this, PVA has no equal.

3 For ease of chopping up worms for adding to ground bait, obtain a pair of 'match fishing' style scissors with multiple blades. There is nothing easier.

4 Plain peacock quills with or without their herl (used for fly tying) are by far the most useful float material around. Simply cut to the desired length with a pair of scissors. Add a half-inch band of colour, fluorescent orange or red to the top of a 3-6 inch section and secure to your line at the base with a band of silicone

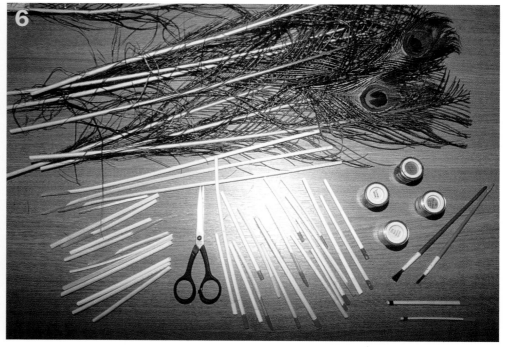

float is 'rising' it is actually 'supporting' (instead of the fish) the single swan shot fixed on the line just a few inches above the hook. So don't wait for the float to lie 'flat' before striking, because by then the fish 'will' be supporting the shot.

6 Half a dozen peacock quills will set you back less than four commercially-made floats, yet when cut up into 4-6 inch sections, they will provide dozens of floats. Simply colour the top half inch of one end in either red or orange fluorescent paint, and fix to the line with a section or two of silicon float rubber.

7 Because peacock quills are so cheap, you won't mind losing floats that pop out of the band when carp or tench go charging through lilies or dense weed beds. It's far better than the line snapping with a 'crack' when the shots either side of a commercially-made waggler restrict a fish's passage through aquatic plants.

8 Keep a small bottle of neat washing up liquid in your kit for occasions (such as 'waggler' fishing) when your line won't sink, and splodge a 'forefinger full' around the line on the reel spool. Wipe your hand thoroughly before baiting up.

9 A small pair of sharp scissors kept close to hand not only saves on tooth enamel, but trims monofilament line neatly. To trim braided lines, you need a pair of 'specialized' braid scissors.

10 Visually locating your fish by stalking is made all the easier by carrying the absolute minimum of tackle. So rather than a box or holdall full of everything you 'might' need, why not wear a lightweight waistcoat housing 'exactly' what you do need. Think about it.

11 In dry conditions when stalking around a lake or along a river bank for extra 'spooky' species, leave the wellies or waders back in

rubber. And to a fish looking upwards through clear water what could look more natural floating in the surface film than a bird quill.

5 Due to its inherent 'buoyancy' (one inch of slim quill will support a BB shot) peacock quill is by far the best float for 'lift fishing' because whilst the

the car. A pair of lightweight 'old trainers' create far less vibrations.

12 For capturing that 'trophy' photo, particularly when you have miles to walk and your camera bag weighs a ton, a small, flat, modern digital camera with a rating of around 4-5 million pixels, that fits snugly into your top pocket, is worth its weight in gold. *See also, Saltwater Tackle Sundries, Tips 6, 7 and 8.*

13 Most digital compacts have a screw thread in the base to accept a tripod. But this is only more clutter to carry around. For just a few quid (from your specialist tackle shop) you can purchase a 'camera thread adaptor' which at one end screws into the base of the camera, and at the other, into a bank stick. So you can easily photograph yourself with the fish of a lifetime, should there be no one else around.

14 If purchasing a new compact digital camera, ensure it has a 'self-timer' mode in the menu. Some give you the choice of taking just one or three pics (with a 10 second delay in between) with just one press of the shutter release button. This feature is most desirable for self-photography because whilst the first shot usually gets wasted due to picking a big fish up and taking time to hold it square onto the camera lens, numbers two and three capture the moment perfectly. Job done.

15 Self photography becomes easier if you sit on your box or chair when displaying your fish to the camera. Set the camera up on the bank stick at around waist height, several feet away, making sure the stick is perfectly upright, so that the bottom of the frame cuts off your legs below the knees. Try a dry run with a pic or two (you're not wasting film with digital cameras remember) positioning your hands to either the right or left (simulating holding the fish) which gives

a better depth of field and ensures the main subject will be in sharp focus. And slowly lift your arms above your knees so you know what level they need to be at and take a pic. If all's well, do it for real.

16 Making up a rod or two the evening before (covering the location and species to be targeted in the morning) and breaking them down again with an elastic band securing the line and joints at each end, for instant erection and use apart from adding the bait, has caught me an awful lot of big fish over the years. In fact only when travelling abroad do I put them in rod bags and into a protective tube.

17 My tackle room is full of varying pre-made outfits, covering fly fishing, lure fishing, pike dead baiting, carp, long trotting etc, etc. So all I have to do is grab the right set-ups and GO.

18 Erecting your ready-rigged rod on the bank within seconds saves not only on time, but also on all that extra noise emanating from carrying a rod holdall, taking rods from their bags, moving about the bank fitting them together etc, which simply tells the fish you have arrived. I say you'll catch more, certainly larger, spookier fish and quicker, by having your rods pre-made. Try it and see.

19 You can even erect a pre-made rod in the dark by holding it up to the sky when fixing joints together to alleviate the line from going around the spigots, and be making the first cast of the day without your quarry being even slightly aware of your presence.

20 To follow on from my way of being ready at the drop of a hat, I also have a selection of different waistcoats, some light, some with thermal linings, each loaded with a different selection of sundry items particular to the species I might be after. A comprehensive seat-type tackle box or bag as such, I do not own.

Lines

end back till the line shows no sign of abrasion and when stretched, immediately returns. If in any doubt, change the line completely for fresh.

3 Whilst incredibly strong in breaking strain for their low diameter, braided lines need to be thoroughly scrutinized regularly (with a magnifying glass if necessary) so that any section which shows the slightest sign of deterioration such as furring or roughness, where it has passed over rocks or tree branches etc, can be instantly discarded. Being much thinner than monofilament (less than half the diameter for any given breaking strain) it takes but a slight 'nick' in a braided line for a breakage to inexplicably occur.

4 Whenever 'inexplicable' and sudden breakages occur whilst float fishing with monofilament, first check your main line by running it between your thumb and forefinger to feel for any roughness that indicates deterioration, caused by rubbing against tough plant stems or rocks, etc. And just in case the problem is with your rod, check all the rings carefully, especially the tip ring for any cracks or abrasive areas.

5 Another way of testing monofilament for deterioration is to hold the line tightly in your hands about two feet apart and firmly pull to test for its degree of elasticity. If it snaps before you think it should, then replace immediately. Pinching large 'locking shots' onto fine monofilament is often the cause of breakage. Either get used to pinching them on 'lightly', or protect the line beneath large shots by sleeving onto the line 5-8mm lengths of fine diameter silicon tubing (used for attaching pole floats) which act as 'padding' when you pinch your shots around them.

6 For making a 'stringer' to retain large fish when abroad such as Nile perch, mahseer, arapaima, or Wels catfish etc, invest in some thick but supple strong,

1 When 'waggler' float fishing in still water it is imperative to 'sink' the line between float and rod tip in order to counteract any draw or sub-surface tow, so you can pull the line 'through' the surface tension, (simply by striking sideways) as opposed to lifting it up 'against' it. Cast a little further than you are baiting the target area therefore, and feather the line down (by using your forefinger against the spool) before dropping the rod tip a few inches beneath the surface and cranking the reel handle like mad for a few turns. This not only 'sinks' but also straightens the line out. New lines benefit from sloshing a little washing up liquid (keep a small bottle handy) around the spool prior to fishing, or you can deliberately purchase lines which sink.

2 It is false economy to fish with line that has been on your reel for so long it has deteriorated either through sunlight (ultra violet rays affect monofilament severely) or such constant use, as most of the line's inherent elasticity has gone. Every time you get caught up on a snag and pull for a break, the last few yards of a monofilament line may have been taken beyond its point of elasticity, rendering it useless. So don't simply tie another hook on the end. Keep cutting the

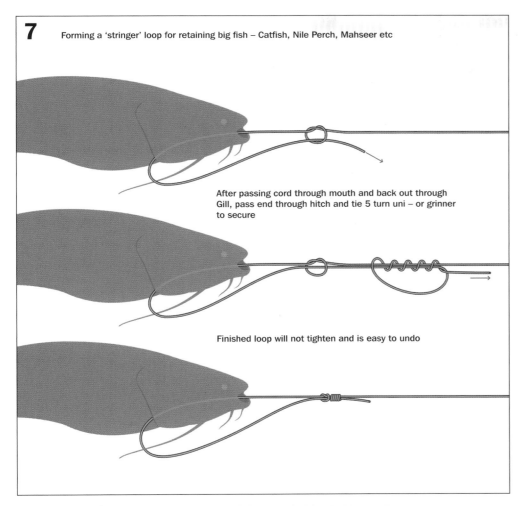

7 Forming a 'stringer' loop for retaining big fish – Catfish, Nile Perch, Mahseer etc

After passing cord through mouth and back out through Gill, pass end through hitch and tie 5 turn uni – or grinner to secure

Finished loop will not tighten and is easy to undo

nylon cord. Parachute lines sold at Army surplus shops will do at a pinch, although catfish specialist shops also supply the ideal material. What is most important is to be able to form a large 'loop' (which passes through the fish's mouth and out through its gill opening) that will not tighten while the fish is retained with the end of the rope tied to a bush, tree or stake.

7 To form the 'stringer' loop, start by tying a single 'hitch' 2-3 feet from the end of the cord. Now thread the cord through the fish's mouth and out through its gill opening. Be careful not to disturb the rakers. Now pass the tab end through the hitch you made and tie a five turn grinner or uni knot around the cord. *See Diagram.* Tighten down against the hitch, and you have a large loop that cannot possible tighten any smaller. Practice a few times to make perfect.

8 The jury will always be 'still out' on the subject of which colour line spooks fish least, because there is in fact no answer. Whatever the colour of your line fish are all too aware that it exists. And thank goodness they do. If they didn't, can you imagine the amount of line bites we would all be continually suffering? Presenting a bait amongst shoal species would be hell, with indications on the float or bobbin happening all the time, as indeed they do when large species such as tench and carp are spawning, or bream are packed so tightly together and in a feeding frenzy, they cannot possibly avoid the line. Truth is that, however painful it may seem, fish do see and are aware of our lines, which is how for most of the time they manage to avoid it.

9 Remember, even the most expensive monofilament line weakens severely and quickly through heat caused by friction as a result of pulling shots or a float (held on by silicon bands) quickly up and down a 'dry' line, or tying knots and pulling on them without adding a lubricant such as saliva.

Lines

your mainline (providing you don't trim the ends too short) acts as a collecting depot for weed and other flood debris that would otherwise work its way down the line and around the terminal rig.

14 When ledgering for pike, zander or eels in tidal river systems - Norfolk's Great Ouse Relief Channel is a prime example - watch out for situations where quite suddenly your line falls back slack as though it has been bitten through above the terminal rig. Close inspection (you can often see and feel 'crimping' along the line) will reveal that it has been 'nipped' through by the sharp shells of Zebra mussels which grow in huge colonies.

15 To alleviate the problems of Zebra mussels, sleeve fine diameter tubing over the last two to three feet of your reel line above the ledger rig which might lay along the river bed and across 'Zebras'.

16 Another way of avoiding the dreaded 'Zebras' is to and angle your rod tip up high (I know it inhibits bite registration) so most of your line is off bottom. Moreover, hit any run immediately. You cannot afford a fish to pull your reel line across the river bed and across 'Zebras'.

17 Following a powerful and lengthy battle with a big carp using monofilament line on a fixed spool reel, you are quite liable to suffer, due to its inherent elasticity, cronic 'line twist' due to it being repeatedly pulled off the spool around a bale arm roller. Braided line incidentally doesn't suffer likewise because it has no elasticity. Sometimes this 'twisting' of monofilament is so bad it's impossible to make another cast, leaving you two options. You either hack off all the twisted line and re-tie your rig, (which is usually best) or you can run all the affected line out along the bank and let it flap about (taking most of the twist

10 It makes economical sense to buy your line in bulk so you don't have to worry whether a spool will be filled sufficiently by just a 100 yard spool. And because bulk line costs less you will be more inclined to change regularly from old to new. But remember to store your bulk spools in the dry and preferably in the dark, because if left open to sunlight the monofilament could spoil through ultra violet rays.

11 When using heavier strains of monofilament abroad in extreme heat, like the harsh and continual sunlight experienced on Egypt's massive Lake Nasser, home of the giant Nile perch, where even rods not in use are in holders open to full sunlight, some brands of mono cam actually start to deteriorate within just a week. So in such conditions it's worth checking their suppleness and elasticity on a daily basis.

12 While braided reel lines have improved certain techniques due to their inherent lack of elasticity and extremely low diameter, exactly these two factors must be kept in mind at all times. For instance: when drift-float fishing for pike, runs can be effectively struck and the line regularly mended against the wind (another advantage is that many braids float well) at distances up to a 100 yards. But 10 minutes later when that big pike has been played close into the margins and when held on a short line, decides to make one last powerful dive beneath the rod tip because it suddenly panicked, as they do, unless you have eased right back on the reel's clutch, one of two things will happen. Either the hooks will be ripped out, or the wire trace or braided line will snap.

13 Whilst thick rubbing leaders are not usually required when ledgering in rivers, for dealing with rocky and particularly snaggy bottoms whilst fishing for barbel for instance, in deep and fast flowing rivers particularly during flood time, incorporate a 20 foot 'thick' mono rubbing leader starting immediately above the hook trace. This accomplishes two things. It will keep the amount of line fractures amongst the rocks to a minimum, whilst the five turn double grinner or uni knot connecting leader to

out) while you wind it back on the reel slowly. This at least eradicates some of the twist.

18 Of course by using either a centre pin or multiplier reel where the line is wound directly onto the spool and not via a bale arm roller, line twist simply doesn't occur.

19 Extreme line twist is also experienced by those who use spinners with blades that rotate at high speed (spoons and plugs

14

20

merely wobble and chug) but there is a way of 'almost' curing this. Simply incorporate a plastic (half moon shape) anti-kink vane or fold over lead into the spinning trace so all the twisting happens between it and the spinner.

20 Avoid using low stretch, (lower diameter for their breaking strain pre-stretched) monofilament lines for fishing at close range, and especially when coupled to a powerful, tip-actioned rod. It's so easy to forget their greatly reduced 'elasticity' and promptly snap up. Far better to use standard, 'stretchy' mono on the reel, and use the benefit of a lower diameter and low stretch mono as your hook length, unless out and out distance fishing, where the benefits of low stretch mono are much appreciated.

Hooks and Rigs

Hooks and Rigs

1 For joining a hook length (usually of a lighter breaking strain) to the main line, when ledgering, many think that a loop-to-loop knot is best. But such a junction creates three separate weak spots, whereas a 'four-turn water knot' creates only one. It's more of a 'weave' really, making it stronger than a standard knot. *See Diagram.*

2 Dubbed the 'knotless-knot' and widely used by those presenting boilies or large pellets on a hair rig, it is a quick, and 'all-in-one-way' of simultaneously attaching the hook and constructing a hair rig. Because the line (it can be tied using either braid or monofilament) merely passes 'through' and 'against' the eye of the hook. However, it should not be used with hooks where the eye is not fully closed, otherwise, the line is prone to fracture in the 'gap' under extreme pressure. Hooks of a 'seamless' construction are available to alleviate this problem.

3 To perform the 'knotless knot' and attach the hook on say 20 inches of hook length material, start by forming a small loop at one end for the hair using a simple overhand knot. Now thread the other end down through the top of the hook's eye, and lay what will be the hair along the shank, ensuring that from the start of the bend, the hair, when pointed upwards, will be exactly the length desired

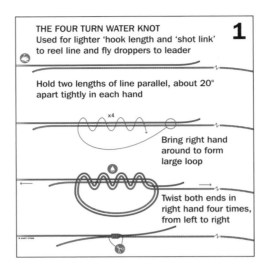

THE FOUR TURN WATER KNOT
Used for lighter 'hook length and 'shot link' to reel line and fly droppers to leader

Hold two lengths of line parallel, about 20" apart tightly in each hand

x4

Bring right hand around to form large loop

Twist both ends in right hand four times, from left to right

to accommodate your boilie. *See Diagram Fig A.* Now, wind the line in tight turns along the shank till you reach the bottom of the hair, and making one turn around it as in *Fig B.* Then wind it back again, passing the end up through the eye of the hook from below the eye, as in *Fig C.* And that's it, except for tying on your trace swivel, 8-12 inches away.

4 Another way of constructing an all-in-one hair rig and attachment of the hook when using 8-15lbs monofilament line with barbel and carp in mind, particularly when float fishing for the latter and you don't want knots at a swivel-junction to greatly reduce the breaking strain, is to use my 'barrel knot and hair' rig shown in *Diagram.* Start by threading the

end of your reel line down through the 'top' of the hook's eye and lay along the shank to form a 10 inch circle of line, with just half an inch of the tab end protruding beyond the bend, as in *Fig A.* Now, taking the right-hand side of the circle, between forefinger and thumb of your right hand, wind around shank and line 8 times going towards the eye, *(as in Fig B)* and finish by pulling through tightly with the tab end. This forms a barrel knot along the shank which can be eased along tight up to the eye before pulling really tight, as shown in *Fig C.* Lastly, tie a simple overhand knot on the tab end to form the loop of your hair rig and trim off, as in *Fig D.* You now do not have a single knot acting as a weak link between rod tip and hook point. If you find the loop finicky to tie on hairs less than 1½inches in length, sleeve a tiny crimp (used for wire traces) over the tab end to form a loop at the desired distance and firmly crimp at each end with round nosed pliers, before trimming off any surplice tab end.

5 For presenting a really large bunch of 'lively' maggots on your hair rig when after carp, tench, chub or barbel etc, the Korda 'Maggot Klip' is a real boon. This non-reflective 'round-shaped' device, slightly larger in diameter than a swan shot has a pointed end for sleeving maggots on without puncturing them which, when full, is retained in a 'brooch-type' mini clip. Your bunch of maggots can then in a jiffy, be added to the loop of your hooks hair rig or attached to a Korda Micro rig swivel.

6 For tying an eyed hook or snap swivel, etc to a braided reel line, my 'uni-clinch' knot is both quick and easy to tie. As can be seen from the *Diagram,* after passing the line through the eye twice and out again through the loop which forms a simple 'clinch', use the tab end to tie a six-turn 'uni' knot around the reel line *(Fig A).* Steadily pull on the tab end till the knot forms a neat 'barrel' *(Fig B),* and then pull slowly and firmly on the reel line itself so the barrel knot slides

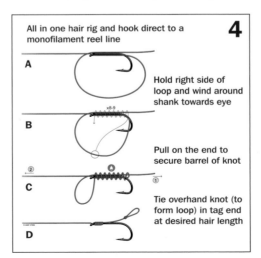

THE KNOTLESS KNOT
For hair-rigging pellets, boilies etc, using braid or mono
3

A — Form loop by making over hand knot at desired hair-rig length threading end of trace through eye of hook

B — Now wind back toward hair (5-7 times)

Wind towards eye, 5-7 times around shank

C — Pass the end 'up' through eye and swivel
'NOT A KNOT IN SIGHT'

All in one hair rig and hook direct to a monofilament reel line
4

A — Hold right side of loop and wind around shank towards eye

B — x8-9

Pull on the end to secure barrel of knot

C — ② ①

Tie overhand knot (to form loop) in tag end at desired hair length

D

Tying hooks or swivels direct to monofilament reel line – use the **MAHSEER KNOT**

Wet with saliva and pull steadily (on the end)

Don't cut tab end too short

down along the reel line tight up against the clinch. Then trim the end *(Fig C)*.

7 For tying all sizes of eyed hooks, from tiny size 18 up to giant 8/0 direct to your monofilament reel line, or adding swivels, there is no more reliable knot, than the 'Mahseer Knot'.

Why? Because the knot itself actually 'stretches' under severe pressure, as opposed to 'constricting', which is the main problem with many 'blood-type' knots. To tie, pass the line 'twice' through the eye which forms a loop. Retain by putting your forefinger through the loop and twist the tag end six times around the line, which forms a second loop. Now pass the tag end through both loops next to the eye, leaving a long tag end. Wet with saliva and pull steadily to bed knot down evenly. Also, pull steadily on long tag end to ensure it is firmly trapped beneath both loops. Trim off tag end, but not too close. Now you can play the most powerful adversary as hard as you like knowing the knot will not inexplicably fracture. *See Diagram.*

8 To tie a spade end hook direct to your reel line is simplicity itself. You certainly do not need a specialized tool. You can actually tie this knot behind your back with your eyes closed, honestly.

Start by laying the line along the shank of the hook (pointing towards the bend) and bring the tag end around in a 10 inch loop, so it protrudes just half an inch beyond the bend. *See Diagram Fig A.* Now, holding the right side of the loop with your right hand (assuming you are right-handed) start winding back up along the shank towards

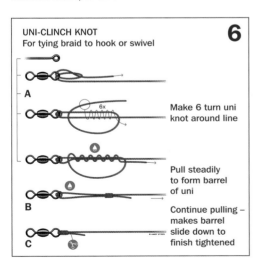

UNI-CLINCH KNOT
For tying braid to hook or swivel

6

A

Make 6 turn uni knot around line

Pull steadily to form barrel of uni

B

Continue pulling – makes barrel slide down to finish tightened

C

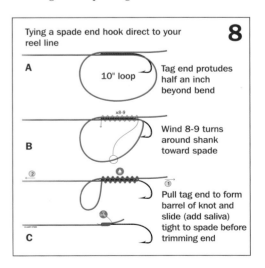

Tying a spade end hook direct to your reel line

8

A — 10" loop — Tag end protudes half an inch beyond bend

B — Wind 8-9 turns around shank toward spade

C — Pull tag end to form barrel of knot and slide (add saliva) tight to spade before trimming end

Hooks and Rigs

reel line and over the tubing, followed by the hook length swivel, (which should be free to rotate) and then another bead, before tying reel line to lead or swivel. For a neat finish, push the end of the tubing over the lead or feeder swivel after tying to the reel line, and to stop it sliding up the line, tie a five turn sliding stop knot from 10-12lbs test power gum above it tight up against the tubing.

11 For the best chance of fish literally setting the hook themselves using the helicopter rig, present all baits from corn to boilies on 'a hair rig'.

12 In line rigs, whether you use an in line lead or an in line frame feeder, benefit from the fact that a carp, tench, barbel or bream virtually hooks itself as it moves away with the bait, and should a line breakage occur it won't become tethered to a snag because it will pull the line back through the lead or feeder.

13 To rig up an in line set up thread on 12-14 inches of fine diameter rubber tubing (which prevents the mainline rubbing against rocky bottoms and the hook trace tangling around the main line) and sleeve into the lead or feeder before tying on the hook trace swivel (usually a size 8) at the front end. This should then push firmly into the lead or frame feeder, making it a 'semi-fixed' and completely safe rig. Finally, tie a five turn stop knot using 10-12lbs test power gum tight up against the top end of the tubing to stop it sliding up the main line.

14 The length of hook link for in line rigs will depend upon to what extent the fish you are after are pressurized. Start with a length of between just 4-6inches, especially if 'method feeder' fishing. But on heavily fished waters a 10 inch hook link will usually create less suspicion. Soft, braided

hook lengths are preferred to stiffer monofilament. But the choice is yours.

15 All baits are best 'hair rigged' when 'bolt rig' ledgering and if using a method 'frame' feeder you can either leave your bait hanging below the feeder or mould the feed around the bait so it is part of the feeder's load. This can prove devastatingly effective, resulting in belting runs.

16 Never forget that the best rig of all and one which creates the least amount of suspicion to a biting fish is simply the baited hook tied direct to your reel line. Nothing more, nothing less. Add just a single swan shot and

the spade end *(Fig B)*. After 8-9 turns hold the knot tight beneath forefinger and thumb of your left hand, whilst pulling steadily on the tag end with your teeth or thumb and forefinger of your right hand. This forms a perfect barrel knot which can then be eased tight up against the spade end, and the tag end trimmed off, as in *Fig* C.

9 A 'helicopter rig', favoured by many carp and tench anglers, is so called because the hook link is free to rotate around the main line above the lead or feeder tied directly to the end. To alleviate tangles, sleeve on 10 inches of fine diameter rubber tubing above the lead, and ensure the hook length is at least a couple of inches shorter.

10 To fit the 'helicopter' hook length first sleeve a tight fitting 'rubber' bead onto the

resistance is created. Add even more shot or a ledger weight and the problems are exaggerated.

17 Nowadays, the choice in patterns of heavily-forged hooks available to carp, tench and barbel anglers to complement bolt-rig ledgering techniques, with neat, well formed eyes, short shanks, micro barbs and super sharp, chemically etched points is simply marvellous. And for the very best in hooks, it's worth going one step further by using patterns that come with a slick 'Teflon' finish, in either gun metal or dull green. This non reflecting coating helps enormously in fooling the spookiest of fish.

18 For several reasons I do not use barb-less hooks and actually prefer anglers visiting my own two-lake carp fishery to use relatively small hooks (sizes 10-8) with micro barbs. I think these, once imbedded, move about less and cut less into the flesh of a carp's mouth especially during a long battle, or one in and out of dense weed, compared to larger, barb-less hooks.

19 No one likes to see grotesque examples of 'parrot-mouthed' carp and tench. And the best way of ensuring this does not happen, is not to be fast asleep in a bivi, or walking round the other side of the lake when fishing close

up to sunken trees, dense lilies, or any other snag that a hooked carp will naturally pull your heavy bolt rig into and become 'stuck', before you can even get to the rod.

20 What actually creates so called 'parrot mouth' fish where either one or both jaw hinges have been obliterated, is down to the 'see-saw' cutting action of large hooks, and to some extent harsh, braided hook lengths, connected to over-heavy leads being literally ripped out of the mouth on heavy line, because the angler did not take control of a hooked fish early enough. Responsibility is the key word when presenting heavy 'bolt rigs'.

Natural

1 If you were left high and dry, miles from nowhere at a super river or lakeland fishery having forgotten the bait, what would you honestly do? Well, if rummaging about turning over logs in search of worms fails to produce, and their isn't a grocer's shop for miles, being able to identify the life cycle of some of our more common aquatic flies would help enormously. Especially that of the 'sedge fly' whose larva are called 'caddis grubs'.

2 To collect these grubs, a foray amongst the shallows, turning over large pieces of flint and sunken logs to which 'caddis' cling in their homemade cases, is the way to obtain a batch for bait. And as the average-sized caddis grub is twice that of a shop-bought maggot, most cyprinid species can be subsequently targeted.

3 To use caddis, each, creamy-coloured, succulent grub has to be carefully removed (using the finger nails of thumb and forefinger) from its protective and intricate case manufactured from twigs and sand particles, while

squeezing gently at the opposite end. And 'hey presto', out it comes. Hook gently through the head with a size 14 hook. After an hour's rummaging about enjoying the rewards of bait collecting you will have collected enough 'caddis grubs' for a morning's long-trotting, or lift-float fishing for tench or carp. Give them a try.

4 If you fancy owning a supply of lobworms on demand for occasions when the ground is frozen solid, or the local tackle shop has run out, why not try gathering your own. The secret for successful 'snitching' is collecting worms from the lawn at night during a mild evening following a good down pour. Then you'll find many of the worms almost completely out of their holes. Those barely out, which require a mini 'tug of war' often break and so, cannot be kept less they contaminate the rest. Remember to creep stealthily and use a wide-beam torch that isn't too harsh. Extreme light and heavy vibrations make worms retreat quickly into their holes. If your garden does not produce or you live in a flat, then simply pop along to the local cricket pitch where for much of the year the grass is kept short. Hang a one

gallon plastic bucket on a cord around your neck which keeps both hands entirely free: one for the torch, the other for picking up worms. Walk slowly and carefully, picking up your feet just like a chicken does, and you will never worry about a supply of lobworms again.

5 To store lobworms for future trips, (the garage is an ideal place because it's cool (lobs last best in temperatures between 35 and 45 degrees F) it's worth all the trouble of constructing a box made from ½ inch plywood. It should be at least 20 inches square and have two lids - top and bottom - with a dozen or so one eighth of an inch diameter holes drilled through each of the sides. The best medium, in which lobs will live quite happily and remain in good condition for at least several months, is dampened, shredded newspaper. Simply tear old newspapers, (you'll need a couple of dozen) into one to two inch strips (strangely, newsprint can only be torn evenly one way) and soak the lot in the sink. Wring the paper out well and place in your worm box together with your supply of lobworms. Remembering every couple of weeks to

turn the box upside down (hence the need for two lids) so the inhabitants keep working through the paper.

6 The term 'worm conditioning' may seem a trifle up market, but try it for yourself using lobworms, which are popped just a dozen or so at a time into a two pint plastic bait box, along with some soaking wet shredded newspaper. Tear the newspaper into one inch strips before soaking and wringing out most (but not all) of the water. Then simply leave in a fridge for at least several weeks. After only one week however your worms will have turned into veritable 'snakes', fatter, stronger and more lively than you have ever fished with before.

7 Cockles may be a 'sea' bait, but when purchased in bulk ready shelled and boiled from the fishmongers stall, they can easily be split up into separate batches and even coloured (use a teaspoon of carp bait dye to a pint or two of cockles and swish around in a bait box together with a cupful of boiling water, and strain off the excess colour) before bagging up and popping straight into the freezer. Quality roach and rudd in addition to tench, bream, chub, barbel and carp etc, all love this bait, which can be presented float fished or ledgered singly on the hook or hair-rigged 2-5 up.

8 Holding vertically a small square-shaped, fine mesh aquarium net hard against the bottom of a brook or

stream, immediately behind a large piece of flint, before lifting it up, will procure all manner of natural baits, Small fish like stone loach, bullheads and even brook lampreys, all much loved by chub, barbel and perch, often shoot straight downstream into the net. So keep a small net in the boot of your car, should you ever be stuck for bait.

9 Specialist pet shops stock all manner of natural baits which cyprinid species love. Mealworms for instance which last much, much longer than unrefrigerated maggots, are available in four sizes from minis to super giants. And how

about waxworms, larvae of the waxmoth. This fat, juicy, quite buoyant, creamy-white grub similar to a wasp grub, (they actually come from the honeycomb of beehives) if carefully hooked through the tail, is a prime trotting bait for roach, dace and chub, while grayling adore them. Waxworms keep for long periods in the tub in which they come packed, if kept at a temperature of between 55-60 degrees F. Even larger still are 'tebos', larvae of a moth imported from Chile which feeds beneath the bark of a Tebos tree, hence its name. Best kept at a temperature of between 45-50 degrees F, they are larger than a wasp grub and will

Natural

attract all cyprinids from specimen-sized dace to carp. Present on a size 12 hook or two up on a size 10.

10 As far as predators like pike and zander are concerned, dead baits are not just dead baits. They can be flavoured (by injecting with various fish oils) and even 'coloured', which really gives them great appeal. Simply put some powdered bait dye into a clean bait box and mix with a little water. Then, gripping by the tail with forceps swish each 'thawed' dead bait about till even in colour, and leave for a while on newspaper for the excess liquid to blot off before re-freezing or using straight away. Alternatively, simply paint on liquid food dye (available from the grocers in amazing colours) with a small brush, straight from the bottle. Pale coloured fish such as sprats, smelt and herrings look amazing in yellow or gold, while any fish coloured in red simply oozes 'colour appeal'. But the choice is yours and the permutations are limited only by your imagination

11 If you love close range 'dapping' for crafty, clear-water chub from amongst the cover of marginal grasses, then locusts, house crickets and grasshoppers are summer baits you just cannot ignore.

Whether you present them downstream on the surface in conjunction with a small floating 'controller' like the 'tenpin' and a greased line, or simply 'dangle' or 'dap' directly beneath the rod tip into gaps in the surface weed, these highly attractive baits available from any specialist pet shop, will catch you chub when others won't. They can be easily kept in an old aquarium (preferably in the kitchen in 75-80 degrees F) with a piece of tightly-fitting gauze on top, and advice on feeding them will be freely given from the pet shop where you bought them.

12 Using 'big' baits for pike, whether live or dead, does not guarantee catching larger specimens, as a jack will grab at a live bait of at least half its own size, while a 20lbs specimen will suck up a sprat from the bottom. In fact presentation is perhaps more important, in that dead baits presented 'static' on the bottom where they are easily hoovered up by larger, pike which tend to be more sedentary in their life style, does overall produce pike of a higher average size than say working small spinners or live baits.

13 Blood worms are so devastatingly effective because they are in most

waters the staple, natural food of all cyprinid species from a three inch rudd, all the way up to a 40lbs carp. But due to their minute size, they can really only be presented on tiny hooks (sizes 22-26) and light lines. So while most big cyprinids tench and carp in particular, actually grow to huge proportions by gorging daily upon vast quantities of bloodworms, they are in no way considered a 'big-fish' bait. The delicate style of 'pole fishing' is tailor made for presenting these 'little red men' which are the larva of the midge fly. And in British freshwaters there are close on 400 different species of midges, which is why they are such a 'major' food item. Plumbing the depth of your swim accurately is imperative because the ideal way of presenting bloodworms is just off bottom. Feed in 'joker' (tiny midge larva) either neat or in damp loam via a pole cup to draw in the fish and present your bloodworm over the top.

14 Worms are not just 'worms'. Each, and there are four popular 'fishing worms' found in British soil, has its own very special uses. The smallest, found in heaps of rotting leaves is the humble 'redworm'. These short, slow-moving worms are much loved by tench, bream, roach, dace and grayling, and because they do not wriggle off the hook are great with barb-less hooks and for baiting the hooks on spinners for added attraction. Slightly larger, is the 'brandling' which is found in manure heaps. A lively, gyrating worm easily recognizable by the yellowy-orange rings around its tail and by the pungent yellow fluid which seeps out as you hook it, the brandling can easily wriggle off the hook if a maggot or caster is not nicked on afterwards. Alternatively after the worm or worms, and a 'bunch' of brandlings are much loved by perch, tench, bream and carp, nick onto the point of the hook and over the barb, a small section of 1/8th of an inch diameter elastic band. Twice the size of a brandling, and therefore a suitable mouthful for cyprinid species of all sizes, plus perch, catfish and eels, is the Dendrobaena, a chunky 3-4 inch red worm

14

17 To keep maggots or casters cool during a long drive, simply pop a frozen 'freezer' pack or two into your bait bucket.

18 To stop free-lined or float-fished, lip-hooked live baits or dead baits flying off on a lengthy cast, simply sleeve onto the hook, after the bait, a ¼ inch section of ¼ inch wide elastic band. Remember to work the hook gently outwards from the top lip so the point is free. You will connect with far more perch or chub in this way because the hook point will be angled in the correct position for striking when the bait is engulfed in the predator's jaws.

19 Whenever 'minnows' become a nuisance and get to your trotted maggots before roach or dace, simply switch over to casters or sweet corn.

20 Minnows, dead ones that is, make a great scatter loose feed when targeting eels, zander, or monster chub during the hours of darkness that are known to exist in still waters. If you forget to catch a supply and freeze down for later use, pop into your local delicatessen or super market and buy a frozen batch of 'whitebait', which is really a tiny sardine. A handful can then be scattered into a few likely, pre-selected swims every other day say for a week, prior to your first session.

that was originally imported from Holland, but which is now commonly bred in this country. Lastly but by no means least because it is in all probability the most versatile, effective worm of all, and I cannot possibly think of a British freshwater species that won't gobble one up, comes the lobworm. *See Tips 4, 5 & 6.*

15 When feeder fishing in silty-bottomed lakes for summer tench and bream, estate lakes in particular that might have over a 100 years of accumulated silt covering the original lake bed, and filling an open end feeder with maggots, sandwiched between a

16

plug of dampened bread crumbs at each end, be aware that within seconds of your feeder touching bottom those maggots will bury into the silt and be lost from sight. The remedy here is to use only freshly killed maggots in the feeder, (which don't crawl away and get lost) by either blanching them in hot water, or placing them in a polythene bag and squeezing out all the air before tying the bag up tightly and placing it in the freezer for at least 24 hours. Job sorted!

16 Elderberries are truly one of the great 'natural' trotting baits for species like dace, roach chub and even barbel, especially when loose feeding with stewed hempseed or tares. Being larger than hempseed they generally sort out a better stamp of roach and dace too. Collect elderberries in the autumn before they become 'over-ripe' and store them in a large (wide-necked) preserving jar containing glycerine or a solution of dilute formalin. Do not pull them directly off the bush or they will squash. Cut off little bunches containing around 20-30 berries and pop straight into the jar. When required, and elderberries are great throughout both summer and winter months, simply give them a good rinse in cold water before use.

20

Manufactured Baits and Lures

1 Here is a great, quick and easy, and most effective way of presenting any trout, carp or other pellet as hook bait, without softening, or threading onto a hair rig. It works with boilies too. Using super-glue, glue a pellet onto a strip of 1/8th of an inch wide elastic band, and trim close leaving enough of a tab at one end to put your hook through. For presenting two-up, either glue two side by side onto the band, or glue the second onto the end of the first. Easy peasy. You can even vary where the pellet sits on the hook by easing the band around the bend, so it hangs immediately below, or ease it around to midway along the shank so it is presented similar to a hair rig.

2 Of course 'commercially' produced 'bait bands' (mini silicon bands) which stretch completely around the pellet also work well with all pellet sizes between 5 and 12 mm. The pellets can simply be pushed into the bait band and positioned on the back of the hook shank in a prime position to ensure a good hook hold. Larger pellets are best drilled and hair-rigged.

3 When casting spoons for pike, zander and even salmon, maintain their 'fluttering' action whatever the

depth, by carrying a selection of the same lure in various weights from ¼ up to an ounce. Then you can wobble large, but 'light' spoons over even shallow, weedy water for pike, or clip on a heavy model (of the same size) for 'counting-down' (at around one foot per second) when working it just a couple of feet above bottom.

4 All manner of soft cheese and meat cubes such as luncheon meat or ham (don't forget turkey, chicken, chipolatas, etc, etc) can be effectively presented simply by pushing the hook through the centre of the cube (cut your cubes roughly to the length of the hook's shank so it can be pulled through) and

rotating it so that the bend and point bed into a corner and disappear out of sight once the line is gently pulled. It is far better however, particularly with 'harder' cubes, to use a 1 inch hair rig, so that the bait is presented 'off' the hook. For instant penetration, it is without question the 'ultimate' confidence setup, when you are 'bolt-rig' or standard ledgering.

5 When preparing hard pellet feed for moulding around a 'method feeder' so they do not break up during the cast, try not to 'over' wet them. Alternatively, make them really 'sticky' by adding the juice from a tin of sweet corn. This not only 'softens' the pellets, but adds that sweet aroma much loved by bream, carp and tench. Once added, stir regularly for 15 minutes till, when squeezed, a ball of pellets sticks together. Adding the corn is yet another option.

6 The 'softest', most pliable 'cheese paste' which chub, barbel, carp and tench all adore is easily made from 'old' bread (from which all the crust has been removed) and a block of Cheddar. Soak the bread, and it must be 'old', in water and wring out well, mashing it between your fingers into a creamy paste. Then grate the cheese finely and take time kneading it into the bread paste. A mix of around two parts bread to one part cheese makes a super paste. For a stronger colour,

knead in a little 'orange' powdered carp bait dye or use Red Leicester in stead of cheddar. And for added aromatic attraction (especially for chub) sprinkle a good helping of grated parmesan cheese over the paste and knead well in.

7 Cheese chunks, particularly those broken from a block of 'rubbery-type' cheese, like Maasdan, Edam or Gouda from Holland, Jarlsberg from Norway, or Subenhard and Danbo from Denmark (explore your local cheese shop)

all make fine 'second' baits to luncheon meat when 'rolling meat' for barbel and chub. They really stay on the hook well.

8 In addition to that irresistible 'wobbling' action, their 'flash' is what attracts predators to spoons. So don't fish firing on only half your cylinders by using tarnished and dull metal lures. Restore to their ultimate brilliance and attraction by using a strong paste-type, or metal polish cleaner and buff up so each reflects the maximum amount of light. And whilst you're at it, replace any bent or rusted treble hooks and split rings. Specially-designed 'split-ring' pliers will stop your finger and thumb nails from splitting, and complete the job in seconds.

9 When looking for an artificial lure that will cast like a bullet, is heavy enough to be counted down to the bottom of deep water where rocks and snags could pose problems, and one that

Manufactured Baits and Lures

will work with equal effectiveness for pike in reservoirs and Scottish lochs to the monster Nile perch of Egypt's Lake Nasser, then synthetic 'rubber shads' have no equal. And because most internal 'lead-heads' like Storm's 'wild eye swim shads' come rigged with just a large single (upward-pointing) hook, as opposed to duos of trebles, they snag up far less than most artificials.

10 Making your own 'designer' paste, allows you to create unique bait that no one else is using (particularly on hard-fished waters) giving you a distinct edge. In a liquidizer, you can pulverize any kind of trout, halibut or carp pellet for instance and reduce it to a fine powder to which raw eggs are added (as a binding agent) before kneading into a ball of pliable paste. All the feed-pellets sold at aquarium and garden centres for koi carp work well, as do such products like, pig pellets, rabbit pellets, even chicken pellets. The only addition (apart from raw eggs) that you might like to try is sprinkling a tablespoon of 'Phillips Yeast Mixture' (a powder available from cage bird shops) over the paste and kneading in. It has a strong, pungent aroma much loved by carp

especially. The ingredients used for making your own boilies also make great pastes simply by kneading in enough eggs. Those with milk derivatives in the base mix, and especially bird food mixes, also work well to which colouring (in the form of powder dye) can also be added. Add a teaspoon of flavouring to a little water and knead into the mix if you so wish. The permutations for paste making are simply endless. It's good (if somewhat messy at times) fun too.

11 Colouring sweet corn could give you an 'edge' over other anglers and 'educated' fish. Start by pouring off all the liquid (great for adding to ground bait or for sticking pellet feed together when 'method-feeder' fishing) and empty the contents of a tin into a poly bag. Add your chosen colour ('Super cook' liquid colourings are great for this) you'll only need a few drops because it is highly concentrated, and then twist the bag to seal it. Now give the bag a good shake, and 'hey presto' your corn is coloured. Use immediately, or freeze for later sessions. Incidentally, if you use a lot of sweet corn, buying large bags of frozen corn from supermarkets, gives you twice as much for

your money as opposed to purchasing in tins. A point well worth remembering. Also worth remembering is that corn is one of the finest baits to use as a 'cocktail', with maggots, a red worm, a meal worm, casters, a small cube of bread crust, etc. The permutations are endless.

12 For presenting 'pop-up' style over dense bottom weed etc, your corn can be sleeved onto a hair rig. Thread a real grain onto the hair first, followed by a buoyant kernel of 'imitation' corn. You can even colour this too. If using a long hook length add an AA shot between 3-10 inches (depending upon weed height) above the bait, thus counterbalancing the buoyancy of the bait. If small species become a nuisance by pecking your corn to bits, use cooked maize instead which is larger and harder. See 'ground baiting' tip 1. It too can be coloured in the same way. But you'll need two kernels of imitation corn to pop up one of maize.

13 The 'old' way of preparing a batch of 'hard' particles like hempseed, (before we knew better) was to boil and simmer the seeds in an old saucepan on the cooker for 30 minutes or so, and completely stink the kitchen out. The modern way, is to first soak the seeds for a couple of days in cold water (and this applies incidentally to the preparation of most particles except for tiger nuts and maize) before straining off the water and putting the seeds into a plastic bucket with a 'rip-off' lid, and then covering with boiling water to a depth of two inches. Press the lid on firmly and allow the seeds to stew and swell in their own juices for a minimum of 24 hours, during which time they will split (showing that tiny white shoot) and darken almost to black.

14 Incidentally, leaving stewed hempseed for two or three days in the bucket almost till it starts fermenting, creates extra pulling power to some species, carp in particular.

Manufactured Baits and Lures

the bank. Wriggling from the silt could be enough eels to last me all winter.

18 I am classifying peanuts as 'manufactured' bait because they do after all, like sweet corn, have to be planted and grown. And when you can obtain some of the American 'jumbo-sized' peanuts, (health food shops have them) there are few more effective particle baits for both tench and carp, used either float fishing with the 'Lift-method' or on a 'bolt-rig' ledger set up'. Either side-hooked or presented two, or even three-up on a hair. I've enjoyed no small amount of success with chub and barbel whilst ledgering with peanuts too. Part of their success is that being 'hard' they deter small nuisance species, and being decidedly 'buoyant' makes then perfect for presenting over or amongst weed beds. To really pop them up however, cut a piece of rig foam to the shape and size of a peanut and place it last on the hair so it floats the others off the bottom.

19 Ready-shelled (un-roasted) standard-sized peanuts are perfect for loose feeding, but both these and the 'Jumbo' hook baits do however need to be properly prepared by first soaking for 24 hours in cold water. Strain off and having put them in a plastic tub with a rip-off lid, cover them to a depth of several inches with boiling water. Put the lid firmly on and leave for 48 hours, after which they will have swollen to twice their size and be ready, after straining off all the excess liquid, for immediate use or bagging up in session-sized batches for popping into the freezer. You can even colour them. *See Tip 11.*

20 If you find difficulty putting stewed hempseed onto the hook, here's how to do it. Find a seed that has only just split open (a little of its white seed protruding) and gently grip between thumb and forefinger to force the split open further, whilst inserting the bend of a fine wire size 14 hook. Wide gape, spade-end hooks are perfect for presenting hempseed.

Or the freshly stewed seeds (always do a sizeable batch) can be split into 'session-sized' portions and popped into the freezer for later use.

15 If you have trouble with dead baits flying off your hooks during the cast and even on the retrieve when targeting pike and zander, remember that when presenting the bait 'static' it's best to first firmly work the barbed point of the top treble on your wire trace (semi barb-less trebles are kinder to both predator and angler) into the sinewy tail root. The muscles here make for a perfect hold. The second treble (barbed prong only) can then be inserted 2-3 inches down the flank. For wobbling dead baits which obviously appear more natural if swimming head first (wish I had a fiver for every pike that has grabbed hold of a static bait being retrieved tail-first) simply reverse the order by working two prongs of the top treble into the baits eye socket, and the barbed prong of the lower treble firmly into the flank. Get used to inspecting the bait following each retrieve and readjust the hooks accordingly when they appear to have worked loose.

16 If you experience soft pastes coming off the hook whilst pole fishing, simply wrap a small plastic cable-tie around the pole (and cut off the tag end to leave an inch or so protruding) several inches above where your hook lies when the rig is laid alongside the pole top. Then you simply hang your baited hook over the tag whilst shipping the pole out without the paste touching the surface.

17 Catching eels during the warmer months on worm or maggot baits intended for other species can become a nuisance. But why not turn such occasions to your advantage, assuming you go fishing for pike and zander during the winter, by taking those eels home (12-18 inch fish are ideal) and freezing down for later use. The head end of an eel especially, due to the amount of blood it contains, and the fact that it casts like a bullet, is one incredibly effective dead bait. Along with the lamprey, eels are in fact my top bait for pike when fishing the Norfolk Broads and their connecting tidal rivers. And I invariably stop the car whenever I am driving beside a fenland drain and see a dredger heaping great piles of silt up along

Ground Baiting

Ground Baiting

1 Both as a hook bait and ground bait for just about every cyprinid species from the heaviest carp to quality-sized roach, maize takes some beating, particularly in these days of bubble-packed, aggressively marketed, 'designer baits' which by comparison are vastly more expensive. A 25 kilo sack of whole or 'plate' maize for instance, will set you back less than one large pack of boilies. But because it is 'hard' it does require careful preparation however.

2 To prepare hard maize, start by soaking the grains (which eventually swell into super, yellowy-orange kernels with a distinct, nutty, wheaty, pop-corn aroma) in water for a few days. Then either pressure cook for 20 minutes, or prepare in the microwave (albeit in small batches) in a shallow bowl of water. The finished (now-split) kernels three times the size of the original, can be hooked on one, two or three up or sleeved onto a hair rig. Cooked maize also forms the base of varying ground baits. It can be added to a breadcrumb-based ground bait for bream or tench fishing (really sinks quickly in deep, fast flowing rivers) or added to seeds and

pulses to form a wonderful particle mix. Buy a sack and experiment. See 'Manufactured baits' *Tip 13*.

3 Liquidized bread is a fabulous loose-feed when using punched-bread or small pieces of crust or flake on the hook for species like dace, roach and chub when rivers are running cold and clear, and you want an alternative attractor to maggots or casters. To prepare a batch remove the crusts from several slices of 'fresh' white bread, and after tearing into pieces, put them all into a food liquidizer and switch on. Literally in a few seconds the bread is reduced by the machine's blades into thousands of tiny, moist particles, which when squeezed gently together can be thrown (underarm) into the head of the swim, where they slowly descend and break up into a 'cascade-like' snow-storm of a cloud. So 'overfeeding' the shoal is never a problem with this loose feed. This is why it works so beautifully in cold conditions.

4 If you want a really 'heavy' ground bait for attracting bream living in deep, fast rivers, which gets down there fast whatever the depth, start with a

base of well-wetted coarse bread crumbs (shop bought) or make up a batch of 'mashed bread' by soaking old bread in water for 20 minutes and then mashing it between your fingers whilst squeezing most of the excess water out. Then add several cupfuls of 'flaked maize' and the same of 'pearl barley', which really stiffen up the mix. To improve it further add a cupful of what you intend using as hook baits, such as chopped worms, stewed wheat, maize, sweet corn, casters or maggots and so on. Finally, knead well into hard 'cricket-balls' for throwing out.

5 Ground baiting 'distant swims' for species like barbel and chub in fast flowing rivers can be achieved in two ways. You can repeatedly use a spod *(see Tip 10)* or a large swim feeder to deposit a bed of bait on the riverbed prior to fishing. Or, you can invest in some PVA (short for Poly Vinyl Alcohol) tape. You can then, using a long 'stringer' baiting needle, thread on up to a dozen or so boilies, cubes of meat, maize or drilled pellets etc, and push them all off the needle onto a length of tape and nick the point of your hook (already baited up hair-rig style) into one end.

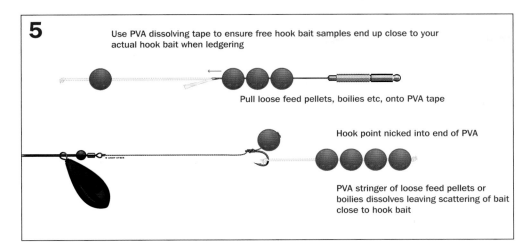

5

Use PVA dissolving tape to ensure free hook bait samples end up close to your actual hook bait when ledgering

Pull loose feed pellets, boilies etc, onto PVA tape

Hook point nicked into end of PVA

PVA stringer of loose feed pellets or boilies dissolves leaving scattering of bait close to hook bait

lake or river bed, an attractive carpet of loose feed (your ground bait really) is spread around it. Remember to add only oils to your loose feed, or you'll melt the mesh or bag before casting. *See also Tip 4.*

9 Don't throw away those old 'floating' casters. Store in a poly bag in the freezer and when you have at least a couple of pints or three, thaw out and utilize by crushing in your hands over a tub of coarse, brown bread crumbs, so all the attractive juices are squeezed out to dampen the crumbs. The myriad of broken brown shells give the ground bait a lovely 'flecked' appearance and if you add hook bait fragments like fresh casters maggots or corn etc, as filling for an open-end feeder, there is little to beat it for bream and tench. You can add the juice from the tin of sweet corn too.

Within minutes of casting out the tape will dissolve leaving a scattering of loose feed right next to your hook bait. *See Diagram.*

6 'Ground baiting' for predators like pike, can work wonders. Choose a still water (obviously not too far from home) where pike exist in good numbers and select a commanding position from which to introduce 'free offerings' every day for a week or so. Such as a long, deep gully between islands, or a promontory reaching into deep water. Those 'cert-looking' swims covering large areas are what to look for.

7 Purchasing fish in bulk for pre-baiting and cutting each into three sections (head-middle and tail-end) before freezing down into packs of a dozen or so pieces (your daily baiting quota of fish pieces) makes economical sense. Or perhaps you already have a freezer full of old baits just waiting to be experimented with. Either way, after a week or so of pre-baiting, try a session, and expect some 'hectic' action. This routine also works well on large rivers particularly at confluences where dykes, drains and other rivers join the main flow. Always great pike and zander movement areas these, that are simply crying out for pre-baiting attention.

8 For ground baiting whilst fishing, there is nothing to beat the addition of a PVA 'stick' made from mesh, or

a clear 'bag' filled with hook bait samples or complementary pellet feed, nicked onto your hook prior to casting out. Because when this synthetic material dissolves within seconds of your bait settling on the

9

FRESHWATER BAITS

Ground Baiting

more or less (give a degree or two either side) the same spot, provided you overhead cast straight out.

11 Remember to only fill the 'spod' to the three-quarter mark. All the bait will then stay in the spod during the cast, with no spills or wastage. There are no prizes for scattering bait all over the lake.

12 To ensure your baited rig ends up in the same spot as your 'spodded bait', clip up your fishing outfit or outfits, to exactly the same distance as on the spod rod, by walking the rigs out along the bank with the reel's bale arm open. It's worth the effort.

13 Catapulting out ground bait is probably the most commonly used method of pre-baiting and feeding up swims beyond throwing range. And provided you follow a few simple rules distances of up to 50 yards can be achieved. Firstly, purchase a proper 'ground bait' catapult fitted with a large, rigid pouch or a plastic 'mesh-type' pouch (which stops the ball from disintegrating when you pull back the elastic) and strong, durable elastic.

14 The secret of catapulting out ground bait is not making the balls of bait too large. Slightly bigger than a golf ball is absolute tops. Otherwise you will achieve neither distance or any degree of accuracy. And do not add loose feed such as maggots to the mix which will split the ball apart when they start to wriggle. Dead maggots are fine. *(See Natural Baits Tip 15.)*

10 The best way to ground bait a distant swim for carp, tench and bream, if you do not have access to a boat, is with a 'spod'. These high-density plastic, rocket-like projectiles can be loaded with all kinds of particles, mini boilies or pellet feed and they will cast to exactly where you wish to place them. But you do need a long, powerful rod (not your fishing rod - something heavier) and strong reel line to cope with the repeated casting and retrieving. Three-quarter fill the spod with bait and cast to the desired spot. Then, before retrieving, pass the line around the line clip on your spool so that each successive cast lands in

15 Boiled rice makes a fine base for 'light' ground baits to which small particles such as mung beans, buck wheat, red dari seeds, stewed wheat and sweet corn may be added. To colour rice yellow, simply add a spoonful of turmeric to the boiling water.

minimum of 24 hours. Then strain off any surplus liquid and your bait is ready.

18 Here's a great tip for preparing just a small batch of wheat to use as hook baits or for mixing in with ground bait on the evening before the morning you go fishing, should you have forgotten to arrange fresh bait. Pour a cupful or two (if you have a large flask) of wheat into a vacuum flask and top up with boiling water. Not right to the top or when the wheat expands, the flask could explode. About three quarters full is about right, leaving a 'space' inside before screwing the cap on. In the morning, empty the contents, now perfectly stewed and nicely swollen showing the white grain inside, and smelling distinctly 'nutty', into a bait tin and you're ready to go.

16 One of the cheapest and most effective bulk, ground bait additives is stewed wheat. You can buy an entire sack for just a few quid, and it's so easy to prepare, both to use as hook bait and for stiffening a crumb-based ground bait.

17 To prepare stewed wheat in bulk, follow the directions for hempseed in manufactured baits *Tip 13*. To colour stewed wheat in yellow, orange or red, it looks great, simply add a spoonful or two of powdered carp bait dye (the colour of your choice) when covering the particles in boiling water in a plastic tub with a rip-off lid. Stir thoroughly before pressing the lid on and leaving for a

19 Black eyed beans are super particle bait which can be easily prepared and coloured, by following the directions given in *Tip 13 of Manufactured Baits and Lures*, for adding to your ground bait mix. Black eyes can be hair rigged or 'side-hooked' and either float fished or ledgered 'bolt-rig' style.

20 Tick beans are a large, shiny dark-brown particle that carp and tench both find irresistible when prepared as for stewed wheat *(Tip 17)* and bait that is totally impervious to the attentions of small, nuisance species. They are thus the perfect ground bait additive. Present two-up on a hair and size 8 hook, when loose feeding with tares and hempseed for barbel. They are deadly.

Bass

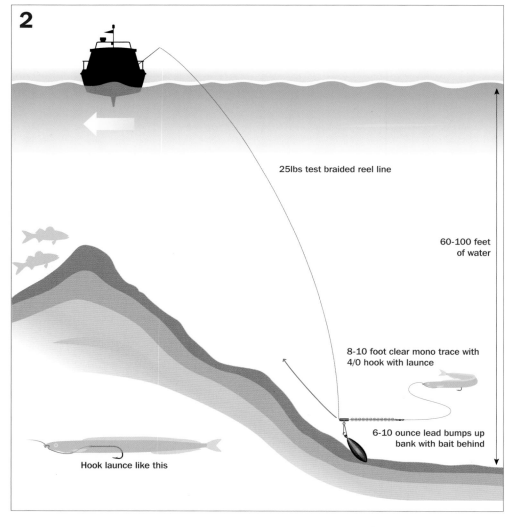

25lbs test braided reel line

60-100 feet of water

8-10 foot clear mono trace with 4/0 hook with launce

6-10 ounce lead bumps up bank with bait behind

Hook launce like this

1 For most boat anglers the nicest way of all to catch bass is by fishing on the drift (with the boat set side on to the tide) and a 6-10 ounce lead (depending upon depth and tide strength) bumping over and up the shingle bank behind the boat towards the top and the shallowest, tip of the bank, called 'the rip' (where waves can be seen breaking) and behind which marauding groups, often of larger bass, love to lurk, waiting to pounce on bait fish that have become disorientated by sheer current force and deviation.

2 The secret of drift fishing, using a non-stretch braided reel line of 20-25lbs test, coupled to a rod with a forgiving tip, is not to allow any more line out once the lead touches bottom at the foot of the bank, long before reaching the rip, or you will simply lose all feeling of your bait's whereabouts due to a huge bow forming between rod tip and lead, as depth reduces rapidly up the sand bank. *See Diagram.*

3 When drifting for bass over banks and rips, use a long (8-10 foot) clear mono hook trace with a 4/0 or 5/0 long shank hook presenting a live launce or Joey mackerel, frozen launce or large king rag worm. Baits are in order of effectiveness here. Bites will then be both bold and

6 Bass can also be taken on the surface with lures, especially 'popping plugs', when during the summer months they patrol close inshore and prey upon small shoal species just below the surface. Use relatively light tackle, (a medium spinning outfit and 10lbs line combo) either from the shore along rocky coastlines or from a small boat worked in and around rocky outcrops. Expect noisy, savage takes on the surface.

7 When trolling for bass using say three rods out from the stern, always ensure the longest line out is on the middle rod. So that when the boat turns to rework a particular area, the middle lure swings away from the other two. If fished short, it will only tangle on the turn.

8 If holding the rod when trolling, do not position it at right angles to the boat. A taking fish will pull the rod round, which because it bends, merely absorbs the hit, resulting in the hooks failing to set. So point the rod tip almost directly at the lure.

9 When trolling for bass near rocks, use a hard coated braided reel line and add (using the Albright knot, *see Freshwater boat fishing 'on the drift and trolling' Tip 10*) a 30 foot, 40 lbs test mono rubbing leader to take any abrasions. One nick in a braided reel line and your specimen bass is history.

10 Remember that a diving plug will run significantly deeper if presented on a low diameter braided reel line, compared to significantly thicker mono of the same breaking strain.

11 Contrary to popular belief, the further behind the boat you allow a diving plug to work, the shallower it will in fact dive.

12 Fly fishing for bass opens up a whole new exciting field of possibilities during the

savage. And there is no necessity of striking hard. Simply wind into your bass when the tip is pulled hard over, occasionally giving a little free line beforehand to 'dithering' biters. On no occasion put your rod down with the bait still over the side.

4 If you want to capitalize on bass from the shore along a rocky coastline, then before even buying or obtaining the bait, plan to walk your beach right at the bottom of a spring tide when all the rock formations and kelp beds are totally exposed. There is simply no better way of determining where to then place your bait (peeler crab is tops) on the next incoming tide, because you will now know the whereabouts of gullies and corridors that bass will use as feeding routes. If you

like, you can even place it on the bottom of a likely rock pool and walk back up the beach whilst paying out line as the tide comes in. This ruse has accounted for many a lunker double-figure bass from rocky coastlines. So study those rock formations carefully at low tide.

5 To locate specimen-sized bass which patrol deep and fast, often narrow gullies between prominent pinnacles of rocks (dangerous spots to fish these in a ripping tide) try stemming the tide with the boat's engine and put out a couple of deep diving plugs from the stern, with the rods in holders. You simply then sit back and wait for one of the rods to keel over. A Rapala CD 18, either in 'blue mackerel', or 'red head', is unquestionably 'the' artificial to use.

Bass

about any eventuality, bass wise, whether casting from a boat or the shore.

13 Those already proficient at long casting will appreciate the greater distances more easily achieved by using 'shooting heads' as opposed to full lines. But either way, whether you explore estuaries as the tide pours in, cast to shoals of bass decimating fry shoals hugging the shoreline or around clear-water harbour entrances, or in a fast boat, following flocks of terns working the surface for bait fish pushed upwards by marauding bass, hooking one, even modest-sized, schoolie bass of up to a couple of pounds in weight, is pure joy.

warmer months. If you go reservoir fly fishing for trout, then you are already well equipped. If not, then a 10 foot, 8-9 weight fly rod coupled to a large diameter 'disc-

drag' reel plus a spare spool or two to provide the choice of 'floating', 'sink-tip' and 'fast-sinking' lines, joined to plenty of braided backing, will cover you for just

14 To attract bass on the fly, go for colour combinations of green and white, blue and white, silver and white, or just a plain white

tying. The best patterns are 'deceiver' and 'clouser minnow' in sizes 4-1/0. Don't be tempted to go larger; your casting distance will only be impaired. To this end use only a short, 3-5 foot clear mono leader.

15 Deep water wrecks often attract small groups of specimen-sized bass, which sometimes fall to pirks or shads worked close to the wreck's super structure. But be ready to heave and haul once you're hooked up. There is absolutely no question of enjoying the fight with a fish hell bent on taking your terminal gear into the nearest ironwork.

16 Another way of accounting for 'wreck' bass, is to set up a drift so the boat lays a little off the wreck, and providing tide and conditions are favourable, actually drift 'along' its length using live 'Joey' mackerel, hooked through the top lip by one prong of a size 1/0 treble hook, on a running lead stopped by bead and swivel above an eight foot long, clear mono leader. You can even pre-empt when a bass is about to take, by the 'throbbing, shuddering vibrations' of the mackerel. And when the rod top suddenly keels over, simply wind into the fish and start pumping, less it finds sanctuary in the wreck.

17 When boat fishing for bass, try never to put your rod down. It will inevitably cost you missed bites and lost fish. Maybe a 'double figure' whopper, the goal of every serious British sea angler.

18 With a double figure bass the target species, it's worth considering to 'night fish' a clear-water harbour, (any of the pretty, Channel Island harbours spring to mind here) using carp-style ledgering tactics (yes, even using electronic bite alarms to register the sudden pick up!) and a fresh, whole mackerel, or 'flapper' for bait. Under the cloak of darkness big bass forage the bottom of the clearest waters alongside harbour walls (so long casts are simply not required)

in order to gorge upon what local commercial 'pot' fishermen have thrown over the side.

19 Piers up and down the country, during the summer months, provide an excellent chance, (without the expense of charter boat costs) of coming to grips with specimen-sized bass. These locations may not look the part, but sheltering in low light values amongst the rusting super structure and wooden pilings where massive shoals of young bait fish gather, wait some powerful adversaries. So don't even think about braided reel lines, or fishing sportingly. At the minimum you need a 30lbs class outfit

that is both light enough to hold for hour upon hour while you're float-fished or free lined live bait does its work, and when hooked up, you need to be totally 'brutal'.

20 Be extremely careful when holding bass, not to be cut by the razor sharp spikes in their first dorsal, and in their anal fin, and by the pointed edge to their gill plates. For a 'trophy' shot, and to remove the hook, hold exactly as you would a pike or zander, by placing four fingers of your left hand into the fish's left gill opening, being careful not to go between the 'rakers', and press down firmly on the outside with your thumb. Easy peasy.

Black Bream

Black Bream

1 The sexes of many sea bream cannot be told apart. But with black bream, males are easily distinguishable from the more 'silvery' females by their really dark vertical bars and especially (more noticeable during the breeding season in the spring) the colourful and striking, bright, aqua-marine 'blue' plumage on its skull around the eyes.

2 You can actually use fresh water tackle to catch this ubiquitous and voracious sea bream. Wherever tides are not too strong and the water shallow, a quiver-tip rod, the kind used for chub and barbel no less, (an Avon-style ledger rod with built-in or push in tip) coupled to an 8-10lbs test reel line, allows these scrappy fighters to really show their mettle. And as the finer reel line (use braid) on a baby multiplier, will permit use of even lighter leads, that characteristically 'dogged' fight of anything over 2lbs, will possibly surprise you.

3 Black bream are commonly encountered when targeting deep water species like conger and ling over rough, honeycombed ground. Again, stepping down to reasonably light tackle, say 15-20lbs test braid and a 12lbs boat rod outfit, with a two hook snood paternoster set up, sporting size 2 wide-gape hooks, will provide hectic and continual sport.

4 Keep the hook snoods short, no longer than say eight inches, or they will tangle, and be prepared to re-bait regularly, or you'll be sitting there with bare hooks.

5 Baits such as small squid heads, tipped with mackerel or razor fish, will keep you more than active, and of course set up a chain reaction deep down there on the bottom while waiting for one of the conger rods to go.

6 Bigger fish like conger or ling, etc are always attracted by the subsequent feeding mêlée enjoyed by small shoal species such as bream and pouting. So it really pays to keep fresh baits going down to the bottom, with at least two or three anglers on board targeting the bream. Specimens to 4lbs plus, are regularly encountered in such situations.

7 As a strong tide slackens keep in touch with the shoal of black bream by reducing lead size to one that only 'just' holds bottom. You can then systematically search down tide from the boat by lifting the rod tip every so often to bump your bait further along the sea floor until bites materialize.

8 During 'neap tides', drifting for black bream over rough ground can provide some exciting and hectic fishing during the spring and summer months. Two and three hook, coloured-jig traces work best, especially if the hooks are tipped with a piece of squid or razor fish. Again, the entire head and tentacles from baby calamari often produce a larger stamp of bream.

9 When bites are felt, allow some free line to peel from the reel for a few seconds until the bream gets the bait well inside its mouth, and the rod tip pulls over firmly. Then lift smartly into the bream, with your thumb on the spool, and knock the reel back into gear once it's hooked. Any delay will encourage the bait to be ejected. But then hang on, captures of two, or even three sizeable bream on the line at once are not unheard of.

10 When the bream are running towards specimen size (3-4lbs fish) do not use more than two hooks, or you will lose more than you boat.

11 Drifts often occur over rough, uneven, rocky and weedy ground, so be prepared to quickly wind up slack, when depth shallows, or to let more line out again in order for the baits to be continually working

at the bottom. Remember to make the bottom loop large enough to go around the lead's diameter for ease of changing.

15 Scientific research has confirmed that black bream are in fact bisexual and protogynous hermaphrodites, which means they start adult life as an egg-bearing female, but end up male.

16 With very few exceptions, only small bream are encountered from the shore. So to really enjoy fish averaging a fair size using light tackle, going offshore is imperative.

17 If specifically targeting bream at anchor, be sure to make up a ground bait/rubby dubby consisting of freshly caught and diced-up or minced fish like mackerel, scad, pouting or garfish, etc contained in an onion sack and attached to the anchor chain.

the sea floor, or just above. If you can keep a close eye on the sonar/fish finder from your fishing position, so much the better.

12 Be careful when holding black bream up for a photo. Their dorsal and anal fins are equipped with strong, sharp spines.

13 As black bream are attracted to and thus most commonly found over large areas of reefs and wartime wrecks due to the prolific amount of natural food in the way of crustaceans and small shoal fishes, losing tackle is par for the course. So have several

two hook snood traces made up and ready to go so you don't lose out on the action while it lasts.

14 Construct a simple trace using around four feet of 30lbs test monofilament. Start by adding the two hook snoods (or droppers), 14-15 inches apart in the middle of the trace, by tying on each using a four turn water knot with short lengths of 30lbs test. Then add the size 2, wide gape hooks, ensuring the snoods are no longer than 7-8 inches. Lastly, tie a simple overhand loop at each end of the trace for quick attachment to a link swivel on your reel line, and a lead

18 Another way of keeping the bream coming once anchored over a prolific mark, is to regularly drop diced-up fish and other bait fragments (keep a bucket handy for this very purpose) down to the sea bed in a large 'bait dropper' rigged for that sole purpose on a separate outfit.

19 Black bream, unlike any other close related bream-type species, (so identification is never in question) are equipped with numerous curved, needle-like teeth inside the outer row in their upper jaw.

20 As black bream are nowhere near as thick on the ground as they once were, take only the odd fish or two for the kitchen and return the rest. They quickly return to the bottom to bite another day. And your children's children might actually get to enjoy their eagerness to feed ravenously and subsequent dogged fight. Wouldn't that be nice?

Coalfish and Garfish

Coalfish and Garfish

1 Though possibly the least common member of the cod family of fishes (next to the haddock) to be encountered around the British Isles, big coalfish characteristically suddenly dive at great speed at any time during the fight, so be prepared to ease up on that clutch if one is suspected.

2 Though caught without any kind of regularity, (in the south) coalfish between 15 and 30lbs are periodically landed around British shores (more commonly from around our south western coastline) from boats drifting over wartime wrecks lying in deep water.

3 Top rig for catching 'wreck' coalfish whilst drifting (also referred to as a 'gilling rig') comprises of a long, 10-18 foot, 20- 25lbs test clear monofilament trace tied to a tubular plastic boom and fixed lead set up, attached to the 25lbs test reel line, (30-40lbs braid has a lower diameter and its non-stretch properties are nicer to fish with) with an artificial on the business end. Such as a small red gill or scallywag rubber lure, (black is a most effective colour in clear water at great depths) jelly worm, twin tail or shad, etc, etc. *See Pollack Diagram 4.*

4 The secret is to lower the artificial 'slowly' down to the wreck in order to avoid tangles, and having bounced the lead off the rusting iron work, to immediately wind up a couple of turns, before starting an 'even' retrieve of slowly winding for say 20 turns of the reel handle, before lowering the rig back down to the wreck again and repeating the procedure. If after a couple of drifts this routine fails to produce a hit, crank it up as fast as you can in an erratic retrieve. But hang on, coalfish sometimes just can't resist such action and hit like an express train.

5 Over wrecks known for 'eating' terminal rigs, instead of clipping your 6-10 ounce weight direct to the lead slider clip, make a 'rotten bottom' from five or six feet of, say, just 12lbs test mono, with an overhand loop at each end, attaching the top loop to the slider clip, and threading the lead onto the lower. This 'lighter link' will then instantly part, jettisoning the lead only should it snag on the wreck.

6 Playing a big coalfish is an exciting experience because no other British deep water species moves so fast and with such agility. A reel with a smooth clutch and fresh line are both, therefore, imperative.

7 Coalfish (also called saithe) is an important commercial fish, netted in trawls and seines by Russian, German and Scandinavian fleets, and is noticeably thicker in the body than its close cousin the pollack, with a distinctive 'white' and 'straight' lateral line, so there should never be any confusion between the two species. Coalfish have pronounced 'forked' tails too.

8 While pollack are a south western species found around the rocky coasts of the British mainland and the western shores of Ireland, the coalfish has a markedly more 'northern' distribution (though a few are taken along the south and south west coasts) from Scotland all the way to the deep water fiords of northern Norway, where it is arguably the most common of all saltwater species and a most prolific and valuable part of the food chain as halibut, cod, haddock and larger coalfish all prey upon young 'coalies'.

9 Coalfish spawn from January through till March in very deep water, the eggs and larvae drifting near the surface till they reach the shallower 'nursery' areas, where vast concentrations of young coalfish emerge to provide the lower end of the food chain for so many cold water species.

10 Did you know that great fun is to be had by catching coalfish on the fly rod? Not whoppers of course, they would be far too powerful for a sporting, 7 or 8 weight, reservoir-trout outfit. Schoolie coalfish in the 1-3lbs range offer the most potential anyway, because

Coalfish and Garfish

13

harbour entrances during the summer months provides the most action. For optimum sport use freshwater tackle.

15 For garfish that can easily be seen through clear water hanging around inside quiet harbours chasing shoals of fry close to the wall, get to really enjoy the leaping qualities of this inquisitive bill fish by using a 13-14 foot freshwater 'waggler' rod coupled to a small fixed spool reel holding just 5lbs test mono. A long 'waggler' style float fixed bottom end only with a band of silicone tubing, provides great visibility, and should be set somewhere between (experiment here) 3-10 feet above a size 14-10 hook, with the bulk shot 2-4 feet above the hook. And on the hook nick a slither of fresh mackerel fillet.

16 To attract garfish and keep them moving in around your hook bait, a blood-based ground bait concocted from fish oils, bran, bread crumbs and finely chopped oily fish like fresh mackerel and fresh blood (ask your butcher) works wonders, though it

they come close inshore to be caught off the rocks and shoal up in vast numbers.

11 The secret is to locate a concentration, and, using a fast-sinking line with a shrimp-pattern fly on the end, sport is assured. A fast, erratic retrieve usually induces the most takes. Within the British Isles, Scottish waters hold the largest concentrations of coalfish.

12 When the coalfish shoals are too far out to target from the rocks with a fly rod, and this applies whether fishing in Norway or Scotland, try casting a 2 ounce pirk on a 12lbs test spinning outfit and counting it

down 10-20 feet before retrieving in an irregular, 'jigging' fashion. Hits are usually both numerous and unbelievably aggressive.

13 For maximum hook-ups when 'jigging' pirks, use a braided reel line of around 20lbs test, with a three foot monofilament, swivelled trace and snap link swivel for quick lure changing.

14 Want a taste of big-game sea fishing? Then consider the highest-jumping, minutest billfish of them all and a real 'gladiator': the humble garfish. And float fishing a few feet below the surface in the warm, upper layers around piers, jetties, breakwaters and

14

16

tends to attract other species like young pollack, coalfish, wrasse and mullet. But that's great; you're talking fun fishing here.

A large 'serving' spoon whipped firmly with strong cord onto 12 inches of garden cane, is indispensable for ladling in this smelly mix.

17 As an alternative to fish strip for tempting garfish, try thin strips of raw steak. Replace regularly when the blood washes out and the meat loses its appeal.

18 To target garfish at distance, from the rougher, often fast, water off harbour walls or whilst standing on the rocks around headlands etc, step up your fresh water outfit to a 12 foot carp or pike rod and fixed spool reel holding 8lbs test mono. You will need a large, cigar-shaped sliding float too, (stopped 3-8 feet above the bait by a bead and five turn sliding stop knot) against which the garfish often hooks itself when running off with your bait, so the first indication of a bite

that you actually see, is a garfish acrobatically jumping away on the end of your line. Therefore, use a lead bullet or barrel lead to cock the float with a cushioning rubber bead between it and the swivel of your hook trace to keep the bait down.

19 When fishing at distance, you may suddenly notice that the float has gone 'flat' indicating a garfish is swimming upwards with the bait. Remember that a three foot hook trace of 10-12lbs mono will help to alleviate those vicious teeth of the garfish from biting your hook off, and bait the size 6 Aberdeen with fresh mackerel strip.

20 If you start running out of mackerel strip, keep one of the garfish and fillet-off a side, which when cut into thin strips, makes for great bait.

18

SALTWATER SPECIES

Cod

Cod

1 Ever wondered why it is in Norway where the world's biggest cod are caught on rod and line from the deep water of the fiords, that huge size 10/0, 12/0 and even larger trebles are attached to even modest-sized pirks? It is quite simply to cut immediately through that 'small cod', coalfish and haddock barrier, all of which can easily engulf standard-sized trebles that come ready-fitted to most pirks. And repeatedly cranking up small to modest sized fish when after the monsters, can make for tiring work. There is of course nothing to stop you following the same principle when specifically targeting the big, summer cod inhabiting southern coast deep water wrecks.

2 Remember when swapping trebles from small to 'huge', to ensure the split ring on your lure is man enough for the job. Special 'split ring opening pliers' (to make life easier) are required for extra strong split rings.

3 When targeting big cod (even big coal fish and pollack) on pirks sporting big trebles, (and this is the

beauty of using giant trebles) should a small coalfish or even an immature cod or pouting become hooked or foul-hooked on the way down, don't wind it straight up out of frustration. Keep lowering your now 'baited' lure down to the bottom or alongside the wreck, knowing that at least one or even two of the hook points will be free, and lift it slowly up and down till the rod tip buckles over. Whereupon a little line needs to be given to ensure the bait and lure are well inside the whopper's jaws, before winding firmly into it. Refrain from actually 'striking' as this could lead to a missed chance. The hooks usually find purchase when the larger cod opens its jaws to eject.

4 To give your pirk even more 'cod appeal', and this trick works especially well with medium to large-sized cod and pollack, (I first saw this used when fishing the famous 'Yellow Reef'

off Denmark's north western coast) add a red or orange, rubber eel to the split ring at the top of your lure. Then, fish which grab at the wrong end, still become hooked. But remember to play each fish carefully less you have just a 'lightly' hooked fish on the rubber eel.

5 If up-tiding for cod in fast tides, to maximize on the area being covered, cast the last rod close up alongside the anchor rope on each side of the boat, with each of the other rods casting progressively further out. Only cast them all out in reverse order, starting with the 'down tide' one. *See Diagram*. In heavily coloured, fast water use a large bait (4-6 lugworms crammed onto a 6/0 hook and tipped with squid) to provide maximum scent trail to cod that are working uptide more by smell than sight. Always allow your 'breakaway' lead to touch bottom and the wires to 'kick-in' by free-spooling sufficient

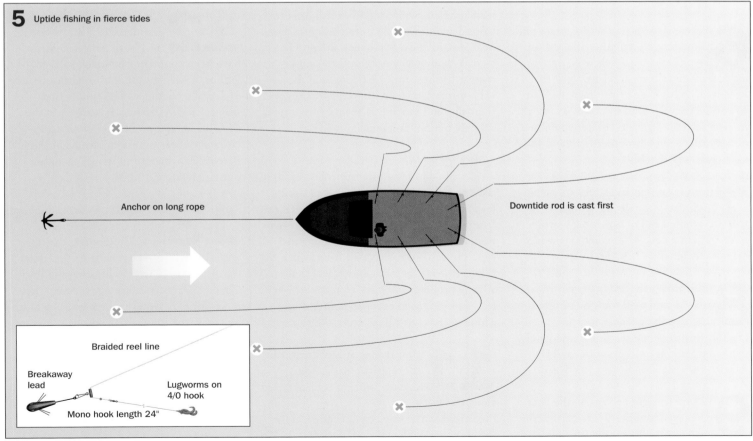

5 Uptide fishing in fierce tides

Anchor on long rope

Downtide rod is cast first

Braided reel line

Breakaway lead

Lugworms on 4/0 hook

Mono hook length 24"

slack line to form a huge 'sub-surface' bow. Otherwise your end rig will simply bump its way all the way down tide to end up immediately down tide from the stern.

6 Never try to 'strike' a bite when up-tiding for cod, whether the rod top keeps knocking, keels over, or suddenly springs back and goes slack to a certain 'drop back' as a fish drags the lead downtide. Simply wind smoothly as fast as you can into the fish and continue winding steadily till the line becomes tight and the rod bends over nicely.

7 Both razor fish and squid are great additions for 'tipping' a hook crammed full of lug or rag worm when targeting cod. Also worth trying is a strip of cuttlefish or mackerel.

8 If up-tiding for cod over very rough ground, add a 30 foot, 60lbs test mono rubbing leader to your 15-20lbs test reel line starting immediately above the lead, in order to withstand the abrasions of rocks, shells and weed, etc.

9 With, say, eight anglers on the boat (the usual number for a charter trip out) all simultaneously up-tiding for cod, with four anglers on each side of the boat, always make sure the down tide rod uses the lightest lead, say a four ounce breakaway. So that it doesn't matter if his lead and bait swings round to fish directly behind and down tide from the stern. The next should fish a five ounce weight. The next, a six ounce weight, and the angler casting furthest up-tide (along side the anchor rope) an eight ounce lead. They will then all stand much less chance of bumping over each other and tangling.

10 When casting out into a strong tide from the beach, to ensure that your baits and leads dig in to end up virtually opposite you (assuming you are using two rods) you may have to walk 50 yards or more along the beach towards the direction from which the tide is flowing, before casting, and then allow a pronounced 'bow' to form between lead and rod tip in order to hold bottom. Think of it as 'up-tiding' from the shore.

11 Cod fishing at night from the shore, particularly from shallow beaches such as those along the east coast, increase your chances three-fold as the shoals will venture closer to shore, under the cloak of darkness, to feed on worms and particularly crabs disorientated by breaking waves disturbing the sand.

12 While it has been reported in past decades that cod along the North American coast have been commercially taken to over 200lbs, nowadays the most realistic chance of actually boating a cod topping that magical 100lbs barrier, exists only in the deep, clear, and prolific fiords of north Norway, where monsters lurking in the Barents Sea migrate to spawn each year during March and April.

13 Summertime during June and July is the most consistent period for coming to grips with the large cod that hang around deep water, war-time wrecks littering the English Channel. And to secure a 'wrecking' trip, most skippers require a firm booking of up to a year, if not longer, in advance. A point well worth considering.

14 Big, fat, lazy old cod show a marked dislike for excessively fast tides, and tend to rest up behind rocks or wrecks during a run at full bore. Slack water can prove productive, but

generally middle-range tides, neaps especially, when drifting deep water wrecks, are much preferred.

15 Like ling, cod do not much like being pumped to the surface too quickly when hooked in deep water. Their extended swim bladder welling up in the throat like a balloon proves this, and they run out of steam long before they reach the surface. Far better to fully enjoy their heavy, dogged fight by pumping them up slowly, (less hooks pull out too) but beware then of a last ditch dive in order to throw the hook when daylight looms, and they are on a short line immediately beneath the boat.

16 Except when they come up to the surface in clear water to chase young coalfish, herring or sprats etc, and I have actually caught numerous small cod in crystal clear Danish waters close to the coastline, on would you believe, diving plugs being trolled at around

three knots, honestly, cod are confirmed bottom feeders. And sport around our British coastline should be considered as such. Unless deep water wreck fishing using lures because the water is so clear, it is best and especially in heavily coloured seas, to appeal largely to their sense of smell, when boat fishing over rough ground, by offering a ledgered bait of lugworm or squid presented hard on the sea bed where they can most easily find it.

17 Where sizeable fish are expected make up a simple end rig with a 25lbs test 4-5 foot mono trace and 4/0 hook tied direct, baited with either squid plus a 'muppet' above, or a good helping of big, black lugworms. We are above all talking aromatic attraction here. And above the trace swivel on the reel line, employ a bead and simple running slider with sufficient lead to keep the bait anchored to the bottom. If the cod are running small, a second hook on a short snood can be added halfway along the trace with a 'change' bait, such as peeler crab tipped with mackerel strip.

18 In these days of ever decreasing returns, don't come back to port with more

gutted cod than you can carry. Allow fish which are bent on diving down to the bottom again the chance to do so. Then everyone will continue to enjoy catching this ever-popular species.

19 With the relatively modern introduction of low diameter braided reel lines now fast establishing a precedent within British sea fishing, for all bottom-fishing, except in the very deepest water and fastest of tides, cod of all sizes are most sportingly taken on a 20lbs outfit. Ok, so you take longer pumping your catch to the surface. So what?

20 In recent years, drawing parallel with the speed at which soft, plastic lures have taken freshwater predator anglers by storm and far into the '21st century', for catching cod over deep water wrecks, especially shoals of cod totally preoccupied with chasing and consuming small shoal fish like sprats etc, there is a growing band of 'wreckers' around who now fish surprisingly light over deep water wrecks, offering the tiniest of artificial 'shads', (just 4-5 inches in length) which due to their tantalizing action account for cod after cod, when all other larger lures, pirks especially, remain unattacked.

Conger Eel

Conger Eel

1 While the uninitiated may be surprised, 'conger addicts' know full well that for its size, bulk and aggressive nature, conger eels have got to be the most 'gentle biters' of all our larger sea species.

2 Even monstrous eels in the 50-100lbs class usually give less of a pull on the rod tip when swallowing down a mackerel flapper, (mind, they do have huge mouths) than a medium-sized black bream or pouting, both of which on some days, continually peck away at large baits intended for conger. Use an uncomplicated rig in the way of a running lead on a lead slider stopped at the hook trace swivel with a large, cushioning bead. The trace itself being 2 foot long and made from 150lbs mono with a 10/0 hook at the business end.

3 The secret when conger fishing, is to disregard all those clanging, tapping, banging and rattle-like registrations on the rod tip. Simply wait for 'slow' and 'positive' indications. Hold the rod, and 'give' a little line to any 'slow' pull. But

don't wait too long before lifting into your eel, less it has already wrapped your trace around the rusting ironwork of the wreck.

4 To distinguish between a small (strap) conger and a freshwater eel is not difficult. Like the freshwater eel, the 'conger's' dorsal, tail and anal fin comprise of one continuous frill that starts immediately behind the prominent, pointed pectoral fins and finishes behind the vent half way along the underside of the body. This same frill starts noticeably further back on freshwater eels, which have protruding lower jaws. This is completely different to the conger's upper jaw, which slightly protrudes the lower. In addition, the eye of the conger is decidedly 'oval', compared to that of the freshwater eel which is round.

5 As most skippers know, the best way of encouraging eels to leave the sanctuary of a wreck and follow the scent trail of your ledgered bait up tide, is to quickly get several hook baits down to the bottom after anchoring up.

6 A freshly caught mackerel 'flappered' and presented on a size 8/0-10/0 hook is the absolute 'top' bait for congers, Hook once only through both lips.

7 Some skippers swear by chunks of cuttlefish for big conger. They are not so easily pecked to bits by small, aggressive shoal species, like black bream and pouting, as a mackerel flapper.

8 When small fish really are a nuisance, pick the largest mackerel in the box and 'cone' it by removing both tail and the first third of its body including head and guts, leaving a solid 'cone' of meat. Hook once only through the narrow end.

9 The jury will always be out as to whether it's best to gaff or net a big conger. Personally, I much prefer to net them as this greatly reduces the amount of blood and slime on deck (no gaff hole to haemorrhage) and the eel can subsequently be easily unhooked and returned simply by lowering it over the side and inverting the net, allowing it to swim back down to the bottom, none the worse for its gluttony.

10 If you have feathered-up more than enough mackerel prior to a conger session, chunk-up a couple of dozen or three fish and put into a carrot sack for attaching to the anchor chain. To conger eels it's like sniffing 'bacon frying' down there, and is particularly effective when congering over rough ground with a large area to attract eels from.

11 To unhook small 'strap' conger, eels of between say 5 and 15lbs, lifting them up to the gunnels and using a T bar, is by far the most efficient way.

12 Keep your hands well away from the jaws of a big conger once it's on deck. With their vice-like grip and twisting body motion, fingers can all too easily be taken down to the bone by a conger eel.

13 Help to hold a large conger up for a 'trophy shot' only when the skipper says it's safe to do so.

14 When good-sized eels are coming thick and fast it pays to have a supply of pre-made, 150 lbs test mono hook traces at the ready. Simply detach the 'mangled' trace from the snap swivel immediately below the lead link (the lead should be removed before hoisting a conger into the boat in case it hits someone) and clip on a fresh one. You can even have a couple of new traces, already baited, standing by on those days when sport is fast and furious.

15 When contemplating ordering a big net to take conger, choose a rigid frame of four feet in diameter, to which six foot long (tapering) one inch diameter mesh net has been fitted. You can than then net the biggest eel tail first and haul it on board.

16 Try to calm down when the skipper indicates that you are connected to a huge eel. Stand feet well apart and 'hinge' at the waist to start every 'pumping' motion whenever there is a possibility of recovering line. Straining constantly against torque is not the way to beat a big eel. It only beats you up quicker than the fish. So remember to lean back comfortably in between 'pumps'. Tighten the clutch right up if using monofilament. In deep water it's almost impossible to break say 50lbs test due to the amount of inherent stretch. But with 'braid' things are entirely different, and you must repeatedly remind yourself that your rod tip is the only 'cushioning' part of your outfit.

17 It often pays to fish lighter outfits amongst the conger baits, whether wrecking or over rough ground, especially when black bream or pollack are averaging on the large side. The feeding frenzy of small shoal fishes especially, will only encourage conger to venture further from their hideouts. And you might well boat a specimen of another species into the bargain. Many a conger

enthusiast has accounted for his PB pollack, black bream or bull huss, whilst conger fishing.

18 If you happen to wind up a bait-robbing pouting when targeting congers, re-hook it through both lips and stab its flanks a few times with a sharp knife to allow those attractive juices to permeate, and lower it straight back down from whence it came. You won't have long to wait before a conger finds it.

19 When is it best to wind and heave into a conger bite? As soon as possible really, getting the rod into a full bend so the eel has difficulty running, is the way to go.

20 In order to prize a big eel quickly away from its lair amongst the honeycombed bottom of rough ground or from the twisted iron work of a wartime wreck, use a large multiplier well-filled, for maximum line recovery.

Dogfishes

2

1 There are three 'angling' dogfishes found around the British Isles, and whilst the tiniest, the lesser spotted is classed as an absolute bait-robbing nuisance by anglers targeting larger species, the greater spotted, better known as Bull huss, but sometimes referred to as a 'nurse hound', are much sought after. Easily told apart from the lesser spotted by its broad nasal flap, which covers each nostril, and warm brown skin overlaid with dark spots of varying size, the Bull huss which is an offshore species, can in fact reach weights over 20lbs.

2 Bull huss favour steeply shelving banks of rough or rocky ground in deep water, often the very same marks frequented by tope, and it is not unusual to catch both from the same anchorage.

3 Of the three, Spur Dogfish are the least commonly caught, although where they do exist, they usually do so in amazing numbers, and are immediately told apart from any other British shark (which of course they are) by the two razor sharp spines or 'spurs' (hence their name) situated at the front of each of their two dorsal fins.

4 Though spur dogs are considered a bottom feeding species, they will in fact feed at any depth. So if ground fishing in 300 feet of water in a Scottish Loch for instance without bites, slowly

bring your bait up 25-50 feet at a time till spur dogs are contacted.

5 When targeting blue sharks in the Atlantic off the east coast of the USA, even in depths of between 250-350 feet, through the clear, blue water, on numerous occasions I have seen spur dogs come right up to within 10-20 feet of the surface to chew on fresh whole mackerel intended for much larger sharks. And they are subsequently considered a real nuisance over on the other side of the pond, even big double figure specimens.

6 To hold a spur dog without fear of getting stabbed by one of its two sharp spines, grip firmly around the head whilst holding its wiry body, belly against your side.

7 Spur dog spines are covered in an anti-coagulant, which means the nasty gash they make in your hand or finger, just wont stop bleeding for quite some time.

8 To specifically target lesser spotted doggies, or spur dogs, (though both species are more commonly caught by accident when after larger bottom-feeding species) a simple two or three hook snood, paternoster trace is ideal.

9 Both of the above species will virtually attack anything edible, from crab to sand eel, but strip baits of mackerel or squid are much preferred.

10 To obtain the most enjoyment from these small sharks, use a 12lbs test boat rod tip with a 20lbs braided reel line, which due to its non-stretch properties will achieve two things. Firstly, each and every bite, no matter how slight will be registered, and secondly, their 'dogged' fight will be much appreciated.

11 When targeting spur dogs in deep water, three hook, luminous jig heads baited with mackerel, squid or cuttlefish, are most effective. The top two are above a plastic tubular boom and lead slider, and the third below. *See Diagram.*

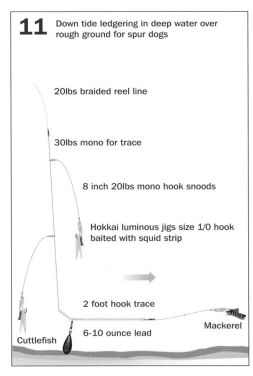

11 Down tide ledgering in deep water over rough ground for spur dogs

20lbs braided reel line

30lbs mono for trace

8 inch 20lbs mono hook snoods

Hokkai luminous jigs size 1/0 hook baited with squid strip

2 foot hook trace

6-10 ounce lead

Mackerel

Cuttlefish

Dogfishes

12 To hold a lesser spotted dogfish firmly for unhooking, grip its head around the gills and tail together in the same hand so it cannot move, while you remove the hook with the other. Otherwise its wiry body will wrap around your forearm and rub the skin off. That dogfish skins were dried and used as sand paper by our forefathers is no fairytale.

13 When fishing at anchor over rough ground where larger 'doggies' like Bull huss are expected, whether using a braided or monofilament reel line, be sure to incorporate a 30 foot 'thick' 40-60lbs test monofilament rubbing leader above your hook trace and lead slider. Use the Albright knot for connecting braid to thick mono *(see Freshwater boat fishing 'on the drift and trolling' Tip 10)* and a double, five turn uni or grinner knot for joining mono to mono.

14 At the business end of a Bull huss hook trace which needs to be 4-5 feet long and constructed from 100lbs mono, (to alleviate bite-offs from their mouth full of teeth) use a 8/0 hook baited with a fresh mackerel flapper. Or a mackerel fillet tipped with a chunk of squid.

15 If the two nasty 'spurs' of the spur dogfish are not enough to distinguish it from all other similar small sharks, note that it has no anal fin. And in this one respect alone, it is also different from all other small British sharks.

16 The spur dogfish is also different in that it is oviparous, hatching sets of 4-6 eggs inside the oviduct. Each is equipped with a large yolk sac which sustains it for a long gestation period of up to 20 months. Whereas other dogfishes lay egg sacs, (from which their young emerge several months later) once eggs inside the female have been fertilized internally by the male.

17 The rare 'black-mouthed' dogfish, similar in size and shape to the lesser-spotted doggie, is seldom caught on rod and line due to the exceedingly deep water in which it lives. It is recognizable by a broad flattened snout with wide-apart nasal flaps and ridge of denticles along the back of its tail.

18 Because lesser-spotted dogfish are at times such a nuisance to anglers targeting larger species, it would be nice to recommend a method or technique by which they are not likely to be caught. Truth is however, when thick on the ground, nothing seems to deter their aggressive feeding, short of fishing a bare hook.

19 Most of use have at some times in our lives have unknowingly eaten at least one species of dogfish. In fish and chip shops up and down the country, they all come under the label of 'rock eel'. 'Shark and chips' just doesn't sound quite the same, does it?

20 To skin a dogfish for eating, make a cut around its body immediately behind the head, and nail it to a fence or gate post. A sharp pull holding the skin with two hands from the edge of the cut will then remove it in one piece.

Ling

Ling

1 Though they are often to be found occupying the same deep water wreck, ling feed quite differently from the usually 'gentle' biting of the conger eel. They can wolf down the largest baits quickly and with ease, so 'hit and haul' immediately the rod top curls over.

2 Anchoring up tide of the wreck as for congers and bumping your bait down tide close to the super structure, using the 'lightest possible' lead, can score well, but you'll need to be constantly swapping to either heavier or lighter leads as the tide progresses or wanes. So hold the rod at all times.

3 A 30lbs class outfit is more than adequate for ling, barring absolute monsters (the 40 and 50lbs leviathans of yesteryear are exactly that and nowadays anything topping 30lbs is indeed a big ling) and a low diameter, non stretch braided reel line of say 30-40lbs test permits the lightest of leads to be used. To alleviate abrasion on the ironwork however, a 30 foot rubbing leader of 50lbs mono is recommended. Join to the braided reel line using a double, five-turn uni or grinner knot.

4 While some wrecks fish productively during the ebb, the most frenzied action with ling usually happens between the first and third hour of the flood tide. So be ready with a selection of freshly cut mackerel and squid bait and spare, pre-made hook traces.

5 Remember, high or low water will be approximately three hours later than your tide table if your boat is more than 12 miles out from the coastline.

6 When fishing wrecks for hefty species such as ling and conger, wearing a protective butt pad into which the rod butt fits and pivots during heavy pumping, is imperative for alleviating stomach and crotch bruising.

7 To specifically target ling when the sonar/fish finder is marking large numbers congregated around the wreck, rig up a two-snood heavy mono paternoster, using a link swivel tied to the end of your rubbing leader. Keep the snoods short with 8/0 hooks on the business ends baited with large strips of mackerel and a coloured plastic squid skirt (Muppet) above. At the bottom of the trace form an overhand loop to which (loop to loop) a 24 inch length of 12-15lbs test mono is added plus your lead, also 'looped' on. So that

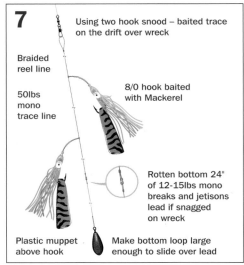

7 Using two hook snood – baited trace on the drift over wreck

Braided reel line

50lbs mono trace line

8/0 hook baited with Mackerel

Rotten bottom 24" of 12-15lbs mono breaks and jetisons lead if snagged on wreck

Plastic muppet above hook

Make bottom loop large enough to slide over lead

should the lead snag or a good fish take you amongst the iron work, the 'rotten-bottom' will break and all you'll forfeit is the lead. *See Diagram.*

8 The technique employed for 'drifting' once the skipper has lined up a drift and issued those immortal words "down you go boys", is to free spool your baits 'smoothly' down to the wreck and once the lead touches down, to wind up a few feet and wait. Gently raising and lowering the rod tip to activate the 'wavering' action of the plastic squid skirts often initiates action.

9 When larger than average-sized ling are on the cards, use one snood and one hook only, (increase hook size to a 10/0) baited with a mackerel flapper.

10 One of the very best baits for a big ling, although they are occasionally caught using un-baited pirks intended for cod, is a good mouthful of cuttlefish. They seem to prefer this to all else.

11 As commercial fishermen have proved, ling can attain weights in excess of 100lbs, a length of over 6 feet and inhabit depths to 200 fathoms. But such monsters to anglers will always remain 'pipe dreams'. The plain truth is that the species is its own worse enemy, because due to its voracity once a newly discovered wreck, the hulk alive with ling, is fished regularly, they are soon cleared up.

12 Though the ling (molva molva) closely resembles a conger eel with its long and slender eel-like body it is in fact more closely related to the cod, which its spineless fins, single barbel beneath the chin and very small scales would tend to indicate anyway.

13 While everyone associates ling with war time wrecks, rough and rocky ground sprouting from deep water, such as around the famous Eddystone Reef is really their natural habitat. War time wrecks are merely man-made reefs.

14 The biggest hauls of ling inhabiting deep water wrecks are made from January

through till March, when the species gathers in huge numbers prior to spawning.

15 As with most species with swim bladders (which inflates on the way up) ling are pumped up more easily following their initial surges down close to the wreck.

16 For targeting big ling inhabiting really deep water over rough ground or wrecks lying in upwards of 250 feet of water, a medium-sized, but heavy baited pirk offers excellent opportunities. Replace the huge treble with a strong 10/0 single and bait with a large strip of mackerel or squid. You will however in all probability haul up more cod than specimen ling.

17 When fishing for ling over rough ground or rocks less than 100 feet deep, night fishing will greatly improve results.

18 When fresh from the sea, particularly from deepwater wrecks or reefs, the ling has most contrasting colouration. Immediately noticeable is the white edging to its powerful dorsal, pelvic and tail fins. Almost a continual fringe and the provider of acceleration from ambush points used for attacking its staple diet of smaller fishes and squids.

19 Whenever a pouting or tiny codling gorges upon baits or a baited pirk intended for ling whilst drifting deep water and can be felt on the line 'jingling' away deep down close to the wreck. Leave it be! If there are any sizeable ling about, your nuisance fish won't last long.

20 Ling are distributed all around our British Isles with by far the greatest concentrations as far as deep water charter boat fishing is concerned, off the west coast of Ireland and in the south west English channel.

Mullet and Mackerel

Mullet and Mackerel

1 The Thick-lipped Grey Mullet (largest of the three British species) is easy to distinguish from the Thin-Lipped due to the first dorsal being two thirds the length of its anal fin, its noticeably 'thicker' upper lip, and because it lacks a dark blotch around the pectoral fin root, which is the characteristic marking of the Thin-Lipped. Thin lipped mullet also sport a yellowish pectoral fin which is not rounded. The Golden-Grey Mullet is similar in shape to the previous two, but is noticeably slimmer in cross section, with a distinctive golden spot on the gill plate.

2 Wherever Thin-lipped Grey Mullet congregate in estuaries, they are real suckers for small Mepps-type spinners (a No 3 is ideal) baited with rag worm. An ultra-light 8-9 foot rod and baby fixed spool reel (filled with just 4lbs test mono) is an ideal combo, guaranteed to produce maximum pleasure from these spirited fish. You'll need to doctor your spinners accordingly (a tip passed on to me by Steve 'stainless steel' Batchelor down in Hampshire when filming mullet for TV) by replacing the weighted brass barrel, (so the spinner works close to the surface) with a line of small glass beads threaded onto the wire stem, and swap the treble hook for

three inches of 8lbs mono and a pennel rig of two size 8 long shank, fine wire single hooks baited with 2-3 inches of rag worm. And try to work the spinner as slowly as possible. When mullet can be felt nipping at the end of the worm, simply keep winding until you hook up. It's a fascinating

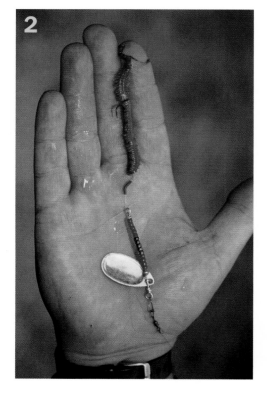

technique that occasionally produces bass, sea trout and even a salmon.

3 Mullet just love bread. Perhaps it is the softness and fluffiness of fresh, white bread flake that is so much like the filamentous weed clinging to the hulls of boats, groynes and harbour walls (upon which these species feed) that make mullet accept bread so easily. For most other popular freshwater baits are usually ignored. Around most marinas and estuary jetties where people feed bread to the ducks and swans, mullet become weaned onto bread and even learn to compete with the birds. So trotting a small piece of bread flake close to the bottom beneath a float on a 4-5lbs reel line is a deadly technique. Remember to pinch the flake on ONLY around the eye of your hook so the rest remains fluffy, and is thus sucked in more confidently. This is most important.

4 Of course you can create your own 'feeding mêlée', even along the most remote part of estuaries and tidal rivers frequented by mullet, by ramming a few old loaves of bread into the soft bankside at water level, just as the river is flooding in. As the bread starts to break up fish will soon follow to its source. Alternatively, put a load of bread scraps into an old keepnet, and stake it out well at low tide within casting distance of where you will be able to stand or wade, and wait for mullet to come in with the tide and find the stream of bread particles released from the keepnet.

5 Catching mullet on the fly rod opens up a whole new branch of enjoyment. But do not chase rainbows by expecting them to suck in a dry fly. Wherever mullet gather along beaches where great hefts of weed get piled up, they feed upon maggots within the rotting weed when it gets carried out to sea. So, 'match the hatch' by tying a size 14 eyed hook to the end of your 4lbs test leader, to which a slither of white (coffee cup) polystyrene has been super- glued (along

the shank) thus representing a maggot. And there is nothing to stop you from even adding a real maggot. It's not cheating. It is 'fly rodding'.

6 To target the large thick-lipped mullet inhabiting deep water harbours, where distance-casting, often into choppy water, makes for rather specialized fishing, make up some special long-tipped 'sliding floats. Simply glue between 12-20 inches of unpainted peacock quill with the herl removed into a 4/5 SSG shot Drennan clear, 'Loafer' float after first removing the float's tip with a razor blade. Then paint the body black and two inches of the tip in red or fire orange.

7 To fish 'long' floats for mullet, which take anywhere between 6-8 SSG shots (you have added a stem to the already buoyant body remember) these bottom-only sliders can be cast 40 yards if necessary (use a 6lbs test reel line) so to

stop one at a pre-selected depth simply tie on a five turn sliding stop knot with a bead between it and the float's bottom eye. Remember to leave the reel's bale arm open after casting to allow the bulk shots (bulked two foot from the hook with a bb half way between) to take your bait down quickly. And there really is only one bait to consider with this method. A pinch of fresh white bread flake on a size 10 hook tied direct.

8 When slider float fishing for deep-water, thick-lipped mullet, loose feed regularly with 'mashed bread'. *See Fresh water Species Chub Tip 8.*

9 As soft, white bread flake is without question the most successful bait for mullet overall, but does stand starkly out from the filamentous 'green' weed they suck from the bottom of boats and harbour walls etc, here's an unusual tip. Have you ever tried 'green' bread flake? Simply bake your own green-coloured loaf. It may not

actually make any significant difference, but if using bait closer to your quarry's natural food gives you more confidence, then it's worth a try. Even if only for the strange looks you'll get from fellow anglers.

10 To make a 'GREEN' 2lbs loaf exactly of the shade you want, obtain a 1¼lb packet of white bread mix and some green powder colouring, as used for making carp baits. Start by dissolving a heaped teaspoon of colouring in ¾ of a pint of hand-hot water, and add slowly to the bread mix in a large bowl and stir well. Knead the dough for five minutes and place in a lightly greased and floured baking tin of the appropriate size. Stretch cling film over the tin and leave in a warm place (the airing cupboard for instance) for 30 minutes until the dough doubles in size. Then place in the middle of a preheated oven set on 450 F/230C gas mark 8 for around 45 minutes. Job done. A 'green' loaf.

Mullet and Mackerel

11 Harbours are the very best locations to fish for mullet because not only are they accustomed to the noise of boats and people in general, they will have been conditioned into accepting food such as bread, which can be used as bait.

12 Some harbours fish best on the flooding tide, others on the ebb. Local knowledge is invaluable, so if you have but a short time at your disposal, ask the locals, or enquire along at the local tackle shop. Purchasing a few essentials remember, has a strange way of producing the very best of advice.

13 The activity of mullet feeding from the muddy estuary bottom and along the numerous adjoining reeks and inlets can be seen at low tide by the distinctive V shaped furrows they characteristically leave in the mud.

14 Securing a substantial supply of fresh mackerel for a day's bottom fishing for tope, bass, congers, ling, or drifting for sharks and so on, is a prerequisite to many a day out boat fishing. When time is of the essence, everyone goes hell for leather in trying to fill a fish box or two, for both hook baits and a bag of rubby dubby to tie around the anchor chain, before heading well offshore. And great fun it all is too. In fact when mackerel are coming thick and fast I'm always like a kid with a new toy, and difficult to prise away. But here's a tip if you are an ardent pike angler. Make sure you keep enough to one side, especially the 'Joeys', (so take your own freezer box along) and stock up for the winter's pike fishing ahead. Those who target catfish will appreciate freshly frozen mackerel too.

15 Whatever branch of sea fishing you pursue, having a store of freshly frozen mackerel at home makes good sense, so that whenever you set foot afloat, you have at least a few baits to be getting on with. They are so useful when cut into thin strips for tipping the hook, and thus adding visual attraction to peeler crab, squid and sand eel, etc when drift fishing for bass, turbot, brill and black bream.

16 When baits are not required by the hundred, but are averaging on the large size and you have time to slow down, get a reservoir fly rod out and fish a single fly on a fast

Mullet and Mackerel

sensation of a mackerel or two having attacked and hooked themselves (due to the weight of the lead) on the way down, repeat (in 10 foot increments) all the way down to the bottom. And remember to let everybody on board know at what depth they were hitting. Then, instead of winding straight up, repeat the procedure in reverse from sea floor to the surface. Systematically working every 'layer' really does produce the goods.

19 Don't discard other species that happen along whilst feathering for mackerel like garfish and scad (horse mackerel) both of which cut into appetizing strips or fillets, but beware of the poisonous weaver fish which looks to all intents and purposes like a freshwater ruffe.

20 Frozen mackerel are also useful for 'chunking' for bass. Using a sharp knife on a cutting board held over the gunnels, cut your mackerel into ½ inch segments and let them drift down tide at regular intervals from an anchored boat. The results can be devastating.

sinking line. The ensuing scrap will make you wish mackerel grew to 20lbs.

17 Another way of really enjoying bait catching is to reduce your set of feathers or jigs to just four, and using a six foot American-style, single handed bait-casting rod and baby multiplier loaded with just 10-12lbs test. A 'full house' then, really makes your wrist ache with joy.

18 Simply lowering a set of feathers over the side and lifting the rod tip up and down when you think they are far enough down is not the most effective way of catching mackerel. Click the reel into free spool, keeping your thumb on the spool and lower the set of lures to a depth of say 10 feet. Stop the spool with your thumb, then raise the rod tip a couple of feet, before allowing another 10 feet to descend. If no joy, and you do not feel that lovely 'jingling'

Plaice and Flounders

Plaice and Flounders

1 Like all flatfish, plaice are attracted to a line of coloured beads (10-20) threaded onto a six foot, 20lbs test, clear mono trace just above a 2/0 fine wire, Aberdeen-type hook that is crammed full of king rag worm. Second bait choice would be lug worms.

2 Incorporating a 'flounder spoon' into the trace a foot or so above the worm bait gives added attraction when plaice fishing. Remember to instantly free-spool line, when the gentle tap, tap, tap of a fish mouthing the worms is felt, so the plaice gets the bait well down when fishing on the drift, before putting the reel back into gear and slowly winding into the fish.

3 Though the British record for flounder is over 5lbs, such specimens are quite rare and anything over 1½lbs is considered not only a worthwhile catch, but also good eating.

4 While the flounder is a 'right-eyed' flatfish like the 'dab', left-eyed' or 'reversed' flounders with both eyes on the left, are in fact quite commonly caught. Unlike all other flatfish, the flounder has a curved line of sharp denticles around the pectoral fin, with more at the base of its wide dorsal and anal fins.

5 Unlike all other British flatfish, flounders migrate into entirely freshwater, and often congregate many miles upstream in the river's first (tidal) weir pool, where they are occasionally

caught on worm and maggot baits intended for coarse species. The occurrence has startled many a fresh water angler.

6 Wide and shallow river estuaries with sandy and muddy bottoms are top spots for flounders (during the summer months) whose natural aggression is harnessed by anglers who incorporate a 'flashy' three inch silver spoon in their terminal rig immediately above the size 4 long shank hook baited with lug or rag worm. Add at least one extra swivel to the spoon and pinch on a small 'fold over' lead immediately in front of the spoon. Both will help to alleviate line twist. This rig incidentally, suffices for both spinning and trolling.

7 To troll for flounders you need to work the baited spoon rig say 30 to 40 feet behind the boat whilst rowing 'with the tide' as slowly as possible, not against it, just fast enough to keep the spoon from fouling bottom. If choosing to fish during the flood for instance, a good plan is to go with the flow to the head of the estuary, and then come back with the ebb to where you first started.

8 If you find yourself without worms, narrow strips of mackerel, herring or sand eel can be used to bait the hook.

9 Whether spinning from the shore or trolling, use a medium strength 8-9 foot spinning outfit and an 8lbs reel line for both, remember that flounders

Plaice and Flounders

congregate in groups, so that when you catch one from a particular area, go over it thoroughly again and again. A nice benefit of both spinning and trolling is that eels are never a problem, as they are when presenting a bait on the bottom.

10 Bottom fishing an estuary can be enjoyed both from the shoreline, or an anchored boat. And using light tackle is the key to enjoying catching flounders, particularly if boat fishing. From the shore however, due to casting long distances, a step up in tackle is required, but be sure the rod has a fine tip for bite registration A simple one or two hook paternoster is all you need, and

because flounders often swim a foot or so above the bottom, try raising your worm bait around 18 inches off the bottom by adding a small poly ball or a tapered (at each end) cork float body, plugged to the hook trace with a short length of bird quill, just a few inches from the hook. Make up 20-24 inch long hook traces to achieve this.

11 Bottom fishing offshore for plaice from an anchored boat, is also preferred to drifting, should the sea bed be made up of clumps of rock or weed as opposed to a clean sandy bottom. Plaice love such areas because they feed on the mussels growing on the sides of the rocks. They swallow small mussels

whole and spit out the shells after crushing the insides to pulp with their powerful throat teeth before swallowing. In addition to a wodge of king rag or lugworm on the hook, (try tipping it with razor fish or a thin strip of squid) other offerings worth trying are hermit crab and peeler crab.

12 When drifting for plaice, so that your bait is dragged 'smoothly' over the sandy bottom behind the boat, use a running lead link above your six foot monofilament hook trace, with a flat and round 'watch-type' lead of somewhere between 5 and 10 ounces, depending upon depth and tide strength. *See Tip 2.*

13 Here's a valuable tip for windy days and strong tides when bites from plaice are few and far between. Slow the boat's drift down in order for fish to grab hold, by putting down a 50lbs weight on a long rope to trail behind the boat. Job sorted!

14 A 12-15lbs class boat rod outfit is all you need for really enjoying catching plaice, with 20lbs braided line filling the multiplier, for maximum sensitivity with the sandy bottom. Don't be tempted to let too much

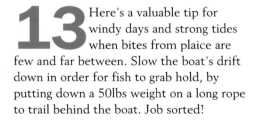

Plaice and Flounders

16 While fishing at slack water between tides is not generally considered 'prime time', by continually raising and lowering the rod top, the bait is given movement, while the lead sends up a cloud of dust every time it is yanked over the sea floor. Plaice find this attractive and will invariably investigate and gobble the bait up aggressively.

17 Plaice taken from the shore are usually caught by accident on worm baits by anglers targeting other species. For those willing to travel however, river mouths in the south west of the country, particularly Devon and Cornwall, offer the very best chance of a reasonable sized plaice from the shore. A light beach caster possessing a fine tip and with a forgiving action is the best tool for the job, in conjunction with a reel holding 15lbs test. A simple two hook (size 2/0 is ideal) paternoster rig baited with king rag worm and a 3-4 ounce lead, completes the combo.

18 Never put your rod down whilst boat drifting for plaice. When bites are few and far between especially, you cannot afford to miss that initial 'knocking' on the rod tip. And this is certainly one fish you cannot rely on to hook itself.

19 Though some skippers like to start plaice fishing from as early as March, the very best time to try drifting for them is during prolonged spells of settled weather in the summer months, when bright sunshine and clear water conditions can actually improve prospects.

20 What is a 'specimen-sized' plaice and the fish to aim for? Well, though the British record stands at over 10lbs, and once upon a time 6lbs plaice were relatively commonplace (no pun intended) nowadays, fish weighing between 3 and 5lbs are very highly regarded. So anyone boating a 4lbs plaice has truly got himself a 'benchmark' fish.

line out when drifting. Upon the lead touching bottom, pay out another 10 feet or so and knock the reel into gear. Remembering to click it into free spool immediately the 'knocking' sensation of a plaice mouthing the bait occurs, or you might pull the worms out of its mouth.

15 Due to the large and distinctive 'orange' spots covering the top of its wide body, and several bony knobs on the ridge of its head, it is, by these two features alone, impossible to confuse the plaice with any other flatfish inhabiting British waters.

JOHN WILSON'S
1001TOPANGLINGTIPS

Pollack

Pollack

1 When is the best time to target a really big pollack? Well, most south and south-west coast skippers who target deep-water wrecks way offshore, rate autumn into early winter fishing the best by far for 15lbs plus specimens. And here lies the secret of drift fishing during 'noticeably slower' neap tides over wrecks: picking the right skipper, who will expect that you book his boat well ahead of time.

2 If pirks are order of the day, and your skipper will know best, opt for a 9½ foot uptide rod coupled to 40-50lbs test braid filling a quality multiplier, preferably fitted with a 'lever' drag, enabling you to instantly reduce drag pressure when a whopper suddenly decides (as they frequently do) to crash dive back down to the wreck; a 'crucial' time when most 'biggies' are subsequently lost.

3 With large pollack in mind, to your braided reel line add an eight foot 'shock' leader of 30lbs mono, to which, via a strong snap swivel, the pirk is attached, that will not only break before the braided reel line should you become hung up on the wreck, but also act as a 'cushion' between lure and the non stretch braid, when your big pollack is just beneath the boat and fancies one 'last-ditch' dive.

4 If working soft plastic shads, jelly worms, twisters or red gills, etc on a long 20-25lbs test clear mono trace below a plastic boom and 6-10 ounce lead, reduce the reel line to 30-40lbs, low diameter braid for a more 'sensitive' presentation. *See Diagram.* But remember that working a big pollack up to the surface using lighter gear will take significantly longer. So be patient, particularly during the early part of the fight.

5 Get used to the extra 'hooking power' provided by using size 10/0-12/0 treble hooks when working large pirks. Trebles that are 'too' small can quickly hook-up with fish of any size from pound plus pouting and immature pollack (that very often get to your lure first) to the specimens specifically targeted. Go for broke.

6 When inextricably snagged up on a wreck whilst drifting, don't risk damage to your rod by over-straining it, or by attempting to break 50, even 30lbs braid even with a gloved hand. Simply put your reel into free spool (under 'thumb'

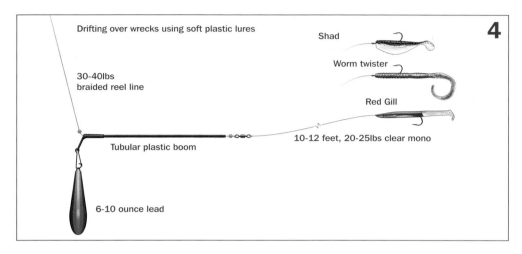

Drifting over wrecks using soft plastic lures

4

Shad

Worm twister

Red Gill

30-40lbs
braided reel line

10-12 feet, 20-25lbs clear mono

Tubular plastic boom

6-10 ounce lead

promotes confident hits which are best not 'struck', but simply 'wound' into. Do not however, be afraid every so often to make an irregular retrieve, or even crank the lure up like a maniac, expecting a savage response, within a split second of stopping winding. In really clear water, variation of retrieve sometimes accounts for those bonus whoppers.

8 Another 'deadly' technique responsible for producing big pollack that live around wrecks is to use tiny, (3-4 inch) soft-bodied shads with internally leaded heads and the hook rigged on top to alleviate snagging, (the kind freshwater anglers use for perch and zander) in conjunction with the normal plastic boom and 4-10 ounce lead set-up, with the artificial presented on 4-8 feet of 15lbs test clear mono.

9 The secret being with these soft bodied shads, as opposed to retrieving the artificial upwards, is to keep in touch with the bottom as the boat

pressure) and wind the line several times (using a figure of eight wrap) around the nearest cleat and let the weight of the boat snap the line. Easy peasy!

7 When working synthetic lures above a wreck, a steady retrieve of around 20 turns of the reel handle (before lowering the lure back down again) usually

5

7

Pollack

drifts along, merely by lifting the rod tip every so often and allowing a little more line out. This is unquestionably a light tackle method best suited to a 20lbs test braided line, baby multiplier and 12-15lbs test tip boat rod, all of which really capitalizes on that tantalizing wiggle of the shad's 'block' or 'twister' tail, where you simply 'wind' into a fish when the rod top pulls over.

10 Anything like a 'harsh' strike when working small synthetic lures such as shads on a braided reel line, is either going to pull the hook out or break the light hook length itself. This technique seems to produce when 'pirking' and 'gilling' does not, possibly because everything around the wreck is preoccupied with feeding upon really small fish such as sprats, which of course these small shad replicate perfectly. So the next time you're out 'wrecking' and the sonar screen is filled with small shoal fish hugging the wreck, but all your 'trusty' artificials fail to produce a hit, try baby shads. They work for cod and bass too.

11 There are few sea anglers about who prefer eating pollack to cod. Indeed, at the end of the day, skippers often find it difficult to even give pollack away. Yet with careful preparation, these fish make a tasty meal.

12 In an effort to remove 'boneless fillets' from the sides of a double figure pollack say, start just behind the skull by running a sharp knife down one flank beside the backbone. After slicing through to the bones at each end, bring the blade through from the tail end, skimming over the rib cage and finishing at the gill. This produces a pair of completely 'boneless' fillets.

13 To perform the impossible, cut your two large fillets into chunks and cook in the oven 'mornay' style with plenty of grated cheese over a white sauce, adding a few peeled prawns into the bargain. You'll then think of pollack in a completely different light.

14 Big pollack often show up over rough ground and of course around wrecks, when conger eels are being targeted from an anchored boat. Keep a spare, lighter outfit handy with a lead that only just holds bottom, and bait an 8/0 hook on a six foot thick mono trace with a fresh mackerel flapper, and every so often bump it well down tide. If kept on the move, any sudden and violent take is likely to be from a marauding pollack. Should you get bitten off however, suspect tope.

15 Targeting pollack from along a rocky, kelp covered, deep water shoreline, (the west coast of Ireland and some parts of Wales abound in such terrain) modest-sized

16

and ledges (sea and weather permitting) where the greatest concentrations of pollack lurk ready to ambush passing bait fish. And the subsequent hit on a speedily retrieved lure, best worked back in a 'jigging' motion, from a double figure fish can almost pull you out of your boots. Again, you need to be continually 'horsing' hooked fish quickly away from their hideouts to ever see them in the boat. Working small pirks deep down amongst jagged pinnacles of rocks is also a prime technique for exploring reefs lying well offshore, where the largest pollack congregate.

19 Float fishing live sand eels (beneath a sliding float rig) from a boat drifting beside a rocky shoreline can also be great fun, with a real chance of contacting those scrappy, double figure whoppers. And if you can feather up some really small Joey mackerel, so much the better. The occasional surprise may be in store too, by the way of the occasional nice bass which love rocky coastlines.

20 Use a large, 'through the middle' sliding float (larger 'pike-style' floats are ideal) stopped by a small bead and a five turn sliding stop knot made from 10-15lbs power gum. Go for a monofilament reel line (you're fishing around rocks, remember) of around 20lbs test, and initially set the float to present the bait at around mid water, but be prepared to fish deeper if runs are not forthcoming. On the business end use a strong round bend 5/0 hook tied to a 25lbs test, three foot hook trace with a lead ball or barrel lead on the reel line above the swivel to keep the bait well down. Hook sand eels once through both lips, and mackerel lightly through both nostrils. Hold the rod throughout, paying out line as the float moves away from the boat, tightening up and pointing the rod at the fish till the line becomes 'humming tight' when the float disappears, before heaving the rod back into the fish, and immediately taking control, less it finds sanctuary amongst the rocks.

specimens say in the 2-8lbs range, can produce some marvellous action. Best lures are small pirks (and it's well to go prepared to lose several) in the 2-4 ounce range that can be cast a fair way out and counted down amongst the rocks, before retrieving in a fast, irregular way suggesting perhaps an injured bait fish. Pollack often hit a lure on the drop (especially 'wedge-shaped' models that tend to sway from side to side) so be ready for any unusual or aggressive indication on the line from the second your lure hits the surface. In addition and indeed before even casting, work out from where you stand on the rocks, the exact spot beside and below the rocks you will need to steer a fish to in order to lift it out.

16 Casting lures for pollack from the shore demands a fairly long, heavy duty spinning rod (a 'bass' beach caster will do at a pinch, providing the reel fitting isn't too high up) coupled to a 'fast retrieve' multiplier filled with 15-18lbs test monofilament. Do not be tempted to use braid; it is far less resistant

to the abrasion of rocks, compared to mono. But what you do need is a 30 foot mono shock/rubbing leader of say 30-40lbs test to withstand constant long casting and contact with jagged rocks. To this tie on a strong snap link swivel for quick lure changing. Join the rubbing leader to the reel line using the reliable five turn, double uni or grinner knot.

17 When extracting pollack from rocky terrain, whilst shore casting, even modest-sized fish, do not allow them to get their heads down and dive too often, or you'll be going home early having run out of lures. Play each fish to the absolute maximum breaking strain of your line, with a very firm clutch setting, and keep pumping the fish up whilst winding furiously. It's 'hit and hold' sport at its very best.

18 Casting towards a rocky, deep water shoreline is even more prolific from a drifting boat. Skippers who specialize in this technique will take you in real close amongst rocky outcrops

Rays

Rays

1 Species like the spotted, undulate, small-eyed, cuckoo and thornback (Britain's most commonly caught ray) more or less fall into one group in so far as tackle and techniques are concerned. All can be caught either down tide or up tide boat fishing.

2 When looking to catch any of the above rays in weak tide runs, stepping down to a 12lbs test outfit with a low diameter braided reel line allows each to really show its mettle. Generally however, a 20lbs class outfit (again, using a braided reel line) and baiting with worm, crab or fish strip cut from the flank of a fresh mackerel or launce, will attract them all, whether down tide, or up tide boat fishing. And in some areas of course they can be taken from the shore. A thickish mono hook trace is required due to the crunching ability of their jaws, with fine wire, but strong hooks, and a lead slider above.

3 If specifically targeting rays, do not be too early in striking. Or indeed strike abruptly. Wait for the ray to 'smother' and get your bait (especially if it's a good mouthful) well into its jaws and the rod tip nodding over positively, before simply winding into the fish and pumping it off the sea bed, all in one long, smooth action.

4 Electric rays, with their flattened, almost 'square-shaped' upper bodies inhabit our seas around the British Isles, but are rarely caught on rod and line.

Rays

They are however easy to recognize as they are the only ray with a 'proper' fish tail.

5 There are two separate species of electric rays to look out for, but certainly not to touch, as a strong jolt of electrical current can be had from touching their pectoral fins. The more commonly caught species (torpedo nobiliana) grows to over 100lbs, whilst the rarely encountered (except for around the Channel Islands) 'marbled electric ray' rarely exceeds 10lbs. Both are now becoming more of an angling possibility around the British Isles as global warming takes hold, and are likely to fall to crab or fish bait presented hard on the sea floor.

6 To add extra pulling power to a crab bait intended for rays, tip the hook with a slither cut from the flank of a fresh sand eel, launce or garfish, to wiggle about enticingly in the tide.

7 Rays such as 'undulates' and 'blondes' are often taken on live sand eels or launce being bumped along over banks of sand and shingle by anglers actually targeting bass or turbot. So be patient if you pull into what seems like the bottom, and see if it moves off, before suspecting a snag (rare over most sand banks) and subsequently pulling for a break.

8 To stand any chance of pumping up a blonde ray (which can average over the 20lbs mark) from the sea bed in deep water and fast tides, where they prefer to live well offshore over banks of shingle and sand, a 50lbs class outfit is recommended. And 2-3lbs of lead is often required simply to keep your mackerel or squid bait nailed to the bottom. They have such immense 'suction' with the sea floor due to the sheer size of their large bodies, and will test your tackle and resolution to the absolute limit.

9 Whilst most species of rays will attempt to go down on and hoover up a 'moving' fish or squid bait, they

JOHN WILSON'S
1001TOPANGLINGTIPS

15

much prefer 'static' food, presented from an anchored boat. Their natural diet of molluscs and crustaceans proves this.

10 Should you catch a sting ray, be extremely careful of its 'sting' which is a pointed, serrated, spine of bone between 3-5 inches in length, covered in a poisonous mucus, and it is 'this' which usually gets left in any wound inflicted. The ensuing pain is not life threatening but most intense for several hours, often accompanied by hallucinations.

11 There are two species of rays possessing poisonous stings inhabiting British seas. The common 'Atlantic sting ray' (Dasyatis Pastinaca) is in shape similar to the blonde ray, but much thicker in the body with a rapidly tapering tail which is equipped with one or two stings situated half way along.

12 To immobilize this particular sting ray from lashing out with its powerful tail which 'bows' and stands upwards like an angry cat in order to ram home its 'sting', simply grab

10

the very end of the tail and wrap once around a 'gloved' hand.

13 The Eagle Ray (Myliobatis Aquila) which has a thick and wide, triangular body with pointed wings, has a long and thin, 'whip-like' tail, with the 'sting' situated at the base of the tail immediately behind its tiny dorsal fin. It is one of the most easily recognizable of all rays.

14 Both British sting rays are 'viviparous', in that they give birth to live young, and are only 'occasionally' caught in the southern half of the British Isles by boat and shore anglers using crab, worm or fish baits presented hard on the sea bed. The British record for both species incidentally, stands at over 60lbs, though in warmer seas around the world the same two species grow to

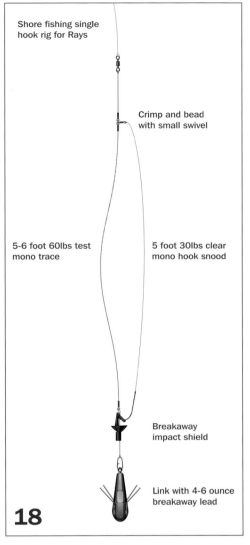

Shore fishing single hook rig for Rays

Crimp and bead with small swivel

5-6 foot 60lbs test mono trace

5 foot 30lbs clear mono hook snood

Breakaway impact shield

Link with 4-6 ounce breakaway lead

18

over three times this size. The top English sting ray 'hot spot' being on the east coast around the shallow waters of St Osyth beach near Clacton, while the top area in Ireland is Tralee Bay.

15 To hold a thornback ray for unhooking which is covered in sharp spikes all over including the tail, grip either side of its cheeks firmly (no spikes in this area) between thumb and forefinger. Being covered in spines, thorns and dense prickles all over, with rasp-like teeth lining its thick, rubbery, skate-like jaws, the thornback should have perhaps been called a skate as apposed to a ray.

16 Generally speaking and because rays do not have canine teeth, a 12 inch nylon

covered wire trace is only necessary when fishing areas of rough, honeycombed ground over which tope might also be expected. Otherwise 'thick' monofilament is the ideal hook trace material.

17 Never 'strike' a ray as such when boat fishing using a braided reel line. Simply 'lift' smoothly into the fish and keep winding till the rod keels over and its full weight is felt.

18 Rays such as thornbacks, small-eyed and even sting rays, can be taken from the shore at night, especially during the warmer months. They each prefer muddy and sandy shorelines. Here is a simple single hook, clipped-down rig with a 5 foot long, 30lbs test mono hook snood that is particularly suited to rays. *See Diagram.* For the main,

6 foot long trace use the same 60lbs test mono as the shock leader,

19 Best baits for rays at night are mackerel and squid strip, juicy soft back or peeler crab, or dead sand eel. King rag worms are also effective.

20 With most rays, larger baits generally produce larger fish. Even a modest-sized thornback or blonde ray will swallow a whole mackerel. So do not be afraid to use a whole side fillet cut from the biggest mackerel in the box. You might be surprised with the result.

Sharks

Sharks

1 By far the most popular of our British sharks, the tope, is equipped with a full set of sharp teeth lining both jaws. But barring the very occasional 'bite off' many boat skippers prefer to use thick monofilament of 150-200lbs test as opposed to wire (its suppleness accounts for more runs especially from fish caught before and released as all are nowadays) and strike all runs instantly, ensuring the hook ends up in one corner of the mouth and is thus easy to extract.

2 Whether float fishing your bait downwind from the boat beneath a float for blue sharks or presenting it directly beneath the boat on a free line with just the addition of a barrel lead, do not be

tempted into using 'over-sized' baits. A single large mackerel or mackerel flapper on a 10/0 or 12/0 hook is mouthful enough, allowing an instant strike without the fear of deep hooking. Even a 250lbs 'blue' (and you would be talking a new British record here) has a comparatively 'small' mouth compared to most other sharks of equal length, except perhaps for the 'long-tailed' thresher shark.

3 In some areas around our British coastline, such as the Thames Estuary for instance, where skipper John Rawle who operates out of Bradwell has

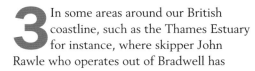

4

pioneered up tiding for tope, 'the' one bait that almost guarantees tope and only tope will grab hold (apart from the occasional really big, double-figure bass) is the head

end of an eel. It is amazingly selective in that it attracts so few nuisance species. Not that anyone is going to think of a whopping great bass as any kind of a nuisance.

4 Targeting blue sharks around our British Isles is much dependent upon sea temperatures. Skippers working off the Welsh coast for instance where the warm waters of the Gulf Stream are just 30 miles out, providing summer temperatures averaging 65 degrees, enjoy a long season from June through till October. So ensure conditions are favourable wherever you decide to fish for blues.

5 When drifting for blue or porbeagle sharks with a good 'slick' going out behind the boat created by a strong concentration of 'rubby dubby' *(See Ground baiting in Saltwater, Tips 1 and 2)* from which birds like shearwaters, storm petrels and various gulls feed upon in the surface film, a sure sign that a shark or several sharks have followed the rubby dubby up to the boat, is when all the birds 'suddenly' get off the water. A great sight!

5

Sharks

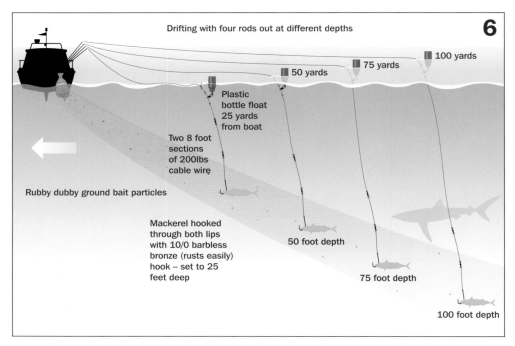

Drifting with four rods out at different depths

6

100 yards

75 yards

50 yards

Plastic bottle float 25 yards from boat

Two 8 foot sections of 200lbs cable wire

Rubby dubby ground bait particles

Mackerel hooked through both lips with 10/0 barbless bronze (rusts easily) hook – set to 25 feet deep

50 foot depth

75 foot depth

100 foot depth

6 If you wish to really enjoy the fight of most blue sharks and the occasional medium-sized porbeagle, don't go above a 30lbs class outfit. Select a combo that does not weigh a ton and go for monofilament over a braided reel line, with 200lbs test cable laid wire trace and 'barbless' size 10/0 'bronze' hook, which will rust and drop out within a few weeks should you be unfortunate in snapping up or are obliged to leave a hook in a fish. To alleviate tangles, fish four outfits back behind the drifting boat, each a different distance out, (say at 25, 50, 75, and 100 yards) and each with the sliding float set to present the bait at varying depths. Say, 25, 50, 75 and 100 feet deep. *See Diagram.*

7 Keep a spare fifth outfit handy, rigged up WITHOUT a float, but ready baited, for targeting fish which suddenly appear from nowhere, as they frequently do, beside the boat attracted by the rubby dubby bags. Such sharks provided they are not scared by the associated moving about and hollering on board (so be quiet) will invariably (if not alarmed) instantly gobble up a mackerel lowered down to them. Alarmed fish might keep going round the boat, occasionally even

nosing the rubby dubby bags, without ever taking whatever you throw at them.

8 Balloons as shark floats are now not being used. They are considered environmentally 'unfriendly' as turtles tend to bite and swallow them. Particularly the 'now endangered' giant leatherback turtle that can weigh as much as a ton, and which comes up from the depths to gorge heavily upon jellyfish near the

7

surface, possibly mistaking a balloon for a jellyfish. A simple polystyrene or plastic bottle-type float that can be detached by unclipping a snap-link swivel (sandwiched between two large beads and stopped at the desired depth by a power gum, five turn sliding stop knot) at the boat is much better.

9 For British anglers wishing to come to grips with a really big 'porbeagle' shark, the North of Scotland and the Faroe Islands, (situated at 62 N north west of Scotland) where specimens topping 400lbs are regularly taken, offer the best opportunities.

10 To tell the difference between a tope and a smooth hound, apart from the fact that tope have canine teeth and smooth hounds do not, remember that the tail of a tope has a large notch on the lower edge of the upper lobe, whereas that of the smooth hound does not.

11 For numbers of porbeagle in the 80-200lbs range, currently, the Welsh coastline off Milford Haven, 30 miles out on the edge of the 'Gulf Stream' between June and September, arguably offers the most prolific fishing around the British Isles.

12 Be certain that your mackerel shark bait goes quickly down to the desired depth by sleeving a heavy barrel lead onto the wire trace immediately above it. Otherwise, it is quite liable to be attacked by gannets, which will repeatedly deep-dive for an easy meal.

13 The largest three sharks found around the British Isles in order of ultimate size potential is the Mako, (1000lbs plus) Thresher, (700-800lbs) and the Porbeagle, (500lbs plus).

14 Whilst waiting for a shark run, it is best to have the reel actually in gear with the

ratchet on, and the drag set lightly, (whether star or lever drag) but sufficient to alleviate an overrun should a fish (as some do) really scream off with the bait.

15 Endeavour, whether fishing for medium sized tope or much larger sharks, to quickly click the ratchet off and gently 'thumb' the spool as soon as a fish starts running off with the bait. Vibrations down the line emanating from a particularly noisy ratchet just might make a 'finicky' shark eject the bait. Just because they are equipped with large canines does not mean they are less sensitive.

16 To rig up for 'down tide' tope fishing using a 20-25lbs reel line (either braid or mono) add a 30 foot, 40lbs test mono rubbing leader (as tope are often encountered hunting over rough and broken ground interspersed with rocks) with a simple lead slider above the hook trace swivel. The six foot hook trace can either be of 'thick' (150-200lbs test mono) straight through with a 10/0 hook crimped to the end. Or, for those worried about the tope's teeth, the last 20 inches or so can be of 50-80lbs braided, nylon covered wire. Top bait is a mackerel flapper. But if nuisance fish arrive on the scene, particularly doggies, which

quickly suck the goodness from a flapper, find a large mackerel and cut in half. Then remove the tail at the root to create a 'cone', which lasts very much longer. Hook once only through the narrow end.

17 There are various ways of loose feeding or chumming to attract tope up to your hook baits. A simple, but 'large' bait dropper attached to a spare rod can be regularly filled with finely chopped mackerel and lowered down. Or a rubby dubby bag (like an old onion sack) can be filled with cut scraps and old baits, and tied around the anchor chain, prior to actually putting the baits out. Or, and this works especially well when the tide is running gently, simply keep chunking up pieces of mackerel on a cutting board with a sharp knife (you need plenty of fresh bait for this) and tossing them over the stern. Or, and this works well even when the tide is really pulling, why not try the 'Carrier Bag' method. *See Saltwater Boat Fishing 'At Anchor', Tips 2 and 3.*

18 Do not wait too long before striking a tope run, or two things will happen. The fish will either eject the bait, or you will have a deeply hooked fish to contend with. Fish with the reel in gear and the clutch lightly

set and the ratchet on, (or tide strength alone will keep your ratchet clicking away if the reel is simply left in free spool) and pick up the rod (pointing the tip at the fish) at the first sign of a run. If the fish is any size at all it will steadily make off with the bait, whereupon you crank the clutch up and when all is 'humming tight' heave the rod back into a full bend.

19 If using a thick mono hook trace for tope, be sure to inspect it following every capture, instantly replacing it if it looks even slightly damaged.

20 When mackerel are in short supply do not discard any small fish as potential bait. Dabs, scad, pouting, pollack, garfish, wrasse and bass will all catch tope. Such an opportunist predator as a shark cannot afford to be choosy.

Skate

Skate

1 Never put your hand close to the enormous mouth of a sizeable common skate. The thick rubbery-lips are covered in backward-pointing rasps (like those on a blackberry bush) and the suction of a mouth that could swallow a rugby ball is truly awesome. They do in fact, amongst other fish, feed upon smaller skate and rays, sucking them in whole.

2 A stand-up 50lbs line class boat outfit is preferred by most skippers for dealing with the power, size, and enormous 'suction' (against the sea bed) of giant skate which can top the 200lbs mark.

3 At the business end, a 1-3lbs lead is attached to a free-running 'tube-type' lead slider stopped against the 5 foot, 250lbs test mono hook trace swivel by a couple of large beads. Above the hook trace is a further 5 foot mono 'uptrace' of the same breaking strain, connected by bead and swivel to the 50lbs reel line which is doubled for several feet. A big skate can measure over seven feet long, and with nasty spines on its tail can actually cut

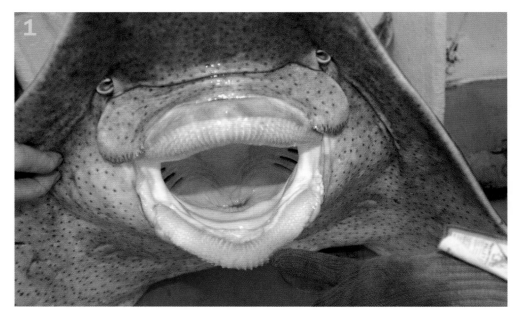

through a 50lbs test reel line. So in effect while your are lowering down a 'short' trace, you have the benefit of 10 feet of 250lbs test mono to alleviate 'cut-offs'.

4 Care must be taken in lowering the bait down to the bottom 'slowly', as tangles cannot be verified easily.

With up to 4lbs of lead required to hold bottom in certain tides, and over 500 feet of line out, no one wants the job of continually checking the baits.

5 A large butt pad that distributes the weight across the groin region is imperative for doing battle with

these huge flatfish, preferably one that has a 'pivoting' rod holder. In addition most skippers will offer their anglers use of a shoulder harness which has clips that attach to lugs on the reel. So in effect, your back takes most of the strain when you lean back and 'pump' instead of your arms.

6 In order to gain line slowly following a big fish's initial, unstoppable run, 6/0-8/0 sized multipliers on which the retrieve can be dropped down a gear simply by pressing a button, are widely used and well advised. This is not a workout for those with back trouble or for the fainthearted. Battles with giant skate of 150lbs upwards, can last an hour or more. And in a really strong tide, possibly over two hours or more.

7 Best baits for sizeable skate are presented on size 10/0 hooks. A large mackerel tipped with squid works most effectively, as does a large squid itself with a body of 12-15 inches. A spur dog/mackerel cocktail is also favoured by many Scottish skippers, who remove the spines and tail of a 3lbs spur dog before mounting it with a squid or mackerel 'skirt' above.

8 Best locations around the British Isles for coming to grips with a 100lbs plus common skate, (second only in

ultimate flatfish size to the Halibut) are off Western Ireland and in the deep sea lochs of Scotland's western Highlands, where the sea

floor shelves to over 600 feet. Prime time being between March and July.

9 Male skate are usually smaller and immediately told apart from females by their two huge 'claspers' (reproductive glands) covering the vent. Eggs are internally fertilized by the male, after which leathery, purse-like egg capsules with horns at each end for attaching to weed or rocks are laid by the female, from which the fully formed young emerge several months later.

10 Don't be tempted to use a braided reel line for hauling up these monstrous flatfish from the deeps. Any subsequent battle will feel uncomfortably 'tight' and particularly arduous for the captor, due to the non-

SALTWATER SPECIES

15

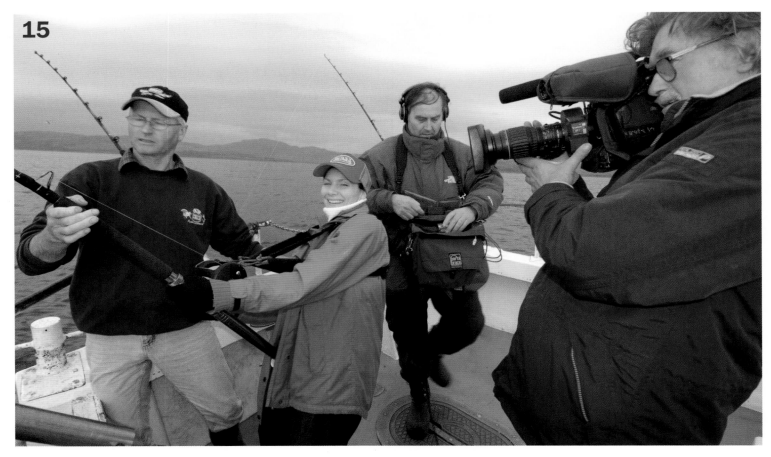

stretch properties of braid. But worst of all is when a big fish nears the boat and decides (as they frequently do) to dive fast back down to the bottom again.

11 Moreover, and this is a real potential problem when fishing with braid, should the line pass beneath the boat, where the rod has to be worked 'around' the hull in order to get a direct line with a skate that has manoeuvred over to the other side of the boat, the chances of a braided reel line scraping against the rough bottom of the hull and instantly fracturing are too great.

12 Giant common skate are certainly a species, as with sharks that benefit from the durability and that all-important 'cushioning' effect provided by the inherent 25 percent stretch in monofilament reel line.

13 Do not leave your rods unattended when targeting big skate, and be sure to set the ratchet and drag to the pull of the tide, in order that an audible warning of a fish smothering the bait and running off are

17

19

on stiff poles are then used (one in each forward corner of each wing) to help haul it overboard through the door, whereupon it is immediately returned after unhooking and the taking of trophy shots.

20 Trust the experience of your skipper when he decides whether conditions on the day, which might look fine to you, are actually conducive for targeting big skate. Excessively strong tides for much of the session could mean the use of leads in excess of 4 and 5lbs, which are certainly no fun to fish with. Nor are winds which would induce the boat to yaw too much and thus make presenting 'static' baits virtually impossible at great depths. Remember that whilst you may well have travelled far for a big skate, if the skipper cannot put his boat to sea, he is not earning a living.

20

instantly heard. Lock hard up, with the drag set too fiercely, and the last sight of your rod will be of it disappearing down into the depths.

14 With so much monofilament line out, it is impossible to effectively 'strike' a skate run as such. When a fish has obviously moved off having swallowed the bait, and this does feel as though you have snagged on the bottom, tighten the drag right up and point the rod at the fish whilst cranking as much line onto the reel as you can till it is literally 'humming tight'. Then, and only then, heave the rod back into a playing position and take stock.

15 Once hooked up to a big skate, stand with your feet apart and lean back a little into the fish. This is easier done if you are wearing a shoulder harness (usually supplied and fitted by the skipper or his mate) because your whole upper body, hinging at the waist, is used to 'pump' the fish upwards. But when it wants to dive, just let it. Straining against such immense torque will only knacker you long before the fish.

16 When a really big skate cannot be levered off the sea bed, an old trick worth trying is to pluck away on a bow-string-tight line with your fingers, like a guitar. The vibrations are felt by the fish which subsequently sometimes moves off. But not always. Another ruse is to drop a heavy lead weight down the line, and to jiggle it about on a slack line once it touches bottom in order to induce the skate to move off.

17 When a big fish becomes hooked, keep a watchful eye on the other rods. It is quite usual for skate to move around in pairs.

18 Other baits worth trying are pollack or coal fish between 2-3lbs, any sized dogfish which is improved by splitting the gut open with a sharp knife to provide a scent trail, and large chunks of cuttlefish.

19 Once a big skate is finally on the surface and its enormous size is appreciated, hauling it on board for unhooking is not so difficult as it would seem, provided the boat has a 'stern door'. Two narrow (2 inch) gape gaffs

Smooth Hounds

Smooth Hounds

1

1 There are in fact two species of this small, athletic shark to be found around our British shores: the 'starry' smooth hound and the 'common' smooth hound, which ironically, is in fact less common than the 'starry'.

2 Both smooth hounds have five gill slits and visible lateral lines, and both are often caught over the same hunting grounds. The 'starry' however, is covered along the back in small, star-shaped white spots. Hence its name. The British record for both species being 28lbs.

3 One of, if not 'the' best bait for catching smooth hounds is a hermit crab, fresh out of its shell. Using a fine wire 3/0-4/0 hook, sleeve on starting at the tail, going all the way through the body and finishing up through one of the legs. And offering it 'up tide' or up tide and across, static on the sea bed over rough ground is by far the best technique for catching them. Present on a running 5 foot mono trace of 40lbs test, above which is a swivel and lead slider holding a 3-6 ounce breakaway lead, depending upon the tide of course. This runs on a 20 foot rubbing leader of 50lbs mono, tied to a reel line of say 25lbs braid, or 18-20lbs mono.

4 As most smooth hounds will average less than 10lbs (double figure fish being 'bench mark' specimens around most parts of the country, particularly if caught from the beach) they should be considered a 'light tackle' fish,

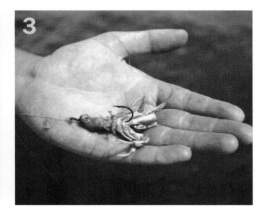

3

unlike the tope, they do not have canine teeth, simply crushing and grinding pads (flat teeth) for demolishing the crustaceans upon which they mostly feed.

8 When casting up tide from an anchored boat, walk down to the stern and cast sideways, with the lead in no way passing 'over' the deck. Horrendous accidents can happen if this strict code of practice is not adhered to.

which incidentally, fights and runs surprisingly well if hooked in shallow water between 15 and 30 feet.

5 Smooth hounds come close inshore during the summer months to feed upon the rich larder of crustaceans found over broken ground interspersed with weed, and for the females to give birth to their live young in litters of up to a dozen or more pups.

6 For those wishing to make contact with specimen-sized smooth hounds, there is no better area than off Selsey Bill in West Sussex during the summer months. Beach fishing for 'smoothies' is also productive between Selsey and Pagham. Several other areas along the south coast also produce big 'smoothies'.

7 For their slender bodies, smooth hounds are equipped with huge, powerful fins (you can see the muscles) actual eye lids allowing them to

fully close their eyes, and a strange, translucent nose, just like the tope. But

Smooth Hounds

9 Smooth hounds are renowned, fast divers when on a short line close to the boat, so don't make a 'stab' at them when netting. Let big fish especially, literally 'swim' into the net, or a frantic, last ditch dive (should the net's frame hit them) could cost you dearly when the trace parts.

10 Shore fishing for smooth hounds is up there with some of the most exciting options available around our British beaches. And night fishing during the summer (June and July are prime months) offers the best opportunity (next to a tope) of coming to

grips with a fast running, double figure shark from the shore.

11 The most productive period is usually a couple of hours before, to a couple or three hours after high water. So be sure to select the night you fish with this tide-span window in mind.

12 A standard surfcaster and multiplier loaded with around 15lbs test and a 50-60lbs shock leader is the ideal combo. Use a single 3/0 'up tide' hook on a 3 foot, 30lbs

test mono trace (clipped up) and 4-6 ounce breakaway lead.

13 Many prefer a 'pulley rig' for catching smooth hounds when casting over rough ground from the beach. It prevents the lead hanging down and possibly snagging bottom as you retrieve a hooked fish.

14 With the 'pulley rig' the single snood paternoster casts like a standard 'clipped down' rig, but upon retrieval with a fish on, it acts like a running ledger.

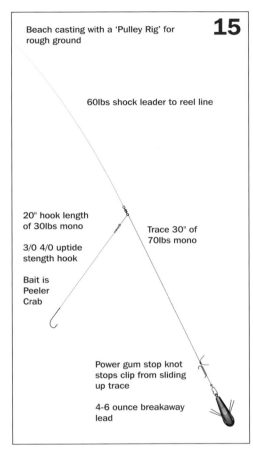

Beach casting with a 'Pulley Rig' for rough ground **15**

60lbs shock leader to reel line

20" hook length of 30lbs mono

3/0 4/0 uptide stength hook

Bait is Peeler Crab

Trace 30" of 70lbs mono

Power gum stop knot stops clip from sliding up trace

4-6 ounce breakaway lead

15 To construct this most effective but simple device tie a strong swivel (say a No 1) onto the end of your shock leader. Then, using several feet of 60lbs mono (same as your shock leader) tie a strong, small swivel to one end and sleeve a small bead up against it. Thread the tag end through the bottom of the larger swivel on your shock leader, and sleeve on a length of tubing (to accept the bait clip) before tying on the lead link. Then slide in the wire bait clip This, the 'main trace' should be around 3 foot long overall. *See Diagram.* To the other end of the small swivel tie on some 30lbs test mono for the hook snood, and add your hook (a 3/0 or 4/0 so that when clipped up, the small swivel and bead lie tight up to the larger swivel, moving the bait clip up or down for adjustment. Lastly, to stop the bait clip tubing from moving upwards under the strain of casting, immediately above it tie on a stop knot using power gum.

16 Rough ground can consume entire rigs cast after cast. Much better to simply jettison just the lead if regularly snagging up. So make a simple 'rotten bottom' for your Pulley rig by forming an overhand loop (to accept the lead) at the end of your main trace instead of the lead link, which is held in place for casting by a panel pin pushed through a piece of buoyant foam rubber. The rotten bottom itself, just several inches of say just 10-12lbs mono, is tied to both the lead and immediately above the overhand loop. The idea is that you have a strong connection between lead and trace for casting, but when the rig hits the surface these become separated (just like the pulley rig itself), leaving a weak link that will break to a firm pull should the lead become snagged.

17 Best bait by far is a big helping of peeler crab, well anchored to the hook with elasticated cotton. Be prepared to change it regularly when spider crabs prove a problem. These crabs which are equipped with long and powerful pincers can all too easily 'crimp' their way along your trace and

hook snood whilst attacking the bait. So get used to 'feeling' along the line with thumb and forefinger before re-baiting.

18 After casting and placing the rod on its rest, with the reel in gear and the ratchet on, slacken back on the clutch so a fish can 'audibly' pull line out when it runs off. But not so light that the waves and tide keep the ratchet 'clicking' continually, giving false hope.

19 Heave into your smooth hound almost immediately after cranking the clutch onto a firm setting and watch out for fish which decide to run fast (as many will) parallel with the beach.

20 A good indication of smooth hounds working their way over your casting area, with the possibility of imminent action, is when the crabs stop pecking at your baits and are conspicuous by their absence. The scalded-cat noise of the reel's ratchet suddenly filling the night air is indeed both startling and music to the ears.

17

Turbot and Brill

1 Turbot and brill share many similarities and even favour the same habitat offshore, of steeply shelving banks of sand and shingle. Both are also thick-set, 'left-sided' flatfish with just a single pectoral fin, a continuous frill around their bodies, and both eyes on the left of the head.

2 Turbot and brill are easily told apart. The brill for instance does not have tubercles along its back, like the turbot, and the first rays of its long dorsal fin or frill, are free of the normal membrane. Unlike turbot, the brill does not have spots on its tail and is a much slimmer fish altogether. The turbot having wide dorsal and anal fin frills, and a large spade-like tail.

3 Should you continually fail to hook up with what seem to be 'positive' bites when drifting with the tide for turbot and brill over shingle banks, though your live launce comes back decidedly 'mauled', even bitten through the back, the one culprit to immediately suspect is the cuttlefish. Cuttlefish attention is usually at its worst when the tide is weak. They can often be felt 'hanging on' for a few seconds during the retrieve. But should you be lucky in actually bringing one up to the boat, try adding a strip of fresh cuttlefish to a mackerel fillet. Big flatfish love such cocktails.

4 'The' most prolific spots around the British Isles for regularly coming to grips with turbot and brill are the vast array of shingle and sand banks off the Channel Islands. Try off Alderney, Guernsey, or Jersey, where local skippers really know their stuff. Prime time is April through till September. Both the south and west coasts of Ireland are good too.

5 When the tides for drifting are not over fierce, using 'freshwater tackle' to catch turbot and brill not only produces more bites, (on account of the more natural bait presentation with lighter lines and traces) but also both fish are vastly more fun to catch than on the average charter, 'boat rod'.

6 To maximize on enjoyment, a 10 or 11 foot carp rod with a test curve of say 2lbs, coupled to a baby multiplier holding a braided reel line of just 12lbs test, is an ideal outfit, which not only

permits the use of lighter leads (the flat leads used for bolt-rig carp and barbel fishing are ideal) for superb presentation, but also really allows these flatfish to show their mettle. Generally however, a 20lbs class, lightweight (you'll be holding the rod throughout) boat rod outfit and small multiplier reel combo loaded with 20-25lbs braid is the perfect combination for drift fishing. Many turbot and brill enthusiasts rig up a tubular plastic boom and lead slider, stopped by a bead against the swivel of a 5-6 foot 20lbs, clear mono hook trace with a 4/0 hook on the business end. But I prefer to use a line of a dozen or so large plastic beads sandwiched between a simple lead slider and hook trace swivel. This rig seems to bump more smoothly over sand and shingle. And I use a 10 foot rubbing leader

of 25lbs mono joining reel line to hook trace. Top baits are launce, sand eels and mackerel strip.

7 The fight of a double figure turbot will give you a scrap to remember. But don't hurry it up from the bottom. The power-dives from turbot can all too easily snap a light reel line. So use the silky-smooth clutch of the small multiplier for the purpose it was devised and really enjoy each battle. Winding smoothly and pumping gently to ease it upwards.

8 Try to strike the bite 'instantly', and you won't connect with many big flatties. Even when using comparatively small baits such as thin fillets

of fresh mackerel or launce, on a 4/0 hook tipped with a piece of squid or razor fish, it is imperative to instantly 'free-spool' line to what feels like a 'taking' fish for a good 10 seconds or so before clicking the multiplier back into gear and lifting the rod tip for confirmation. Then, and only then, wind slowly into the fish.

9 There is no doubt that drift fishing is a fascinating technique to perfect over offshore rips, where bottom depths over a series of sand and shingle banks may very between 20 and over a 100 feet of water. As with all boat fishing at sea, success depends largely on the expertise of the skipper who, having selected a good set of tides (usually springs) will set his craft to drift steadily over the banks along particular

Turbot and Brill

routes. And to do this a certain amount of wind is desirable.

10 When the boat is drifting 'too' fast, some skippers put a 50lbs weight down to the sea bed and drag it along behind. Others rely on their customers using heavy leads to ensure that their baits are dragged along 'steadily' over the sand and shingle sea bed where turbot and brill lie in wait for small shoal fishes to pass by, often on the down-tide side of the bank just over the 'lip'. If the rod top does not continually 'knock' as the lead bumps off bottom, you are not dragging bottom. So clip on a heavier lead.

11 A braided reel line (around 20-25lbs test) is essential for maximum 'sensitivity' when feeling for that distinctive 'judder' on the rod tip and often 'savage' take to follow, from a large flatfish. To get the bait down to the bottom, free line must be paid out quickly but smoothly, less the five foot hook trace tangles above the lead.

12 Some anglers like to incorporate a 'flashing attractor' spoon in their trace set-up, usually a foot or so in front of the bait. Remember, turbot especially, are most aggressive predators equipped with huge mouths and enormous 'sucking' power.

13 Occasionally big turbot are caught by anglers wreck fishing for congers. They like to lie up in the 'scour' holes at each end of the wreck, caused by the tides continually hitting the sides and scouring out deep hideouts. Top skippers endeavour to anchor up to favour such holes when a really big turbot or two might be on the cards, and the congers or ling are not playing ball.

14 To stand a fair chance of landing 'wreck turbot' that just could weigh up to 20 or even 30lbs, you'll need more substantial tackle than when drifting snag-free sand banks: a 30lbs outfit no less, with a 'thick' monofilament, 5-6 foot trace sporting a single 6/0 hook, below a running ledger set up. Tie the lead to the slider using a 'rotten bottom' so it will jettison if caught up with the superstructure.

15 Good baits for wreck turbot are large launce or a large mackerel fillet, a mackerel flapper' or a fresh pouting. Big turbot are equipped with a huge mouth so don't mess about.

16 When that big turbot or brill finally lies flat on the surface next to the boat ready to be hauled out, don't be tempted to use a gaff. A net ensures your prize won't slip back in.

17 Both brill and turbot tend to 'group-up' over rich feeding areas, so when a couple or three fish come to the boat in quick succession, expect action yourself. And if not, check your bait is still there or not covered in weed.

18 While drift fishing over banks of sand and shingle is the accepted way of locating brill and turbot because more ground is covered than by anchoring up, there are times when good hauls are made from a boat anchored over deep depressions, by skippers who know their marks intimately.

19 Because turbot eggs and larvae (a single female can lay up to 10 million eggs) float with the currents for several months before coming to rest on the sea floor, the species is spread

over a wide coastal territory around the British Isles. Though mostly due to certain areas being over fished, they are not caught everywhere. Along the east coast for instance, the species is particularly thin on the ground.

20 There are two other left-sided flatfish that might just be mistaken for a small brill. The tiny 'Top Knot' which has an unusually wide, brown body covered in dark brown blotches, and the rather slim-bodied 'Megrim' (a more likely catch) which has a large head and eyes and a slightly protruding lower jaw.

Wrasse and Shad

Wrasse and Shad

1

1 Don't keep losing all your terminal gear each and every cast when extracting wrasse from shorelines where rocks and heavy kelp cover your entire casting area. Adding a 'rotten' bottom which breaks when you pull hard to jettison the lead only, is the way to overcome what could turn out to be a costly affair.

2 To construct a 'rotten-bottom' rig, use a 30lbs test reel line and add 20 foot of 50lbs test monofilament to act as a 'rubbing leader'. To this attach a strong swivel and a 3 foot trace of 50lbs test. In the middle tie a blood dropper loop and add your single 4/0 hook on an 18 inch 30lbs test snood, and at the end tie on a 'butchers S' hook clip. *See Diagram.* Add 6 inches of 15lbs test connecting hook link to lead stem eye, and hang your lead on the hook, via an oval split ring which takes the strain of casting, but releases upon impact

with the bottom. When caught up in the kelp or rocks, simply pull steadily for the 15lbs test 'rotten bottom' to part, and then reel in quickly less it snags again.

3 To economize on the cost of leads when targeting wrasse at close range from a rocky shoreline, knowing full well that the majority will never come

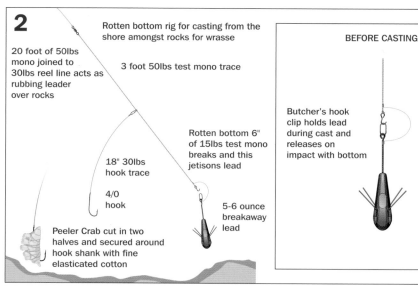

2

Rotten bottom rig for casting from the shore amongst rocks for wrasse

20 foot of 50lbs mono joined to 30lbs reel line acts as rubbing leader over rocks

3 foot 50lbs test mono trace

18" 30lbs hook trace

4/0 hook

Rotten bottom 6" of 15lbs test mono breaks and this jetisons lead

5-6 ounce breakaway lead

Peeler Crab cut in two halves and secured around hook shank with fine elasticated cotton

BEFORE CASTING

Butcher's hook clip holds lead during cast and releases on impact with bottom

back, use old spark plugs. Your local garage should oblige.

4 Though both species of shad, the Allis and the Twait, migrate into rivers to breed in fresh water around the British Isles, they spend much of their time at sea. And whilst the former, the Allis shad is now rarely encountered, the smaller, Twait shad is predictable, in so far as those wanting to catch one, by gathering at the same locations far up river each year for their spawning cycle.

5 Massive concentrations of Twaite shad gather just below the huge weir on the River Severn at Tewkesbury, and at the junction of where the River Wye converges with the River Monnow, usually

at the end of May each year, and as such are prime 'Shad' locations, but for a short time only.

6 The Allis shad is in fact classed as an endangered species, protected under the wildlife and Countryside Act of 1981, whereby attempting to catch one is an offence.

7 My top tip for Twaite shad fishing is to fish 'ultra light' using a super-light spinning rod coupled to a baby fixed spool reel and 4lbs line, with a 00 sized vibratory spinner on the business end. The shad is very silvery, similar to the tarpon in its overall appearance, and size for size, exerts as much energy in its repeated leaping and head shaking.

8 You can also catch shad on a lightweight, 7-8 foot 4 weight fly rod outfit coupled to a floating or sink-tip line. Best patterns are fry-like imitations such as 'zonkers', etc presented in the standard way of casting downstream and across, and retrieving from the 'dangle' in short erratic bursts.

9

another species however, resplendent in its livery of bright blue and orange-yellow. Rarely topping 2lbs, the male 'Cuckoo' is arguably one of the most strikingly coloured of all British sea fishes. Females are more drably painted.

11 The tiny 'Corkwing' wrasse grows to less than half the size of the Cuckoo and its fully scaled body is a mixture of greeny-brown. Distinguishing features are a crescent-shaped, dark mark behind the eye and another darkish mark in the middle of the tail root.

12 When sea conditions are calm, (particularly during the first two hours of the flood tide) float fishing for wrasse from a rugged, rocky coastline into gaps and ravines between pinnacles of rocks or reefs, is great fun using either a stepped-up 12 foot pike or carp rod and multiplier outfit, with a 15-20lbs reel line. This may seem over-heavy for a fish which averages just 2 to 3lbs, but it is the habitat of rocks and weed in which wrasse choose to live that ultimately dictates tackle strength.

13 A slim, 'through the middle' sliding float stopped with a 4mm bead and mono (same as reel line) stop knot and set to present the bait just above bottom weed or rocks is ideal. At the business end tie a small, strong swivel to the reel line with a barrel lead threaded on above to take the bait down quickly and cock the float. To the other end of the swivel add 20 inches of reel line and tie on a size 6- 2/0 (depending upon bait size) strong hook.

14 Hook patterns used for big carp are ideal for wrasse fishing and will take the strain of lifting fish out, while the lighter and longer shank of an Aberdeen-style hook, finds good purchase and (due to the long shank) is not so easily bitten off. For an overall pattern taking both shank length and

9 There are actually three species of wrasse commonly caught by anglers around the British Isles, although as colour variations of the biggest, the 'Ballan wrasse' (which can reach double figures) are enormous, due to the type, colour and make up of habitat they frequent, it would

appear there are several different species at the very least.

10 There is no chance of mistaking the noticeably more slender (than 'Ballans') but flamboyant male, 'Cuckoo wrasse' for

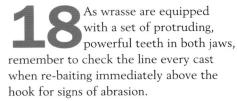

18 As wrasse are equipped with a set of protruding, powerful teeth in both jaws, remember to check the line every cast when re-baiting immediately above the hook for signs of abrasion.

19 To stand a chance of a big wrasse, say 5lbs or upwards, don't be afraid of presenting really 'big' bait like a whole, large crab that would perhaps seem ridiculous. The jaws of any sizeable wrasse however will make short work of it, and your fingers, if you are not careful when unhooking. Their 'crushing' power is immense.

strength into account, it's hard to better an 'up tide' style hook, which in some patterns is available in smaller sizes.

15 Top baits for wrasse are peeler and soft crab, king rag worm, mussels, cockles, scallops and limpet, in that order. And don't be afraid to ground bait by continually lobbing in fragments of your hook bait. It works wonders when rock fishing at close range.

16 There is no 'playing' wrasse as such, because upon being hooked they immediately dive for darkness where they feel safe, and do their best to take your line into caverns where they live. So from the outset, wind and pump

like mad to stop the wrasse from finding a hidey-hole. And don't ease up till it's lying on the surface ready to be hauled out.

17 Another reason for strong arm tactics and tackle to match when targeting wrasse, is that spots where fishing is best, are often so high above the surface, short of having a drop net handy, (always advisable) lifting them out by holding the line or with the rod itself, is the only way of seeing them on dry land for unhooking.

20 Lowering your bait down amongst the rocks (with the lead attached via a 'rotten bottom) from a boat drifting slowly along close to vertical cliffs can produce some splendid and often, hectic sport. In such locations you can never afford to put the rod down or even relax your mind, always anticipating the sudden bite and subsequent 'dive' from a good fish.

At Anchor

1 Should you find yourself boat fishing for sharks 'at anchor' in 'coloured water' anywhere around the world, (this works great for small sharks like tope) one way of putting out an attractive sub-surface 'slick', is of course to tie a carrot-sack full of fish scraps to the anchor. Or, there is the 'carrier-bag' method.

2 To work the 'carrier bag' method, use a heavy, spare rod, and thread the 50-80lbs test line through the bottom of a heavy duty, polythene carrier bag and add a heavy boat lead of say 1½-2lbs.Then wrap a couple of strong elastic bands around the bottom of the bag and lead so it cannot pull through. Now, having diced up and minced a whole batch of fresh oily fish to which extra fish oils have been added, half fill the bag with the mixture and quickly lower over the stern with your reel set in free spool, and wait for it to touch bottom.

3 Immediately, and this is the 'secret' of this technique, as the bag descends, water pressure folds the

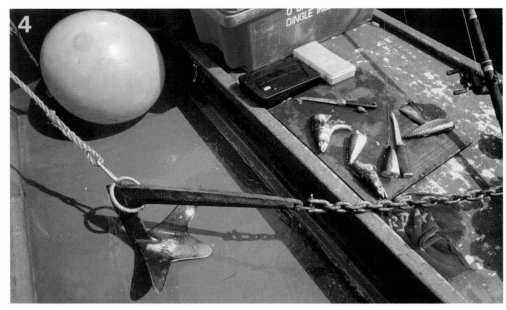

top of the bag 'like magic' over the contents, which can not release till it hits bottom, after which you give a couple of heavy tugs on the rod tip. This 'inverts' the bag, which is easily retrieved, its contents now attracting sharks situated down tide, and another 'helping' is lowered. It is so very simple yet so effective.

4 When anchoring over particularly rough ground, the most effective method of retrieving the anchor is by using an 'Alderney' ring, which runs freely along the anchor stem and is connected by rope to a buoy at the surface. When up-anchoring you then simply pull on the buoy line while motoring up tide, using the engine's power to haul the anchor free from the bottom.

5 As a general rule of thumb always pay out in rope, 2-3 times the depth beneath the boat in order for the anchor to dig well in at a shallow angle.

6 Even in weak tide flows, your bait can be made to work a long way down tide and thus explore a large area of the sea bed, simply by using the lightest weight that will hold bottom. To search once the lead has touched down, lift the rod tip smartly and allow line to be taken smoothly from the multiplier, having clicked it into free spool, (using gentle thumb pressure against the spool) causing the lead to bounce a few yards down tide.

7 When 'bumping' bottom as it is generally called, hold the rod throughout and watch the tip for indications which, if using a monofilament

9

only requires less lead to hold bottom, but also permits more sensitivity due to its lack of stretch. Bites therefore, compared to monofilament, actually seem amplified, and are easier to interpret.

8 With a fierce tide running, the only way of making your lead hold 'static' on the sea floor is to let out several more yards of line once the lead has touched down, in order for an exaggerated 'bow' to form in the line between rod tip and lead. If you are still unsure whether the lead is on the bottom or not, and is merely 'floating' and hanging in the tide, study the rod tip carefully. The rod tip will be vibrating gently (due to the trace and bait spinning way off bottom) if the lead has not found purchase. Due to the stretch in monofilament, touching bottom in a strong tide race is not always easy to determine, (and becomes harder to judge the further down tide you allow the rig to fish) while if using a braided, non stretch reel line, there is little confusion.

9 Keep terminal rigs as simple as possible when ledgering directly down tide, with a lead slider threaded onto the reel line and stopped against the hook trace swivel by a plastic 'cushioning' bead or two. Leads can then be changed both easily and fast, to suit various stages of the tide. Don't fish with any more lead on the line than the tide flow dictates.

10 Up tide boat fishing, formerly called simply 'boat casting' was pioneered during the early 1970s by skippers Bob Cox and John Rawle fishing the shallow waters of the Thames estuary out of Bradwell marina. Their catches, which included no less than 66 thornbacks in an afternoon and 180 bass in just two hours up tide casting, influenced boat anglers all around the British Isles into fishing more sportingly.

11 The deadly effectiveness of 'up tiding', results from the fact that as a shoal of fish

line will seemingly diminish in their ferocity the further down tide your bait travels, due to the inherent stretch of mono. A braided reel line due to its reduced diameter not

10

divides to avoid an anchored craft overhead, especially in really clear or shallow water, casting uptide and across, it puts baits in front of fish on each side of the boat that down tide fishing cannot. Plain and simple.

12 The most functional end rig for 'up tiding' consists of a running lead slider (to take a 'breakaway' 3-8 ounce lead) stopped on the reel line (mono or braid) by a single bead and swivel, to which a 3-7 foot mono hook trace is tied at the opposite end.

13 For species like bass where bait movement is desirable, it pays to use as long a trace as you can comfortably cast, by placing the baited hook over one of the leads wires. This then separates upon hitting the surface.

14 If targeting bottom feeders such as cod, rays and smooth hounds, a 3-4 foot hook trace is quite sufficient.

15 When up tiding over rough ground, it is advisable to add 30 foot of say 40lbs test mono to your 15lbs mono or 25lbs braided reel line to act as both a 'rubbing' leader and shock leader when punching out an 8

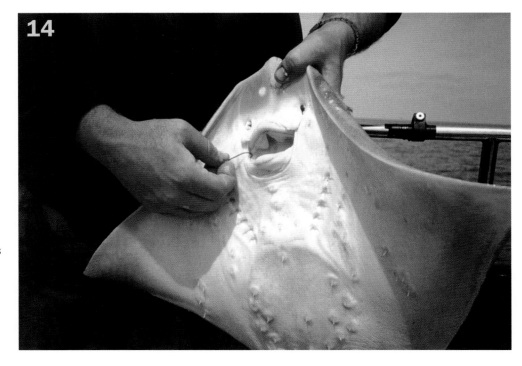

ounce lead, say. Incidentally, weights beyond this are just not practical.

16 For strong tides and deep water a 'fixed wire' bomb is required for the bait to hold station. But for most situations in shallow water and modest tides, the breakaway lead reigns supreme.

17 When casting up tide, yell to everyone on board that you are about to cast and never do so with your rig hanging from inside the boat. A sideways and upwards cast from well outside the deck (standing at the boats stern) is safer for all.

18 Immediately your lead touches the sea floor and digs in when up tiding, free spool sufficient line to form an exaggerated subsurface bow. It may seem totally outrageous, but this is the only way of ever holding your bait static on the bottom. Let insufficient line out, and your lead will be bounced down tide by sheer current force against the line. Whereas with a 'bow' only the acute part of the bow is affected by current drag.

19 When out afloat and due to bad weather and a badly rocking boat, repeatedly opening and closing, even getting to, your

main tackle box becomes a chore, it's worth keeping some swivels, beads, lead sliders, split rings etc, and a pair of sharp wire cutters that will suffice for cutting and trimming through any diameter wire, braid or mono, in the top pocket of your jacket or salopette (bib and brace).

20 A lightweight, waterproof salopette is an invaluable item of top clothing when boat fishing, especially when messing around with congers eels. As it goes entirely over your top shirt and trousers, back at the car you simply peel it off straight into a bin liner, and drive home dry and not smelling of eels.

On the Drift and Trolling

On the Drift and Trolling

1 A trick used by experienced skippers who regularly 'drift' to catch big flatfish like plaice, is to put out on a long rope, a 50lbs weight, which in difficult conditions slows the boat's drift down just enough in order for their customers baits to be 'sniffed out', sucked in and swallowed.

2 Don't react immediately to a bite from flatfish when 'drifting'. Pay out line freely for several seconds (count to five slowly) so it can get the bait well into its mouth before putting the reel back into gear and winding slowly and smoothly into the fish.

3 Lead choice can prove important when drifting over clean sand and shingle banks for big flatfish. Those circular, studded 'watch' leads are favoured because they bump easily over the sea floor whilst kicking up puffs of sand, thus attracting fish to the bait. Keep a selection of varying sizes handy to accommodate changing conditions. In light seas, the freshwater, 'nobbly' equivalents, called 'gripper' leads, are ideal.

4 A simple no nonsense rig for drifting with plaice, brill or turbot in mind, can be made by stopping a lead slider-boom (with a cushioning bead between) against the swivel of a 4-6 foot mono hook trace. For extra attraction incorporate a spoon into the trace six inches above a size 1/0 hook baited with king rag worm. Where turbot are expected bait a 3/0 hook with fresh strips of mackerel or launce, but don't be surprised if a pollack or bass also finds such baits appealing.

5 When way offshore and about to start drifting for blue sharks on a day that promises little wind (so essential for moving the boat along in order to spread a slick of 'rubby dubby' which sharks can follow up to the baits) put a couple of rubby dubby sacks over the stern and troll them slowly along for a while to put 'aroma' into the water, before starting to drift.

6 While in the clear, shallow waters around Denmark's east coast, cod (yes cod!) along with numbers of sea trout, are regularly caught on trolled lures, bass and pollack are really, (apart from the

6

very occasional sea trout) the only two species around the British Isles that respond to 'trolling tactics'.

7 Drifting over and along wartime wrecks which litter the English Channel offers the best opportunity for anglers on charter trips to come to grips with big cod, ling, pollack, bass and even the occasional coal fish, not to mention numbers of smaller, but hard battling fighters such as the black bream.

8 In order to book up the best sets of tides for drift fishing over wartime wrecks lying in deep water, which are the 'slower' neap tides, you may have to confirm a trip with your skipper at least one calendar year in advance.

9 For targeting cod and pollack whilst drifting over deep water wrecks you need a 9-9½ foot 'up tide'-style rod, with plenty of power in the butt, yet a relatively soft tip. This is to alleviate lightly hooked fish (as so many are when hooked on pirks) from slipping the hook immediately upon hooking, and when close to the boat thrashing about on a short line.

10 A multiplier is by far the best tool for drifting, as it indeed is for all modes of sea fishing. When fishing at great depths, say over

80-100 feet, a low diameter, braided reel line makes life so much easier. Being of low or virtually no stretch, every knock and bite, no matter how gentle, is transmitted to the rod, and of course every lift and jerk you make with the rod is transmitted directly to the lure. So its action is not lessened as with monofilament.

11 Remember that if you jerk the rod upwards four or five feet to 'activate' a pirk bumping a wreck deep down in over 200 feet of water using monofilament line that under pressure stretches up to 25 percent, how far do you think your pirk moves? Exactly.

9

On the Drift and Trolling

12 After jerking the rod tip upwards to raise the pirk, drop it quickly so the artificial zig zags down to the end of its drop on a free line for maximum visual attraction to cod and pollack, which often hit, just before it is jerked upwards again.

13 Be sure to incorporate a 'weaker' trace, when wreck fishing on the drift, of a lighter breaking strain that will break easier than your braided reel line, so that if caught on the rusting ironwork, you simply wind the reel line in a figure of eight wrap around the nearest cleat and let the weight of the boat snap it off. If using a 40lbs test braided reel line for instance, use a 6-8 foot length of 28-30lbs mono between lure and the swivel joining braid to mono. Then the mono will fracture every time.

14 If you run out of tubular plastic booms when drifting over sand banks for species like plaice, turbot and bass etc, a most effective rig can be made simply by threading a dozen or so large beads onto the reel line between the lead slider and hook trace swivel. Nothing more. Actually I much prefer this 'bead' rig because it rolls better up steep-sided banks and tangles less.

15 When trolling for spooky species in shallow water, bass in particular, it's worth investing in a silent 'electric' motor. For catching bass in clear water, a percentage of which might have been already been caught and released, if you tend to repeatedly work the same shoreline or feature, you need all the help modern technology can provide.

16 A point to remember about drift fishing close to wrecks, is maintaining as 'vertical' a line as possible between rod tip and end rig, which sometimes means using slightly more lead or a heavier pirk than would seem necessary. Otherwise, trailing an excessive amount of line behind the boat, due to the angle at which it streams out, could pull your rig easily into snags.

17 When drifting over a wreck in a fair tide or strong wind for cod or pollack using pirks, you sometimes have just one or two chances of lowering the artificial 'straight down' and 'jigging', before the line streams out and it becomes impossible to maintain a 'vertical' line. It is then far better to quickly retrieve and drop immediately down again, or simply wait for the skipper to motor up tide and make another drift.

18 One solution to the problems of maintaining a vertical line as in *Tips 16 and 17*, is at the

15

wreck in the tide flow and you are obliged to retrieve.

19 By quick, manoeuvring between three and four anglers all working off the stern, each can benefit from casting up tide and moving (to the left or right as the case may be) while their pirk is descending, as the next angler makes his cast, and so on. You need to get into a definite 'routine' for this to be executed effectively, and not to panic when somebody snags up on the ironwork.

20 As your largest, potential PB cod spirals up through the clear water depths and seems to be growing in size the further it rises, soon to be ready for netting, remember to ease back significantly on that clutch. Lightly hooked fish especially, need but one flick of their tail when on a short, unforgiving line close to the boat. So be ready just in case.

very start of the drift when still a fair way off the wreck (casting from the stern) to literally 'cast' your pirk 40-50 yards up tide (using a smooth underarm swing) so by the time it reaches bottom it is virtually in a straight line down to the wreck. And make the most of that first 'crucial' lift and fall of your lure. In exceptionally deep water, one 'jigging action' is sometimes all you will get before the lure streams away from the

20

Rods and Reels

1 When trolling lures, set your multiplier on a firm clutch setting, so that on impact with the lure the hooks are driven home hard into the fish. Something that will not always happen with a loosely set clutch. You can then slacken the clutch off progressively as the fish nears the boat on a short line. In case it decides to make one last ditch dive.

2 Generally speaking 'up tide' style rods of around 9-9½ feet long are ideal for working pirks over deep water, wartime wrecks. Beware of models rated to take up to 10 ounce leads for up tiding because these could be far too stiff in the tip. To alleviate repeatedly pulling the hooks from lightly-hooked fish, and on non stretch braided lines this problem is only compounded, go for a rod with enough beef in the butt section but with a 'forgiving' tip which allows the rod to fold into a nice curve with a big fish on.

3 An ideal up tiding rod used for working lures over wrecks should also have a fairly short distance between reel fitting and butt end, (22-23 inches from end cap to the middle of the reel fitting is ideal) preferably with a slip-on rubber end cap to fit over a gimbel fitting which helps avoid groin bruising should you choose 'not' to wear a butt pad. There is nothing more uncomfortable than having constantly to be 'over-reaching' when winding in, because the reel fitting is too high.

4 Whatever the boat rod, get used to NOT winding the swivel on your hook or lure trace all the way up into the tip ring. The force is enough to fracture the exceedingly hard, yet brittle 'inner' of most modern tip rings. To jog your memory, thread a bright red bead onto the reel line immediately above the swivel. It acts as both reminder and safety factor as the bead will act as a barrier between swivel and tip ring.

5 To cover a multitude of boat-fishing styles and techniques, a lightweight 'system' type, carbon boat rod that

comes with a choice of three different tips (12-20 and 30lbs class) that each fit into the same butt to make up a 7 foot rod, means you need to carry less rods around.

6 If your shore fishing requirements are varied, it's worth considering a 'twin-tip' style shore rod, where the basic tip covers larger species, and the 'lighter' tip has a far more sensitive and finer tip to indicate bite registrations from flatfish, etc.

7 Once you get home from a sea fishing trip, even if some of your rods have not actually been used, but

12

have been on the boat or beach and open to the salt air, spray them all well under a fresh water hose before putting away, paying particular attention to rings and the screw reel fitting.

8 Reels too, need to be washed thoroughly under pressure of a fresh water hose to eradicate every single trace of salt, otherwise corrosion will set in. It's the very first thing I do upon returning home.

9 For smoothness of casting with a multiplier reel, especially when trying to achieve long distances from the shore, be sure to set 'the drop' before casting. This means adjusting the spool for casting by tightening the knob at the end of the reel so whatever size weight is about to be cast, can 'just' about drop to the sand under its own weight with the reel in free spool.

10 If you wish to use braid on a fixed spool reel when spinning for bass and pollack etc, go for a quality model, one with a 'precision oscillation system that has a neat,

cotton reel-like line lay. Such reels are not cheap but a joy to use.

11 When you see reel numbers like 6000 and 7000 etc, this relates to the model size and its capacity, first used by the ABU

13

Company, but which over the years has been adopted as a benchmark guide by many other manufacturers. Anything within the 6000-6500 range for instance usually relates to casting with 15-18lbs test monofilament. While with the 7000 series, heavier lines of 25-30lbs are recommended. The 9000 and 10,000 series handle monofilament lines up to 35-40lbs test. Braided lines do not enter into these ratings, but being of a vastly reduced diameter, each reel will hold more braid than it will mono.

12 For targeting bass or pollack from areas of rugged and rocky coastline such as along the west coast of Ireland, don't assume your heavy fresh water spinning or carp rod will suffice because the size of the fish expected won't be anywhere near that of heavy weight carp. Just a 5 or 6lbs pollack will make a mockery of a carp rod amongst the kelp and rocks. A light bass beach caster would be a better choice.

13 When purchasing a multiplier reel to perform 'heavyweight' functions and battles with

SALTWATER TACKLE

14

hard and fast fighting fish, do not choose one with a 'level wind'. The force of either monofilament or braid being ripped from the spool under a firm drag setting could rip the mechanism from its tracking due to an acute angle forming from each end of the spool to where the line passes through the guard.

14 Do not use an ancient, plastic-spooled multiplier obtained second hand for the rigors of boat fishing. Under the severe constriction of tightly wound monofilament, plastic spools will collapse and shatter.

15 To assist in the winding up of really large fish, some boat fishing multipliers are fitted with a lower gear which either cuts in automatically, or can be operated simply by pushing in a button. Though they cost more, such reels are indispensable for deep water adversaries like giant skate, conger eels and sharks.

16 It pays to send multiplier reels back to the manufacturer regularly for servicing if used on a regular basis. The cost against a new reel should your old one become unusable prematurely is minimal.

17 When purchasing a new fixed spool reel for shore casting, do not be mesmerized by the amount of ball bearings claimed by the manufacturers, which of course 'do' matter in a multiplier because they contribute to its casting performance. Look more at the actual line lay function of a fixed spool, because how the line is wound onto the spool, greatly affects how it comes off. In top of the range

18

models with smooth, oscillating line lay and multi bearings, you do of course get both.

18 When choosing a multiplier for both pirking and bottom fishing in deep water where big fish are on the cards, two factors are worth special consideration. Does the reel have a large line capacity and is its spool diameter sufficiently wide enough to recover line quickly? Is it fitted with a 'lever drag' which allows you to instantly pile on pressure to stop a big fish from making the wreck, but to back off just as quickly should a fish suddenly dive as it nears the boat? Something which big cod and congers do with surprising speed.

19 To slow down small shore casting multipliers, you can either swap the oil for thicker, and, or, re-fit the reel's centrifugal brake blocks, assuming you removed them to cast further.

20 If you are looking for a small multiplier purposefully to lure fish for species like bass, coal fish and pollack etc, choose a narrow spool model which makes continual casting and 'thumbing' an absolute joy.

20

SALTWATER TACKLE

Sundries

'downwards' while you simultaneously pull upwards and 'jerk' to shake the conger off with your right. It is a technique which benefits from regular use.

3 The best T bars are manufactured by Stainless Steel Engineering in Hampshire, Tel 01590 674988.

4 Keep a roll of plastic bin liners permanently in the boot of your car. They are not only imperative for holding your gutted fish to take home, but also things like sopping wet and smelly or slimy clothing which if left un-bagged will stink the car out for days. Good for wet and muddy boots too.

5 As opposed to plain wellies or trainers, the traction gained on a wet and slippery deck from wearing specialized waterproof 'deck boots' (designed for the yachting market) is enormous and well worth the investment.

1 One piece of kit no self-respecting sea angler, particularly boat anglers, should ever set off fishing without is the T Bar disgorger. Rather than having to bring small to medium-sized conger eels or ling into the boat for instance for unhooking, with all the resulting chaos, not to mention slime, (so far as congers are concerned) both can be effectively and quickly unhooked outside the boat as can most others species destined to be released.

2 To unhook congers over the side (assuming you are right-handed) grip the hook trace firmly in your left hand while hooking the 'curl' of the T bar over the hook length and running it down to as near the hook as possible. The trace in your left hand is then held sharply

4

6 For those quick 'trophy photos' when fish are coming in thick and fast, a small, flat, 'press and point'-type digital camera housed in the top pocket, is indispensable. A rating of 4/5 million pixels will produce stunning results, even when printed off on your own computer. Many of the photos in this book were in fact captured using my little Casio digital camera which is just 4 million pixels. Simply because at the time I did not have sufficient time or inclination to unwrap my Nikon D200 from its protective bag. If you do not already own one, ensure the miniature digital model you go for has a large monitor screen of around 2-2.5cm, for ease of both 'taking' and 'viewing' your pics.

7 To use these small cameras which can be passed over to anyone in order to capture 'your' PB, get the 'taker' to hold the camera out in front for viewing, rather than look through the viewfinder, and take all your pics using the 'fill-in-flash' mode. I keep mine set permanently in this mode. On all but the brightest of days and the most evenly-lit

subject, results will look infinitely more striking, and 'crisper' for using fill-in-flash.

8 Don't be tempted to obtain as many images as you possibly can for the size of memory card housed in the camera. It's best to take fewer pics per memory card, (you can of course keep a 'second' memory card just in case) and all

of top quality, so set the camera's memory to 'fine' quality. And don't settle for less. *See also Fresh water Tackle Sundries Tips 12, 13, 14 and 15.*

9 For a powerful rechargeable headlight kit to see exactly what you are doing on the beach, whether baiting up or landing a fat cod, it's worth

6

SALTWATER TACKLE

Sundries

10

investing the price of just one new reel, in a Samalite HL 100. Complete with a Nickel Metal Hydroxide Battery that takes up to a 1000 recharge cycles, housed in an adjustable and comfortable power belt, this unique head light comes complete with mains charger and the choice of a wide angle or flood-spot light beam lamp. Information from SMP Electronics on 01276 855166.

10 For spreading the load evenly across your groin area, investing in a good quality butt pad makes not only good sense, but also allows you to fully enjoy the fight of the larger salt water species, sharks and skate in particular. Models with a pivoting gimbel to accommodate the 'slotted' rod butt are recommended for ease of 'pumping'.

11 What is 'pumping'? Well it is the means by which even the largest, heaviest, most powerful adversary, can eventually be brought along side the boat. The secret is to 'never' wind against torque. All this does is beat you up, not the fish. When a big fish wants to run, let it, under maximum drag of course. And when it slows up, coming almost to a standstill, then, and only then, start 'pumping' the rod first by lowering the tip and then by raising it, gaining line all the time by winding, whilst lowering the rod tip and repeating the technique.

12 To make a few protective 'thummies', invaluable for gripping the spool of a multiplier tightly when distance casting, purchase a pair of rubberized-plastic (linen-lined) industrial gloves and cut the fingers

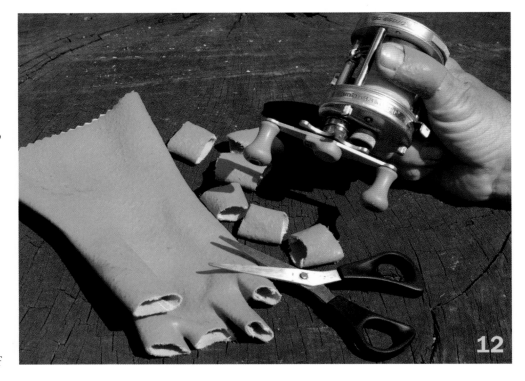

off in 1-1¼ inch sections. Some are bound to fit the thumb (covering the joint) of your right hand.

13 To ensure your carbon, spigot-joint rod comes apart easily, simply rub candle wax on the male part of the spigot. It will not only minimize wear, but also not get stuck in the first place.

14 If your spigot-joint rod does become 'stuck' and impossible to separate into its 'two' joints, then plunge into and leave in cold water for a while if conditions are hot. Or, if conditions are freezing, do the opposite. Eventually, the two joints will come apart, by getting a friend to grip one end and gently 'twisting' whilst pulling, as you pull and 'twist' in the opposite direction.

15 Whether pier, beach fishing or up tide casting from an anchored boat, using the right 'break-out' style lead is of enormous importance. Rather than having to cart along the 'kitchen sink', leads with interchangeable heads, such as the 'Gemini' sinker range are extremely handy. These also come available in 'fixed grip' wires.

16 Don't endure packets of rusting rigs and tangles in your tackle box any longer. Buy a purpose-designed rig wallet and the larger the better. Spray its zip regularly with WD 40.

17 To protect your index finger when holding the line tight to the rod for long distance casting using a fixed spool reel, invest in a leather finger protector (also called a hudkin) which comes with an elasticated strap for holding it in position.

18 For rod tips that stand out like a 'beacon' in the dark, use 'battery-operated' tip

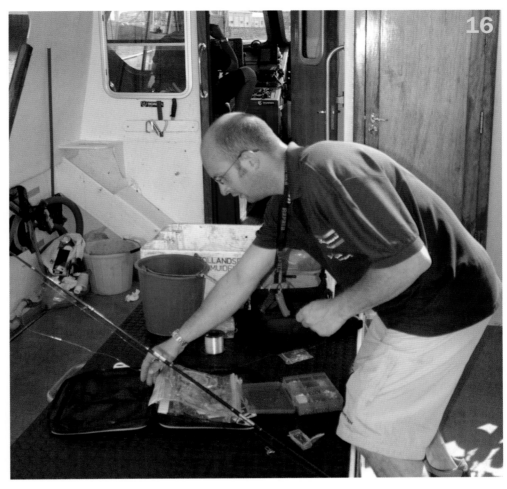

lights. These are available in either red or blue. The red ones come complete with mini rubber bands for rod tip attachment, while the blue lights are taped on both sides.

19 If you like adventure fishing such as rock hopping and being continually on the move for species like wrasse, garfish, mullet, pollack or bass etc, a multi-pocketed 'hip

pack' from the Rapala stable, which secures neatly around the waist via a wide, padded belt and houses just about every tackle item you might need including artificial lures and bait, allows you to keep your hands free for climbing with just your rod to hold. It completely does away for the need of a tackle box.

20 Also invaluable, whether you fish from the beach, rocks or from a boat, is a lightweight waistcoat, for wearing over your top coat or smock. Again, it does away with the need for several separate boxes or bags in that small items you might need to locate several times during a session, like scissors, wire cutters, forceps, T Bar, swivels, beads, hooks, trace material and so on, are all easily stored and more importantly, come immediately to hand.

SALTWATER TACKLE

Lines

Lines

1 Though initially devised for the rigors of big game fishing in the Bahamas, hence the name of 'Bimini Twist,' this is a useful knot for both fly fishing and beach fishing in addition to general sea fishing situations, particularly trolling, where maximizing on a monofilament line's breaking strain is imperative. The knot, because it 'stretches' and which tests as strong as the line itself may seem complicated, is not difficult to tie. Start by doubling the last two feet of line and with your right hand in the end of the loop making 30 twists (Fig A), whilst holding the other ends tight in your left hand. This makes one continual twist. *See Diagram.*

2 Now put your foot up onto a chair and put the loop over the end of your shoe. Keep your hands wide apart and pull gently, which compacts the twist (Fig B). Put your right forefinger into the loop beneath the twist, while allowing the tab end to wrap down over the initial twist towards the loop, Hold both ends tightly through this process, as in Fig C. Still holding everything tight, make a half hitch with the tag end around one side of the loop. This 'locks' the twist. Then repeat around the opposite side of the loop. To finish off, make one large half hitch around both sides of the loop, followed by four on the inside working up towards the junction. Lastly, pull tight using saliva to bed the hitches down neatly and trim off the tag end to within ⅛th of an inch of the knot (Fig D, E, F, G, H & I). Your 'Bimini Twist' is finished.

3 For joining low diameter braided reel line to a thick monofilament trace or leader, the 'Albright Knot' is ideal, making an incredibly small and neat knot which passes easily through rod rings. Start by doubling the end of thick mono which in effect becomes a loop. Push the tag end of braid through loop and start winding back around loop, working towards where the braid entered for 13 turns. Now push tag end through loop (the same side from which it entered) and gently pull to bed knot down ensuring coils do not wrap over each other. Remove surplus end of mono loop, and the knot is finished. *See Freshwater boat fishing on the drift and trolling, Tip 10.*

4 Remember that due to ultra violet rays which can still affect monofilament line even on a cloudy day, check your line regularly when reels are in constant use and open to the atmosphere. Some brands appear to deteriorate much quicker than others, particularly when left out on the beach or boat day after day.

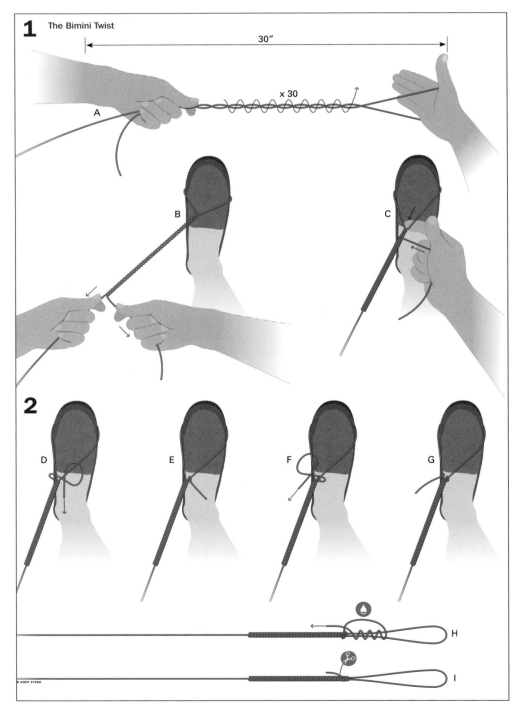

1 The Bimini Twist

30"

x 30

A

B

C

2

D

E

F

G

H

I

© ANDY STEER

5 For joining braid and mono of similar diameters together, or for braid to braid or mono to mono (so long as the diameter of each is similar) the ideal knot is the 'Double Uni', or 'Grinner'. Start by overlapping the ends of the two lines held parallel by around 20 inches and hold tightly together. With one tag end form Uni-knot circle *(as in Diagram)* and twist five times around the two lines. After wetting with saliva, pull tag end to snug knot into a neat barrel around line. Now repeat the procedure with the opposite tag end and form second Uni or Grinner knot and pull firmly to make a neat barrel. Lastly, after wetting each line between the two knots with saliva, steadily pull on both lines till the two knots come together to form one. Trim off the surplus tag ends and the knot is complete.

6 Remember these dos and don'ts when tying knots with monofilament 1.Always wet the line with saliva before bedding down a knot and pulling tight. 2. Always pull slowly when tying knots. 3. Friction causes heat which weakens monofilament. 4. Never cut the tag end too short.

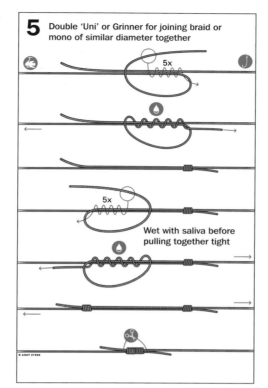

5 Double 'Uni' or Grinner for joining braid or mono of similar diameter together

5x

Wet with saliva before pulling together tight

© ANDY STEER

7 For adding a 'thick' (50-100lbs test) monofilament hook trace or shock leader to a much thinner reel line (say 20-30 lbs test) where a swivel is either not wanted or is not practical (because the knot may need to go back and forward through rod rings) start by tying a 'Bimini Twist' with the reel line. *See Tip 1.* Now tie a double overhand knot in the thick line and thread just an inch of the loop of your 'Bimini Twist' on the reel line through same side as tag end of thick line (Fig A). Pull hard on thick line with pliers to fully tighten the double overhand knot. This will weaken that first inch of your Bimini Loop (Fig B) so wet with saliva and pull loop all the way through. Now, using the entire loop tie a five turn Uni or Grinner knot, and after wetting again, pull tight and hard up against the double overhand knot (Fig C). Lastly, trim off ends of loop and the double overhand knot, but not too closely (Fig D).

8 The same, 'above knot' may be used for adding a shock leader to much lighter line when beach casting. And to ensure the knot will pass easily through

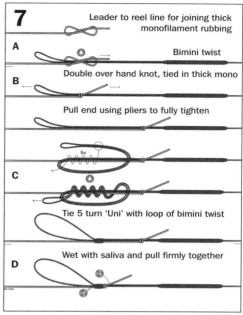

7 Leader to reel line for joining thick monofilament rubbing

A Bimini twist

B Double over hand knot, tied in thick mono

Pull end using pliers to fully tighten

C 5x

Tie 5 turn 'Uni' with loop of bimini twist

Wet with saliva and pull firmly together

D

level wind mechanisms, tie just a single overhand or clinch, for the Bimini to bed up against. The same knot may also be tied without the Bimini on the reel line. But it will of course not be so strong.

Lines

11

9 When making 3-6 foot trolling or bottom traces from thick monofilament, reduce its 'memory' before tying knots, by looping around a cleat and pulling firmly and steadily on each end for 20-30 seconds till it stays limp.

10 For ease of seeing and untangling in the dark (compared to 'clear' monofilament) construct your beach casting shock leader using brightly coloured mono, either yellow or red. But use clear mono for the actual trace.

11 Most good skippers, whether at anchor or on the drift, do not allow their guests to use a mixture of both mono and braided reel lines. The resulting tangles can be horrendous.

12 Because coils of braided line tend to dig into one another under casting pressure and during the retrieve if used on a multiplier for beach fishing, regular bird nests will result. So go for a good quality fixed spool reel where the line lay eliminates snarl-ups and coils digging into each other.

13 When beach casting there is a simple formula for the strength of 'shock leader'

required (so your lead doesn't snap off and possibly hit someone along the beach when winding your rod up) and it is based on the weight of your lead. It is, 10lbs of breaking strain for every ounce of lead to be cast. So for a 4 ounce weight use a minimum of 40lbs test mono. For a 5 ounce-50lbs, a 6 ounce-60lbs, and so on.

14 The length of a 'shock leader' should be no more than your casting drop, plus the distance from tip ring to reel, plus just five to six times around the reel. Usually around 20-21 feet long. This is to ensure the leader knot leaves the reel at the very earliest.

15 When shore casting with a fixed spool reel make sure the drag is screwed up tight, or line slip might result from a powerful cast.

16 To join a shock leader to your reel line, use the 'beach casters knot' which comprises of a half hitch tied in the end of the leader, plus a five turn 'grinner' or 'uni'. Start with the half hitch, leaving a six inch tag end.

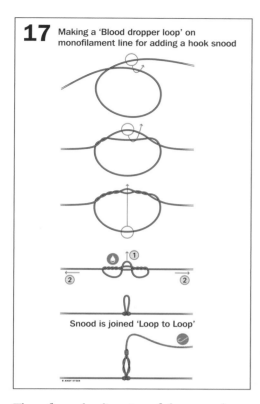

17 Making a 'Blood dropper loop' on monofilament line for adding a hook snood

Snood is joined 'Loop to Loop'

Then, from the direction of the tag end push the reel line through the loop. Tighten the loop by finger pressure only, with just a few inches of reel line coming out the other side. *See Tip 7 Diagram.* Now fully tighten the half hitch (using pliers on the tag end) which will weaken the reel line, so pull a foot or so of new line through, and make four turns around the leader, then bring the reel line back to form a loop with the end facing away from the half hitch. Now make five turns inside the loop and after adding saliva for lubrication, partially tighten the knot. Then slide the knot down tight up against the half hitch and (adding more saliva) pull tightly and evenly on the reel line through the half hitch. Lastly, trim off both tag ends fairly close.

17 For adding a hook snood anywhere along your trace line, consider the 'blood dropper loop'. Start by twisting the trace line into a large loop and by using thumb and forefinger of both hands twist the top of the loop around itself three times. Then pull the bottom of the loop through the middle of the twists to form a 'dropper' loop. And pull tight slowly. Job done. *See Diagram.* Your actual hook trace can now be added (loop to loop) to the blood dropper loop.

18 Braided reel lines do not wear or deteriorate as rapidly as monofilament, even though their colour may fade, and at least a year's fishing (maybe two) of regular use should be expected. Be careful however with extremely fine diameter 'micro braids' of 8-15 lbs test, which because they are so much thinner than monofilament equivalents, require regular inspection for nicks or abrasion.

19 When filling up your multiplier with fresh braid, put the plastic spool of braided line in a bucket containing three or four inches of fresh water and wind onto your reel with the plastic spool spinning, so the braid is wound on both wet and firmly, (run it 'begrudgingly' through a 'gloved' hand in front of the reel) so it beds down tightly. This is most important, because if braid is wound on loosely, the first good fish will pull it between coils and cause a 'lock-up'.

20 If you are not satisfied that your braided reel line is wound on 'tight' enough, run it all out behind the boat on the way out to a day's fishing and wind it back in again. Don't be tempted to tie anything on the end, because with a couple of hundred yards of line trailing behind a fast moving boat, the pressure of winding in anything but the line itself would prove too much.

SALTWATER TACKLE

Hooks and Rigs

Hooks and Rigs

1 To see clearly your hook and rig when fishing into darkness and especially for baiting up or undoing tangles, invest in one of the miniature, yet powerful multi-LED (light emitting diodes) headlamps which run on slim, AAA batteries. They are now so light in weight you even forget you're wearing one.

2 For presenting large fish fillets or a small whole squid, opt for the superior hooking power of a 'two hook' pennell rig, which involves tying one hook to the end of the snood or trace, with a second hook sliding (by its eye) above. The upper hook can be secured at the desired distance below the lower by simply wrapping the line around the shank five or six turns.

3 To construct a 'fixed' pennell rig first thread the line through the eye of the upper hook and tie on using a 'spade end' knot *(see Diagram of Fresh water Hooks and Rigs Tip 8)* and then add the lower (at the distance desired) using a 'grinner' or 'uni' knot.

4 Pennell rigs work best in conjunction with forged 'up tide' style round bend hooks.

7 Keep your larger hooks honed to perfection by regularly using a Rapala fine grit, aluminium oxide sharpening stone. Blunt hooks cost you dearly.

8 Do not however, attempt to sharpen chemically-sharpened hooks, especially in the smaller sizes because the wire at the point is invariably reduced anyway. And you will end up with a blunter hook.

9 Do not remove hooks from their protective packets and store in a compartmented box, as every time you open it at sea, or on the beach, salt air will enter and start the rusting process. Over a period of time, even those sprayed with WD 40 fall victim to the salt. Keep them in your rig wallet and take out a packet at a time.

10 Unlike coarse fish which are continually being caught and released, sea fish rarely associate the presence of a hook with danger. So if you are unsure about hook size when using a particular bait, always go 'larger' rather than smaller, for maximizing on the chances of hooking up. And don't worry about 'hiding' the hook.

11 The reason for fish coming off or not being hooked in the first place is often because the bait has 'slipped' down and masked the point. So either secure a good mouthful of fillet with elasticated cotton, (leaving the hook point clear) or use a two-hook 'pennell' rig which holds a bait such as a small to medium sized whole squid, out straight so it cannot 'wodge' down.

12 Whether beach or boat fishing, never use small to medium sized hooks for more than one session. They are cheap enough. And blunting due to hooking and un-hooking, and from contact with the sea floor, not to mention 'corrosion', are reasons enough.

5 For tying on hooks, spinning traces or swivels direct to a braided reel line, use my 'uni-clinch' knot, described in the *Fresh water Rigs and Hooks Diagram, Tip 6.*

6 For snipping off tag ends close to their knots, use either a small pair of wire cutters, or a stainless steel Rapala 'clipper', which is similar to a pair of nail clippers, with razor sharp cutting edges.

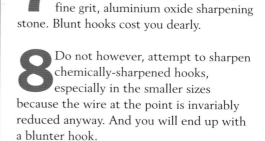

Hooks and Rigs

13 Gauge the size and strength of hook you use not only to bait size, but also to the size of the largest fish you could conceivably catch from the mark being fished. So don't for instance, present a mackerel flapper over a deep water wreck where congers are the target species on a 6/0 fine wire 'Aberdeen' style hook. It will quickly straighten under pressure. Conversely, you will hook and boat more black bream using small but strong fine wire hooks, than a thick-wire O'Shaughnessy of identical size. It's horses for courses.

14 For trouble-free pier and beach fishing go for a simple 'two-hooks clipped down rig'. *See Diagram*. When small species are targeted such as whiting, dab and sole etc, use size 1 hooks, but for smooth hounds, cod or rays etc, size 2/0 are imperative. The entire trace is less than four feet long and constructed from 60lbs mono, with a 'Breakaway' impact shield 4 inches above the lead link. Breaking strain of the two hook snoods is 20-25lbs mono with 10lbs test (red) power gum for the stop knots.

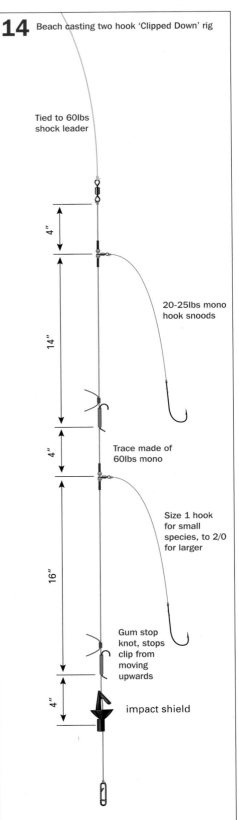

14 Beach casting two hook 'Clipped Down' rig

Tied to 60lbs shock leader

4"

14"

20-25lbs mono hook snoods

4"

Trace made of 60lbs mono

Size 1 hook for small species, to 2/0 for larger

16"

Gum stop knot, stops clip from moving upwards

4"

impact shield

15 Always have several replacement traces made up for a beach fishing session. There is never enough time when actually fishing, especially in the dark or when finger tips are freezing. Traces and rigs are best made up at home when you have time to be meticulous with knots and crimps.

16 It makes sense to copy shop-bought traces that you like and to even incorporate modifications of your own, such as using larger or different patterns of hooks etc. Once hooks, snoods, beads and crimps are all in place, remember to stretch out the trace simulating the weight of a casting lead (using a couple of panel pins knocked into a length of wood) and make exact adjustments to the clips.

17 Avoid using brightly coloured monofilament for hook snoods. Clear, limp, memory-free monos such as 'Amnesia' are recommended.

18 If adding a 'rotten bottom' to your shore trace to minimize tackle losses, take extra care when casting. Leads designed to be jettisoned are not as reliable as one fixed directly to the end of the trace.

19 When threading monofilament through the narrow tubing of plastic booms or rubber eels, cut the end off at an angle to make it feed better, or attach to fine, but stiff wire and pull through.

20 Oversize swivels are a thing of the past for most situations at sea, especially for rig making as they collect weed far easier. Most shore fishing rigs for instance require swivels in sizes between 1 and 3, which are more than sufficient in their relative breaking strains.

17

SALTWATER TACKLE

Natural

1 Gathering fresh, live bait for bass or pollack fishing in the way of launce (greater sand eel) and Joey mackerel, is a very important, sometimes 'laborious' part of the day's fishing. But rather than continually hauling up 'full houses' of bait, why not make it more sporting, and thus more enjoyable. Simply use a 'lightweight' outfit to feather up with. I just love using my little 'American bait casting outfit' for mackerel and launce. And reduce the amount of tiny jigs above a small pirk when fish are thick on the ground, from six to just four. Even with just a couple or three mackerel coming up on say 12lbs test line on a baby multiplying reel, it feels as though arms are being wrenched out of their sockets. Lovely stuff!

2 When offering live launch or mackerel for pollack or bass watch the rod tip closely. The bait will usually panic as a predator approaches causing the tip to judder and jingle violently. But wait for it to hoop over before winding into the fish. Resist the temptation to actually strike. With a non stretch braided reel line especially, this could result in the hook being ripped out.

3 Keep live baits caught feathering such as mackerel and launch in an aerated bucket or tank with portable pump and air stone. Have a separate bucket handy for those which come up foul hooked or bleeding, which if introduced into your main tank will shorten the life of the others.

4 Though the tough root of the mussel is small, it helps secure this 'soft' bait if the hook is passed through it. Mussels work particularly well if frozen. Secure well with elasticated cotton. Chopped-up mussels add extra attraction when used as loose feed if targeting species like wrasse with a couple of mussels on the hook.

5 For optimum results, a peeler crab must be just about to shed its shell. This is what fish aiming to feed upon

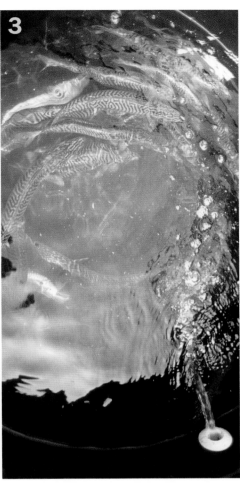

sea, (fresh mackerel oozes blood and its skin is tough) pass the hook point in and out of the bait a few times, then wrap well with elasticated cotton.

10 For most decent-sized fish, boxed and frozen 'calamari', the commercial name for squid, provides anglers with enormous choice in bait size, which casts well, holds together well and has immense 'drawing powers' whether you present the squid whole (5-9 inches long) or cut into strips. Just like mackerel, always have a box in your freezer.

11 Remember not to thaw out an entire box of squid. It quickly deteriorates in warm weather. Keep in a cool box so the bait is in tip top condition for baiting up.

them are looking for: a juicy, aromatic meal. So ensure your tackle dealer sells you crabs that are just about to shed.

6 For binding peelers on, use modern, fine diameter, elasticated cotton which doesn't put fish off.

7 The most reliable method of hooking peeler crab, (whether using whole or half a crab) is to thread the hook (fine wire-up tide-style hooks are best) through the body via its leg sockets and secure using fine diameter elasticated cotton.

8 You can easily test a crab to see if it's ready to peel by pressing under the shell behind its legs. If a small crack starts to appear, your crab is indeed ready.

9 To present soft fish like herring, sprats or frozen mackerel which when thawed out is nothing like the firm, flesh of the same fish fresh from the

Natural

12

baits and is most economical on your supply of live sand eels.

15 Frozen sand eel may look perfectly well after a long drift, but the fact is, they will have lost much of their effective scent and juices, so change for fresh bait following every drift if you have sufficient supply.

16 That the attractive juices from king rag worm are strong is proved by the fact that should they enter a cut on your hand, it hurts. Drop into sand to provide additional grip for baiting up, and always offer a good 'mouthful'.

17 A 3/0 or 4/0 hook baited with king rag worm is improved by the tipping of a slither cut from the flank of a sand eel or mackerel, or you can add half a peeler crab or a baby squid head.

18 Always change lugworm baits after every cast whether they look ok or not. Do not simply add another worm or two. It is false economy. Their vital attractive juices quickly wash out in a strong tide flow whether beach or boat fishing. If beach fishing and using bait clips you will need a bait stop which needs to be pulled down the hook snood in order to secure the threaded worms.

12 Ensure your hook or hooks (a pennell rig works well with squid) are not masked by presenting 'too big' a bait. So don't simply add more squid when retrieving obviously 'chewed' bait. Take the old, washed-out squid off and replace with fresh.

13 To reveal that attractive 'white' succulent flesh of the squid, grip the two small fins at the top of its body and pull firmly down whilst twisting. It then peels off easily.

14 If baiting with live sand eels when drifting over sandbanks for bass, remember between drifts, while the skipper guns the boat up tide to commence another drift, to put your hooked-bait into a bucket of fresh salt water. This saves re-hooking or changing

19 When threading lug worms onto a fine wire hook (imperative when presenting worms) make sure it is threaded through the centre of the worm, and try to avoid 'loops' where the hook missed, because fish can easily grip these to pull it off.

20 Because the head end is the 'juiciest', it makes sense to thread on lugworms 'tail-first'. Always use a long shank hook.

14

16

19

SALTWATER

Artificial

Artificial

1 Were anyone (shudder the thought) restricted to just one artificial lure for fishing in saltwater the world over, what would it be? Well, a Rapala CD (sinking countdown) 14cm or 18cm, probably the larger of the two, in either blue mackerel or hot orange, would be hard to beat. These wooden lures have an irresistible action, are super-strong in construction and come fitted with robust trebles and split rings. Both sizes catch bass, pollack, all the tunas, barracuda, wahoo, big jacks, tarpon, even sailfish, etc. And you could use it successfully in freshwater for giant lake trout, pike muskellunge, Nile perch, tiger fish, peacock bass and catfish. Need I say more?

2 To save on broken fingernails when opening split rings on artificial lures, to replace or change over from one strength treble or large single to another, it's well worth investing in a pair of 'split-ring' pliers. A great tool for what can otherwise turn into a difficult, even painful job.

3 To reduce the chances of the treble hook on your pirk snagging the ironwork when working deep water wrecks, especially those festooned with commercial netting, simply cut off one of the hooks, or take the treble off and replace with a large single.

4 When steadily retrieving red gill or scallywag rubber lures up from wrecks, don't be tempted to strike, whether a firm hit or tiny pluck. Just keep winding till the rod top hoops over and the clutch starts slipping. Otherwise, the hook might be ripped out if you make a strike.

5 Try not to slow a lure down when lowering it down to a wreck. Otherwise, you could waste time with an unwanted mackerel or scad. Nuisance fish hooked or foul hooked as the case may be (and you are not to know of course so it's always a gamble) close to the wreck however, offer more promising prospects. So leave them on for a while.

6 It's always worth keeping a varied and comprehensive selection of made-up sets of 'carded' sea rig jigs, in addition to sets of basic 'mackerel feathers', in your trace wallet. Tiny lumiflash and super flash lures, mini shrimps, etc are invaluable whenever there is a chance of feathering up fresh sand eels or launce.

7 Sets of larger, multi-shrimp or luminous, Hokkai lures will sometimes outfish plain old mackerel feathers. So it's wise to have a

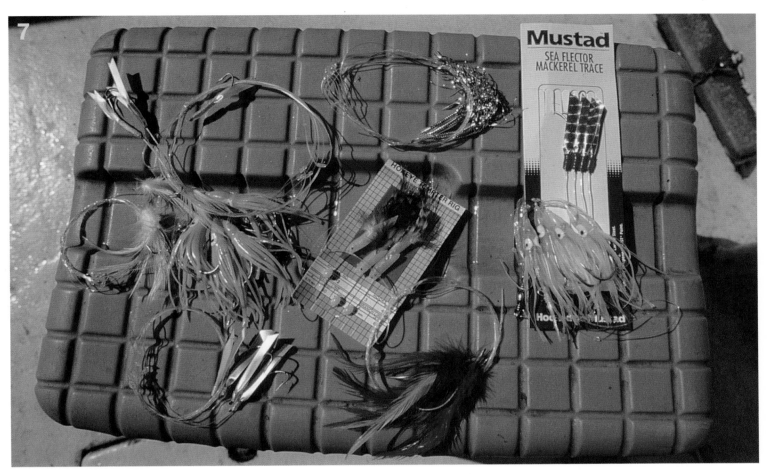

few alternative sets of 4-6 hook rigs available when gathering bait gets tough, and the shoals of mackerel are few and far between.

8 You never really know what's going to grab hold when jigging sets of feathers or mini-lures. I once hooked into a porbeagle shark not far off Weymouth whilst trying to secure enough mackerel for a day's bass fishing over a wreck. So be sure to have sufficient backing on your reel if fishing 'light'. No, I never saw the shark; it ran out over 200 yards of braid, before chewing through the 40lbs mono trace.

9 In areas over rough, rocky and weed-covered ground, replace the lead weight on your set of lures with a 'flashy' pirk, in case there are a few decent pollack or bass down there amongst the bait

fish. Bonus fish are always welcome when gathering fresh bait, and fight well on the lighter outfits best used for feathering.

10 Chromium-plated, flat-sided pirks called 'yanns' can prove unbelievably effective for bass

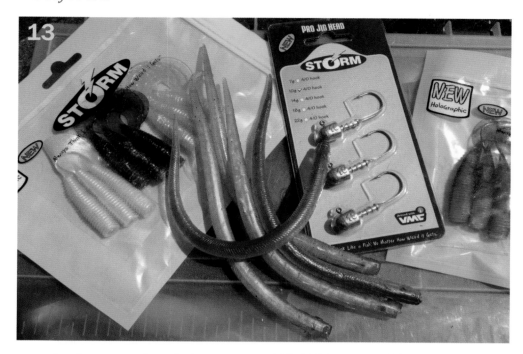

13 Plastic worms are now available in all manner of shapes, sizes and scents. The WildEye Naturistic 'sand eels' from the Storm stable, for instance, come in a wide range of colours and in lengths from 10-30 cm. They look and even 'feel' like the real deal. So when fresh bait is hard to come by, having some in your trace wallet could save the day.

14 For presenting the above, and all other makes and types of plastic and rubber worms and eels such as red gills and scallywags, shads, twin-tails, etc to species such as coal fish, cod, bass and pollack, rig up a 10-12 foot mono hook trace of around 20-25lbs test, with a black, tubular boom and lead slider above, stopped by a cushioning bead against the trace swivel. *See pollack Tip 4.*

15 Referred to by many anglers, particularly charter boat 'skippers' as a 'gilling' rig (because it was originally devised for presenting Red Gill rubber sand eels) the above is a rig that will catch cod and pollack around deep water wrecks on days when they seem loath to hit pirks.

occupying deep areas where the bottom is nothing but pinnacles and corridors of jagged rocks, where no other tackle set-up stands a chance. Weighing between 3 and 5 ounces, yanns are worked in a 'jigging' fashion and allowed to 'flutter' tantalisingly on the drop amongst the rocks, which is where naturally, most of the hits from bass come.

(5/0-8/0) hook to each by pushing the loop through the eye and down over the bend, and after baiting each with a fresh fillet of mackerel, you have a great working trace for species like cod, pollack and ling especially. Tie an overhand loop at the top end for joining to the reel line via a snap link swivel, and a large loop at the bottom to accommodate your lead or pirk.

11 Called 'muppets' by most sea anglers, coloured, plastic squid skirts are threaded on the line above a pirk, a fish fillet, or a worm bait to provide added visual attraction. Being made from a soft, rubbery plastic they do not seem alien to fish, and so it's worth always keeping a few in your trace wallet.

12 To make up an inexpensive, simple two-hook snood trace using muppets on four feet of 40-50lbs mono (ideal for drifting over snaggy, deep water wrecks) form two blood dropper loops of around 4-5 inches long, (see salt water tackle lines' Tip 17) around 18-20 inches apart in the middle. Make a small hole in the head of each muppet and push the snood loops through. Add a large

16 The secret with 'gilling', having lowered your artificial down to the wreck and once the lead has touched down, and immediately wound up a few feet to clear the ironwork, is to then retrieve slowly and evenly, counting say 10 to 12 turns of the reel handle before lowering the lure down again. Only this time count to maybe 15 turns. And on the next 20, till you find the 'taking' depth. Which can not only vary from session to session but also from hour to hour. So be prepared to constantly experiment when action is slow.

17 If there is no response from winding the lure up at an even pace when 'gilling', suddenly wind twice as fast and in an irregular manner. But hang on should a big pollack or coal fish think your lure is worth chasing. Many a large 'bonus' fish has come in this way.

18 Synthetic rubber and soft plastic 'shads' with holographic, flash foil bodies, are arguably the most effective of all artificial lures currently available. Fitted with naturalistic bodies impregnated with attractive oils and internally leaded, with either block, or curl tails, shads account for enormous numbers of cod, pollack, coal fish and bass over rough ground and deep water wrecks.

19 Though marketed specifically for the fresh water scene, to target pike, perch and zander, the comprehensive and colourful range of shad-like artificials, with their scented, realistically moulded body shapes, are literally taking deep water wreck-fishing situations apart. Storm Lures, for instance, manufacture soft, plastic, look-alikes in, anchovy, sardine, herring and mackerel plus several fresh water fish formats. All of which will fool cod, bass, and pollack, etc into hitting hard. A braided reel line is essential, for working these lures effectively.

20 Also worth trying are artificial 'swimming crabs' and naturalistic shrimps. The latter being actually 'shrimp-scented'. These can be worked close to the bottom around piers, break waters and harbour entrances using a 'sporting' heavy freshwater outfit, for maximum enjoyment.

19

SALTWATER BAITS

Ground Baiting

1 Not actually 'ground baiting' as such because no amount of 'rubby dubby' ever ends up on the sea floor (and it's not intended to) but this 'specially prepared' concoction, and every skipper has his own special mix, (simply referred to as 'chum' over on the other side of the pond) is of paramount importance for attracting sharks to a drifting boat.

2 To make a great 'rubby dubby' base, use a concoction comprising of minced mackerel and bran (which soaks up the juices and flutters down through clear water attractively) plus concentrated fish oils, all mixed together in a 10-30 gallon tub.

3 The rubby dubby is greatly improved by the addition of fresh blood (the local butcher will usually oblige) which is still further improved, if left overnight to 'ferment' a little. Fine, white sand is also sometimes added to the mix to produce that 'cloud' effect.

4 Once the skipper has steadied the boat, worked out the 'drift' and turned off the engines, between two and four onion sacks (it's one hell of a smelly and messy job) are filled with the 'smelly' mix and lowered over the side on ropes and tied off at around the boats waterline, in order that the constant rocking of the boat plus wash from the waves, steadily release behind the boat, a stream of rubby dubby particles, which actually creates a visible 'slick' on the surface that can be seen for miles. It's then a matter of waiting for the sharks to show up.

5 Don't automatically throw the heads and tails of your fresh fish baits over the side. They can be diced up to use as loose feed, lowered down to the bottom (if pier or boat fishing) in a bait dropper, or minced finer for a rubby-dubby bag to go around the anchor chain. There's time enough, and hopefully bait enough for feeding the sea gulls on the trip home.

6 For mincing up fish heads and bits, look out at car boot and jumble sales for an old steel meat 'mincer' with a built in clamp. They may be old fashioned but for turning bait remnants into useable 'chum' they are invaluable.

7 To target the mullet of intimate tidal rivers, fish which make their way in with the tide to feed upon bottom algae, you can easily wean them onto

4

dubby, is to use a large mortar and pestle. But afterwards don't attempt to use it for anything but fishing bait.

10 In the Channel Islands a most effective in-shore rubby dubby to complement float fishing tactics, is called 'shirvy', and concocted from a finely diced mix of red meat and oily fish to which bottled fish oil and bran is added. It should have the consistency of chilli con carne once all mashed up in a bucket.

11 'Shirvy' stinks so much (don't get it over your clothes, or in a mad moment even think about throwing it in by hand) it needs to be ladled-in at regular intervals from the rocks

or harbour wall with the aid of a large dessert spoon whipped firmly onto a section of garden cane. Its powers for attracting species like coal fish, pollack, mackerel, wrasse, garfish and mullet however, are legendary.

12 An alternative ground bait for attracting species like bream, bass, garfish, mackerel and mullet, etc when fishing from rocks or from piers during the summer months, is stale bread mixed with boiled fish.

13 If fish are not available to boil up for the ground bait mentioned above, simply add a tin or two of sardines or pilchards to the mashed, stale bread. Pier anglers will

10

accepting bead flake on the hook by ground baiting with mashed bread. Old loaves simply pushed into the mud or into bank sides soon break up to release a steady stream of attractive particles.

8 When float fishing from rocks, headlands and harbour entrances for species like mullet, pollack and garfish etc, a ground bait consisting of minced fresh fish (garfish, mackerel, sprats or herrings, etc plus a liberal helping of pilchard or herring oil and all bound together with bran), will keep fish moving up onto your bait.

9 An effective, if somewhat messy way of reducing diced-up fish like mackerel into a base for rubby

SALTWATER BAITS

Ground Baiting

species like bass and pollack. Having gathered a good supply of fresh mackerel or launce (greater sand eel), cut them into ¾ inch 'chunks' (hence the term) on a cutting board positioned on the stern gunnel, and allow them to drift down tide.

15 For filling with chopped fish or shell fish remnants etc, and either using as a baited weight or dropped down independently loaded with your favourite ground bait, the 'Portugese' designed, Hiro Bait (steel meshed) Cage, which comes in four sizes between 200g-1100g, is perfect when targeting shoal species such as mullet or black bream.

16 Though designed originally for fresh water 'barbel' anglers for dropping down up to half a pint of hempseed at a time in fast flowing rivers, 'giant' bait droppers are perfect for inshore and estuary boat anglers wishing to continually ground bait with finely diced fish. Keep one ready-rigged to a spare rod for instant use.

benefit from putting the mix into a small mesh bag (a carrot sack is perfect) for hanging on a rope alongside the stanchions.

14 When tides are not too strong 'chunking' is a most effective way of ground baiting for

17 An excellent addition to any ground bait for sea fishing is what delicatessens sell as whitebait, which are usually young herrings, sprats, or sardines. Their silvery bodies provide enormous 'flash appeal' to any mix.

18 Whitebait is particularly useful (mix with white sand which adds sparkle and helps bind it together for throwing) to attract species like bass, pollack and mackerel to the boat, after which spinning or jigging with small pirks and shads, or free lining with small fish or triangular-cut fish strip will score heavily, especially in clear water.

19 Ground baiting to African beach anglers targeting bronze whaler sharks along Namibia's 'Skeleton Coast' first catch a gully shark and slit it from vent to throat before staking it out at the water line. On a good day, sharks start arriving within minutes attracted by the trail of blood and juices washed into the sea by incoming waves.

20 I am not for one minute suggesting British shore anglers should follow the above practice, but there is nothing to stop those targeting bass along rocky coastlines, or smooth hounds that venture close in shore during June and July, to fill an onion sack with fish and crab remnants and stake it out at low tide just before the flood.

19

SALTWATER BAITS

John Wilson's
1001
TOPANGLINGTIPS